Llewellyn's

Herbal Almanac

2006

Editing/Design: Michael Fallon
Interior Art: © Mary Azarian
Cover Photos: © Digital Vision, © Brand X,
© Digital Stock, © Photodisc
Cover Design: Lisa Novak

You can order annuals and books
from *New Worlds*, Llewellyn's
magazine catalog. To request a free copy
call toll-free: 1-877-NEW WRLD, or visit our
website at http://subscriptions.llewellyn.com.

ISBN 0-7387-0151-3
Llewellyn Worldwide
P.O. Box 64383, Dept. 0-7387-0151-3
St. Paul, MN 55164

Table of Contents

Growing and Gathering Herbs

Culinary Herbs

Herbs for Health

Herbs for Beauty

Herb Crafts

Herb History, Myth, and Magic

Introduction to Llewellyn's
Herbal Almanac

Welcome to 2006, faithful reader, and a new edition of Llewellyn's *Herbal Almanac*. It's a new year and time to take a look again at the current research on, and ever-expanding use of, herbs as medicine, as culinary spice, as cosmetic, and as magical item. This year in particular we tap into some of the deeper aspects of herbal knowledge—using herbs to promote a healthy prostate; making a Celtic nine-herb charm; growing herbs hydroponically; and using African body butters. And we bring to these pages some of the most innovative and original thinkers and writers on herbs.

This focus on the old ways—on times when men and women around the world knew and understood the power of herbs—is important today. Terrorists, water and energy shortages, hatred, internecine battles, militant religious fervor, war, all seem to be holding sway over the good things in life—beauty, good food, health, love, and friendship. While we don't want to assign blame or cast any other aspersions, this state of affairs perhaps is not surprising considering so many of us—each one of us—is out of touch with the beauty, magic, and health-giving properties of the natural world. Many of us spend much of our lives rushing about in a technological bubble—striving to make money and living life in fast-forward. We forget to focus on the parts of life that can bring us back into balance and harmony.

Still, the news is not all bad. People are still striving to make us all more aware of the magical, beautiful ways that herbs can affect our lives. In the 2006 edition of the *Herbal Almanac*, the various authors pay tribute to the ideals of magic and beauty and balance as they relate to the health-giving and beautifying properties of herbs. This may sound a bit far-fetched, but after all it does not take much imagination to see that a traditional English garden will bring some much-needed beauty to our lives, that making a remembrance potpourri to honor the past will calm the soul, and that learning some new chocolate recipes will bring to you some health and peace of mind.

Herbs are the perfect complement to the power of the mind, an ancient tool whose time has come back around to help us restore balance in our lives. More and more people are using them, growing and gathering them, and studying them for their enlivening and healing properties. We, the editors and authors of this volume, encourage the treatment of the whole organism—of the person and of the planet—with herbal magic. One person at a time, using ancient wisdom, we can make a new world.

Note: The old-fashioned remedies in this book are historical references used for teaching purposes only. The recipes are not for commercial use or profit. The contents are not meant to diagnose, treat, prescribe, or substitute consultation with a licensed health-care professional. Herbs, whether used internally or externally, should be introduced in small amounts to allow the body to adjust and to detect possible allergies. Please consult a standard reference source or an expert herbalist to learn more about the possible effects of certain herbs. You must take care not to replace regular medical treatment with the use of herbs. Herbal treatment is intended primarily to complement modern health care. Always seek professional help if you suffer from illness. Also, take care to read all warning labels before taking any herbs or starting on an extended herbal regimen. Always consult an herbal professional before beginning any sort of medical treatment—this is particularly true for pregnant women.

Herbs are powerful things; be sure you are using that power to achieve balance. Llewellyn Worldwide does not participate in, endorse, or have any authority or responsibility concerning private business transactions between its authors and the public.

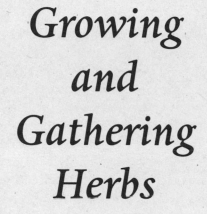

Growing
and
Gathering
Herbs

Using Native Plants to Attract Butterflies

~ by Laurel Reufner ~

B utterflies bring us hope. Along with their practical use as pollinators for our gardens, they offer a bit of moving grace and beauty when we cross their path, lifting our spirits. They seem so fragile, and yet their continued existence in an increasingly hostile world is encouraging considering our own struggle to survive.

While butterflies indeed seem quite fragile, they aren't quite as delicate as we've been led to believe. In fact, a little help from us, by way of our gardens, goes a long way to ensure their continued survival. Often very adaptable, butterflies are drawn to a wide variety of nectar-filled plants. And plants native to your region attract not only native butterflies that prefer those plants, but help preserve a small bit of what makes your area unique.

If you are truly interested in starting a butterfly garden, there are a few garden additions to consider. Try adding a water source. Believe it or not, butterflies love mud puddles—they gain valuable minerals from the dirt while "puddling." To make a puddle area, simply sink a shallow plastic container in the ground, fill it with dirt, and keep it wet. You'll have happy butterflies. A birdbath filled with water and some strategically placed flat rocks allow your garden visitors to get a drink and sun themselves at the same time.

Like all insects, butterflies are cold-blooded and need the warmth of the Sun to be able to fly. It is therefore a good idea to give them somewhere to hide during the winter weather. This can easily be provided by way of small wood and twig piles or sometimes even some nice, thick mulch. These both will add needed shelter and safety in the harsher months.

Some Native Butterfly Plants

The following plants are all native to North America. Many of them are prairie plants that may be endangered, so adding them to your garden does some double good. Growing plants native to your area usually means they are more adapted to your growing environment and are therefore much more likely to thrive.

Mention butterflies and many folks think of milkweed and monarchs, so that's where we'll start our discussion of plants. This family contains something for nearly every soil type and every lighting situation except perhaps full shade.

Monarch caterpillars seem to prefer the leaves of the red milkweed (*Asclepias incarnate*) over other plants in the family. These plants prefer moist to wet, although not necessarily muddy, soil. Red milkweed plants produce striking red and pink blossoms around Midsummer that last only through July. Although the rare Sullivant's milkweed (*Asclepias sullivantii*) may not be as tasty as its red-flowered friend, it is more easily controlled in a garden because it does not spread by rhizomes like the rest of the family.

Many of us are familiar, at least by sight, with the common milkweed (*Asclepias syriaca*). Its pink and yellow flowers produce a lot of nectar, making it a butterfly favorite. It is probably the most versatile of the family when it comes to growing conditions. Common milkweed will grow in the largest variety of soils and can thrive even in partial sunlight. It can be grown easily from seed, producing sweet-scented flowers around Midsummer. However, once established, syriaca spreads easily by rhizomes, so be careful where you plant it.

An absolutely beautiful member of the milkweed family is the butterflyweed (*Asclepias tuberose*), which has a profusion of orange and yellow flowers from June until September. While many species of Asclepias can get quite tall (three to five feet), butterflyweed reaches a maximum of three feet in height. It is gorgeous in cut flower arrangements as well. Able to tolerate dry conditions, butterflyweed needs full sunlight and well-drained soil to grow well. Also, don't try to transplant this one once it is established. Damaging its long taproot will kill it.

While many of the plants mentioned in this article are considered versatile, nothing comes close to the amazing versatility of the aster family. An aster variety can be found for full sunlight to full shade, for dry, damp, or moist soil, and for any soil type. New England aster (*Aster novae-angliae*) is one of the most gorgeous in the family, growing from three to six feet tall, with brilliant purple blooms right up into October. New England asters prefer full sunlight and moist soil, but will handle partial shade.

Big leaf aster (*Aster macrophyllus*), meanwhile, is a much shorter cousin that grows only one to two feet high. Like a mint, it spreads via underground rhizomes and is an excellent ground cover in difficult areas, such as those shady spots or a hillside. Smooth aster (*Aster laevis*) produces pale blue-purple blooms that last into October as well. Reaching a height of two to four feet, smooth aster is hardy, cold-tolerant, and thrives in almost any soil type. It is a long-lived plant, making it an excellent perennial for the busy gardener.

For copious fall blooms, try growing some of the many goldenrod varieties. Most of these plants do best in full sunlight and in well-drained soil. Unless they are likely to trigger your allergies, they are worth the garden space. Especially worth mentioning is the Ohio goldenrod *(Solidago ohioensis)*, a compact plant with beautiful foliage that will, come August, become covered in beautiful orange and yellow flower heads. Reaching only three to four feet in height, it would be a wonderful complement to butterflyweed.

A couple of other full sunlight varieties worth mentioning are the stiff goldenrod *(Solidago rigida)* and showy goldenrod *(Solidago speciosa)*. Both of these flowers are nice additions in dried flower arrangements. Rigida can reach a height of nearly five feet and is popular with both birds and butterflies, especially monarchs. Speciosa only reaches three feet at most, and nearly one third of that is the flower head!

Don't despair if you want to try adding goldenrod to your garden but only have shady or woodland space in which to plant. Anise-scented goldenrod *(Solidago odora)* prefers shady areas and dry, sandy soils. Crush some of the leaves lightly in your hands and you'll quickly see how this plant got its name. Birds enjoy this short plant, as do butterflies.

If blue-stemmed goldenrod *(Solidago caesia)* lives up to its description, it's certainly worth creating a spot for it in your garden. Come August, millions of tiny yellow flowers cover the gently arching stems. This particular plant grows two to three feet in height and needs well-drained humus soil. You can grow it in full sunlight to partial shade, and, as an added bonus, it also attracts hummingbirds.

Add a conversational piece to your garden while also helping preserve a rare prairie plant and the Baltimore checkerspot butterfly by planting the unusual white turtlehead *(Chelone glabra)*. You will have to plant this variety in a damp portion of your garden. The flowers of this unique plant actually resemble, yes, a turtle's head. White turtlehead will take full to partial sunlight, and it grows to heights between two and four feet. Its white flowers would probably look lovely in a Moon garden as well.

Plant prairie dock *(Silphium terebinthinaceum)* where it has some room to stretch for the sky, as this plant, when flowering, can reach a height of ten feet. Its short leaves, however, remind one of elephant's ears. Around July, the plant blooms, sending up bunches of flower heads resembling miniature sunflowers atop long, bare stalks. These plants are true perennials, often living for decades if not disturbed or damaged. It will grow in clay, sandy, or loamy damp soil, and, like sunflowers, it is a Sun worshipper.

Coneflower is another popular family of plants for both the herb and flower garden. These plants prefer full sunlight and medium to dry soil. Many will even grow in clay, sandy, and loamy soils. Purple coneflower *(Echinacea purpurea)* and Ozark coneflower *(Echinacea paradoxa)* are perhaps two of the most striking, each with showy flower heads. If you are just as interested in herbal properties as is attracting butterflies, try growing the narrow-leaf purple coneflower *(Echinacea angustifolia)* or its cousin the pale-purple coneflower *(Echinacea pallida)*. Both are native to western prairie areas and are tough, drought-resistant plants. Both are high in the medicinal properties prized by herbalists.

While its name might indicate otherwise, orange coneflower *(Rudbeckia fulgida)* is not part of the Echinacea family. This brightly flowered plant belongs to the black-eyed susan family. Growing to a height of between two to four feet in full to partial shade, this flower is very popular with the butterflies. Try planting it with prairie blazingstar or joe pye weed for a beautiful, blooming mix.

Some relatives of orange coneflower to consider include the original black-eyed susan *(Rudbeckia hirta)*. It is quick growing, self sowing, and hard to kill except for the true black-thumbs among us. Grow from seed or transplant to get a jump-start on blooming plants. (Hirta doesn't usually bloom until the second year.) Plants reach heights of one to three feet in good soil, but it will grow in clay-based ground, full to partial shade, and is absolutely beautiful. If you want the addition of heat tolerance, try sweet black-eyed susan *(Rudbeckia subtomentosa)*, the show-off of the family. This plant is tall, able to reach a height of around six feet, and has tons of flowers to catch your attention.

The blazingstar varieties are beautiful, full of purple-pink blooms from August to September. One of the best things about this family of flowers is that they are attractive to not just butterflies, but also to birds and hummingbirds. There are several members of this family worth considering for your garden, including the prairie blazingstar *(Liatris pycnostachya)*. This particular flower enjoys full sunlight and slightly moist soil. Its tall flower spikes also make an excellent cut or dried flower for arrangements. Dense blazingstar *(Liatris spicata)* is another attention-getter in the flowerbed. This variety likes moist, marshy soil of clay, loam, or sand. Give it what it needs and you'll see late-season blooms that last until it frosts.

Rough blazingstar *(Liatris aspera)* is so named because its large flowers are rather shaggy looking, as though they need haircuts. Aspera prefers dry, sandy soil, but will also do well in well-drained loamy dirt. It's a rather unassuming plant until the flowers bloom; then it goes from drab to spectacular. Another shaggy-looking blazingstar is the northern blazingstar *(Liatris borealis)*, which has growing demands similar to those of the rough blazingstar.

Finally, there is the meadow blazingstar *(Liatris ligulistylis)*, which has brilliant, deep purple-pink flowers similar in appearance to the northern blazingstar. It needs rich, moist, loamy soils and full sunlight. If you like monarch butterflies or goldfinches, this is a must-have plant for you.

We next turn our attention to the joe pye group of plants. Joe pye weed *(Eupatorium maculatum)* is nearly as attractive to butterflies as butterflyweed. Full sunlight and moist, rich soil will keep this plant the happiest. It grows to a height of between four to six feet and is perfect for the edges of ponds and streams. Not only butterflies, but bumblebees also love this plant. Tall joe pye weed *(Eupatorium fistulosum)* is the family patriarch, growing to an impressive eight feet in height with profuse, deep purple-pink flowers that begin growing in August. It has the same growing requirements as joe pye weed, and it adapts easily to a cultivated environment. Flower-wise, sweet joe pye weed *(Eupatorium purpureum)* is similar to its Sun-loving cousins, but can also tolerate woodland shade and drier soil. Monarchs and swallow-tails also love this plant.

Boneset *(Eupatorium perfoliatum)* is another good plant for the herbalist butterfly lover to have in their gardens. Easy to grow, boneset loves moist, marshy areas, full sunlight, and a variety of soil types. Where much of the joe pye weed family has purple-pink flowers, boneset's blooms are white and look like tiny lacy doilies atop the stems. The leaves are also joined at the base, where they attach to the stem of the plant so that it looks as though the stem is growing right up through them.

Mistflower *(Eupatorium coelestinum)* has a unique stem structure similar to that of boneset, although its flowers are smaller. This is a short plant that will grow in full sunlight to partial shade, preferably in moist soil. It has a longer bloom time than the other Eupatoriums mentioned, lasting from July through October and the first frost.

Bergamot *(Monarda fistulosa)* is another versatile native plant for the garden. Many different butterflies and hummingbirds enjoy nectar from its blooms, and its sturdy stems are used by indigo buntings for nest building. Bergamot is a good flavoring for teas. It is easily grown and will tolerate a variety of soil types that are damp or dry. Grow it in full sunlight or try it in some partially shaded areas. As a final bonus, the dried seed heads can be used for feeding birds or in flower arrangements.

Grow a bit of history in your flower garden with New Jersey tea *(Ceanothus americanus)*, the plant colonists used as a tea substitute in the days following the Boston Tea Party. New Jersey tea is full of white fluffy flower heads that are enjoyed by butterfly and hummingbird alike. More shrub than flower, the plant grows to about three feet tall by three feet across, in full to partial sunlight, sand or loam, and in dry to damp soils. It grows slowly, so be patient with it and in return it will provide decades of enjoyment.

There are so many other beautiful native plants to consider for a butterfly garden, but space constraints limit what can be discussed in this article. Some final plants to investigate and consider include steeplebush *(Spiraea tomentose)*, lavender hyssop *(Agastache foeniculum)*, lanceleaf and stiff coreopsis *(Coreopsis lanceolata* and *C. palmate* respectively), as well as various vervain, lupine, clover, and Columbine varieties.

In researching this topic, it was surprising to learn that many of the beautiful aster family are native to North America. So is the breathtaking and beautiful passion flower *(Passiflora incarnate)*. Surprisingly, both chicory and Queen Anne's lace are imports from Europe. They're so prevalent in the countryside that it's easy to just assume they started out here.

Native plants are often beautiful yet practical additions to your flower garden, helping not just butterflies but also birds, hummingbirds, and the native environment. Furthermore, learning more about these plants teaches us more about our history. Two good places to start your explorations online are the Prairie Nursery, located at www.prairienursery.com, and Companion Plants at www.companionplants.com. *All About Weeds*, by Edwin Rollin Spencer (Dover Publications, 1974), is an opinionated, fascinating read, while both *Butterfly Gardens* by the Xerces Society and the Smithsonian Institution (Sierra Club Books, 1998) and *Stokes Butterfly Book* by Donald and Lillian Stokes and Ernest Williams (Little, Brown, 1991) are good sources of information on both plant selection and the mechanics of butterfly gardening.

Growing Herbs in a Hydroponic System

⤜ by Sheri Richerson ⤛

Growing herbs on a windowsill, in the yard, or in a greenhouse environment can be both rewarding and challenging. There's a whole new set of rules to learn about light exposure, pest problems, and starting seeds. And, when you try hydroponic gardening, the learning curve can get somewhat steeper.

Still, once you get the hang of hydroponic gardening it's worth the extra effort. After you get accustomed to adjusting the pH and regularly attending to your system, the plants will grow and flourish in a way that just doesn't happen with soil-based plants.

When you grow herbs hydroponically, you can expect a higher output not only in quantity but also in quality. Properly grown hydroponic herbs are provided with everything they need to thrive. This is very unlike typical soil-grown plants. Hydroponic-grown herbs grow at a faster rate, with higher production and better quality than soil-grown plants. When done correctly, hydroponic growing yields herbs that are finer in quality than soil-grown herbs. They have a stronger flavor and produce more oils. A test done on basil grown in soil and in a hydroponic unit showed that the hydroponically grown basil had a 40 percent increase in flavor over the soil-grown basil.

Growing herbs in a hydroponic system requires a bit of knowledge about plant preferences. For example, choose a nutrient solution with numbers that are simple and regular—such as 5-5-5 or 10-10-10. A nutrient solution that is too rich will produce herbs that lack flavor. There will also be a decrease in the amount of oil produced.

Herbs that are easy to grow and respond well to a hydroponic environment include basil, mint—which is not as invasive when contained in a pot—chamomile, oregano, calendula, St. John's wort, lavender, lemon balm, feverfew, horehound, lemon balm, fennel, yarrow, rosemary, sage, and French tarragon.

No Soil, New Rules

Growing plants in a hydroponic system for the first time can present some unexpected challenges. If you've always gardened in soil, forget the old rules and get ready for some new ones.

To begin with, starting seeds destined for hydroponic systems involves more than just sticking the seed in soil and waiting for it to germinate. This requires a day or two of preparation. Starting seeds in rockwool cubes provides a definite advantage over seeds germinated in soil, because there's less of a problem with damping off and the seedlings generally are stronger and healthier.

Since soil isn't used in hydroponic growing, pest infestations are reduced. It is pretty hard for pests to lay eggs in some types of hydroponic growing media, such as expanded clay and rockwool.

It's almost impossible for the media to be tainted before beginning to grow, unlike soil, which can be contaminated with insect eggs or pathogens before the point of purchase. Expanded clay and rockwool is heated to thousands of degrees in the manufacturing process, which practically ensures that insects, eggs, or mold spores aren't present at the time of packaging.

Learning to control the pH level of the nutrient solution for hydroponic growing can be a challenge. You need to check pH levels on a daily basis. Although this may sound like a time-consuming chore, it actually only takes about five minutes a day per system. While pH is nothing new to gardeners, soil-based pH levels are slow to change, and the wrong pH isn't nearly as toxic to soil-based plants over a short period of time as in hydroponic systems. According to Brian Baca, proprietor of Albuquerque Hydroponics & Lighting, when pH is out of balance, mineral elements in the solution may not be fully available to plants. This is sometimes called "lockout." Perfectly healthy plants can begin to die off within a few hours due to pH imbalance. In hydroponic gardening, there doesn't seem to be a way to save these plants once their demise begins, although saving a plant that is severely wilted is sometimes possible in soil-based gardening.

There are a number of hazards to be aware of with hydroponic growing. Whitefly can be a problem in soil-grown plants, but I've found that this insect pest really loves plants in a hydroponic environment. The infestation and damage on hydroponic plants compared to soil-based plants is much greater. Systemic and chemical insecticides aren't used as often with hydroponic systems as they are with soil-grown plants. When growing edible plants hydroponically, you cannot use many of the pest control products available on the market. Traditional home remedies, such as using liquid dishwashing detergent, don't seem to help much either, so be prepared to come up with a plan for combating infestations. One possible solution is to use products that contain neem oil. Beneficial insects and natural predators can also be used to combat problems.

One solution to a pest problem is to remove the plants from the system and do a complete flush. First, remove the expanded clay Grorocks and pots from the system. Then run a solution of 5 percent hydrogen peroxide through the system continually for twenty-four hours. Then rinse the Grorocks in warm water until the water running out of the system is completely clear. Allow the rocks to drain overnight, leaving the system on to flush the interior parts.

The next day, run clear water through the system for a couple of hours to ensure that any remaining hydrogen peroxide is removed. Then drain the system and refill it with fresh water and nutrient solution. You can use a 5 percent bleach solution, if you prefer; however, hydrogen peroxide won't harm the plants as much as bleach if any solution is left behind in the system.

You may decide to use an insecticidal soap that has been approved for use on vegetables to take care of any eggs or adult pests that still remain. Always make sure to follow the directions on the manufacturer's label should you decide to go this route. Remember that spraying once won't eliminate the problem, and many products aren't approved for indoor or edible plant use.

Living, Learning, and Still Growing

Once the pest problem is remedied, you may decide to add new plants to your hydroponic system or simply keep the ones that have been treated.

In the beginning, try growing two plants in soil and two in the hydroponic system. It is important that these be the same plant and the same size. For example, try two cinnamon basil plants, one in soil and one in the hydroponic unit. You may be disappointed that there aren't any noticeable differences during the first few weeks. However, about six weeks into the growing cycle, you will begin to see differences in plant size, growth rate, and foliage. The plant leaves in the hydroponic system should be larger and more abundant than those grown in soil. The plants should also be healthier.

Here are a few items worth noting during your initial hydroponic experiences. For the most part, don't try to start seeds directly in the system. Rockwool tends to minimize the amount of shock a plant experiences during transplanting in comparison to bare-rooting into the system.

One big bonus to hydroponic gardening is that the fertilizer is always available to the plants—as long as the pH is in balance. The plants just take up what's needed, as it's needed. Also, the nutrient solution contains all of the elements necessary for optimal plant growth—elements that may or may not be present in different types of soil.

This may be why hydroponic plants show such increased vigor. It has to do with nutrients. Seedlings grown in soil also increased their leaf size with the addition of a hydroponic nutrient solution. If you begin adding nutrients to soil-grown plants, you should notice a dramatic increase in leaf size and growth rate.

Even flowers, vegetables, and fruit respond positively to being grown in a hydroponic environment. Numerous gardeners who grow hydroponic fruit, vegetables, and flowers have reported that their yields have doubled and even tripled simply by switching to hydroponics.

System Notes

You may want to test different commercially available hydroponic systems geared toward hobbyists or simply build your own system. Here are a few issues worth relating.

First of all, pump systems can malfunction and cause plant death in a few short hours. Most systems don't offer any sort of warning device. Some systems do have a water reservoir so plants that have long enough roots to reach the reservoir have a chance for survival in the event of pump failure. Other systems operate on a pump system but don't utilize a water reservoir. If the pump fails, it will stop providing the nutrient solution to the plant, which will cause the plant roots to begin to dehydrate and die.

In such cases, an expanded amount of clay rocks should hold enough moisture content to keep the plants alive for about ninety minutes. So, if you can remedy the problem in this time frame, you can most likely save the plant.

There are also systems designed to use a wicking system so the plant can draw water and nutrients as needed. This system is a bit more complicated to check up on since you can never actually see the water running. However, the vibration of the pump can be felt, or the wicking can be inspected to see if it's damp. Should this system malfunction, you could always submerge the plants—pots and all—into a container filled with nutrient solution for the short time that it would take to get the pump replaced or even water the plants by hand a couple times a day. The drawback to some of these systems is that the pump is usually substandard in size.

Christian Martensen, in the Customer Service Wholesale Department at Hydrofarm, strongly recommends Emily's Garden for beginners. The reason is that you can set the system to your particular requirements. You will need to check the water level and, as long as you keep the reservoir filled, it works. Should your pump fail unexpectedly, an aquarium pump will work. However, make sure that it's the same capacity as the original pump—this is important for the proper operation of the system.

One nice aspect of pumping systems is self-containment. Basically, systems look like flowerpots with small tubes running up the sides. The pump is situated on the floor covered by a base that supports the pot. This gives the grower the option of growing hydroponically indoors without the tubing and other somewhat unattractive accessories that are part of larger systems. Many wicking systems also make excellent indoor systems because of their compact size.

If you have the room and want to grow more plants—and don't care about numerous irrigation tubes and buckets—there are larger systems that do a fantastic job and offer the option of growing larger—as well as a larger number of—plants.

Ideally, the perfect environment for any hydroponic system is in a greenhouse because of the increased amount of sunlight. Should you decide to use your hydroponic system indoors, there are a number of suppliers who do offer special lighting setups. In the proper climate, hydroponic growing can be done anywhere with sufficient light.

Propagation Tips

Most herbs, including basil, sage, thyme, rosemary, French tarragon, thyme, lavender, oregano, and mint, grow easily from cuttings. Some of these plants do not come true from seed, so if you want the exact plant that you have it is best to take cuttings, dip them in rooting gel, and place the cuttings in the rockwool cube or other hydroponic medium.

Some herb plants—such as chives, woodruff, tansy, lady's mantle, and catnip—can be divided. If you choose to divide plants that you already have, be sure to carefully wash the roots— especially if they were previously soil-grown. To do this, simply shake the soil off the roots, fill a container with warm water, and dip the roots into it. You can cut off approximately one-eighth to one-quarter of the root system but be sure to have a weak solution of nutrient solution made up to set the plant into if you choose to trim the roots. Trimming the roots will help the plant to grow and adjust to its new environment a bit better and is a common practice at nurseries when potting up plants. Allow the plant to sit in the nutrient solution for about ten minutes before placing it in a large rockwool cube or other chosen media. Some of the other media options include Oasis foam and composted tree bark cubes.

Finally, you can choose to start some herbs from seed. A wide variety of seeds are available for medicinal, culinary, and magical herbs. Plants such as belladonna, mandrake, wolfsbane, and sweet grass can all be started from seed. This is sometimes the easiest way to obtain otherwise hard-to-find plants.

Starting seeds that will later be grown hydroponically should begin in a media designed for hydroponic use. The two most important things to keep in mind when choosing a seed-starting media for a hydroponic system is that it must be able to maintain the correct moisture level and promote strong root growth in order to be successful.

Step-By-Step Seed-Starting Using Rockwool

To start this process, buy some rockwool cubes from your favorite hydroponic supplier. You will also need to select some seeds to grow. Beginners may want to start with plants such as herbs, tomatoes, or peppers.

Once you have the rockwool cubes, fill a gallon container with water and use a pH test kit to get an accurate pH reading. If the reading is over 5.5, you will need to add some "pH down." If it's lower than 5.5, you'll need to add some "pH up." When adding the diluted acid or alkali solutions, the best advice is to go slowly. You don't want to add too much at once. For example, if the pH of your water is between 6.0 and 6.5, begin with just one-eighth of a teaspoon of pH down. If you find that it isn't enough, add another eighth teaspoon and so on until you get the correct reading.

Once you have properly balanced water at a pH of 5.5, put the rockwool cubes into a waterproof container that's large enough so that the cubes can be completely covered with the water. Pour the water into the container with the rockwool cubes and let soak for twenty-four hours. This is an important step. Rockwool is naturally alkaline. Soaking the cubes will bring the pH up to a more neutral reading.

After the rockwool has soaked, drain the container. Once the excess liquid has drained off, the seeds can be sown. One option is to soak the seeds in a Superthrive solution for an hour beforehand to promote better germination. You will likely find that you will have excellent germination rates by simply planting the seeds directly in the prepunched holes in the tops of the rockwool cubes. Plant two or three seeds per cube. Once the seeds have germinated and grown a bit, remove all but the strongest seedling from each cube.

Place the planted cubes in a container that will allow them to sit in the pH-adjusted water. The water should be kept at a depth of approximately one-fifth of the cube. A gentle bottom heat of 75–80 degrees F can help promote faster germination and seedling growth. During this stage, check the pH every day. It should remain at 5.5 throughout the germination process.

After the seedling has two sets of true leaves, begin feeding the plant with a mild vegetative solution. To make this solution, take a gallon of water and add the proper amount of nutrient concentrate according to the label's instructions. Mix it up and wait for a half hour before testing the pH, which should now be at 6–6.5. If not, follow the previous directions for adjusting the pH. You will get optimum accuracy if you wait thirty minutes after adding the pH adjuster to the solution.

The procedure for mixing the diluted vegetative nutrient solution will vary from product to product. Simply follow the directions on the nutrient container and consult your garden store if in doubt. A general guideline would be to start with the mildest formula, then increase the concentration every week or so. It is always better to start mild, even too mild, and increase the concentration as needed. Once a garden is burned, it can take two weeks to recover—if it recovers at all. Once the plants are actively growing, the conductivity of the nutrient solution should be slightly increased every five to seven days.

At least every three days, remove the cubes from the container and clean the trays. Then replace the cubes and add fresh, diluted vegetative nutrient solution. Continue this process throughout the germination and seedling stage. It's important to check the pH every time you use the solution. You can water soil-based plants with any leftover solution and make a fresh batch for your rockwool cubes as needed.

When the roots are approximately one-half inch long on the outside of the rockwool cube, transplant it into the hydroponic system. Continue to increase gradually the conductivity of the nutrient solution every few days until the desired level for the particular crop being grown is reached. The maximum ratio should be no more than four teaspoons per gallon of water.

Continuing Education

With hydroponic herb growing, you would never guess that growing a plant could be so complex and so rewarding at the same time. Once you get the hang of growing plants in a hydroponic environment, you won't want to go back to gardening in soil.

Regardless of which herbs you choose—culinary, medicinal, or magical—most herbs, flowers, vegetables, and other plants will respond quite well to being grown in a hydroponic environment. Growing herbs in this manner will allow you to garden year round, indoors or outdoors.

In addition, with the increased demand for locally grown fresh produce, growing herbs hydroponically may allow you to pick up a little extra cash on the side from local grocers, restaurants, or even people in your neighborhood.

If you haven't tried hydroponic gardening, give it a shot. Your plants will thank you for it.

Fairies in the Herb Garden

❧ by Ellen Dugan ❧

Through the flower, I talk to the Infinite . . .

It is the invisible world.

It is that small voice that calls up the fairies.

—George Washington Carver

The wisewomen and cunning men of old believed in them. Every race and culture had their own stories about them. While the spelling of the word fairy may be varied, it's true that their names and titles are also many: faeries, the Fae, the Good People, and the people under the hill. There are the Good Folks, elves, nature spirits, elemental spirits, the little people, brownies, gnomes, sylphs, undines, pixies, sprites, and devas. To believe that the fairies really exist is a personal thing. Over the years I have discovered that the fairies have been the ones to convince me of their presence in the garden, not the other way around.

How to Know?

How do you know when you've encountered the fairies? Well, you'll have to tune into your senses and see what they tell you. There are always signs. A few examples would be: a nearby plant quivers for no reason while you work in the herb garden; you can't shake the sensation that something is walking through your hair, but there really isn't anything there at all; you feel yourself walk through spiderwebs in an open area; and, most importantly, you are absolutely convinced that you are not alone while working with your herbs and flowers.

No matter what size or style of your herb garden there is always a nature spirit that watches over it, revealing him- or herself in an unpredictable way. When you sense a personality in the garden—congratulations, you have fairies.

If you still aren't sure—and it's likely you will be for some time—there are several more official ways to identify fairy activity. You can start by looking for a mushroom ring. Traditionally, these fairy rings can be anywhere from a foot or so to several feet in dimension, and they are thought to be a gateway to the fairy realms. The rings seem to appear overnight and will last for several days before they fade away. According to tradition, by the way, stepping inside the ring will put you in immediate contact with the fairy kingdom.

Flowers blooming out of season is another excellent clue to the presence of fairies. When violets bloom in the fall or a summer rose suddenly breaks out in a rare autumn display of flowers, then you know. Recognize and accept these events as gifts from the fairies.

Flowers with unusual color combinations or petal counts are another tip-off. This spring, I bought a large single foxglove plant to add to my enchanted gardens. A few weeks later the flower stalks started to set with lovely purple blooms, just as advertised. Then, when the next flower stalk began to open up much to my surprise it was pure white. This caused a thorough inspection of the plant. How odd, I thought, it was certainly one plant, not a combination of two. Hmmm . . .

When the third flower stalk opened up a week later, I held my breath and discovered that these blossoms were a soft combination of white and dark purple—and they all came from the same mother plant. How strange and wonderful. Later in the fall as the temperatures began to cool that lone foxglove started blooming again. Sure enough: Again it was white for the first flower stalk and soft purple for the second.

Another hint that the fairies have come to stay is when established plants morph into double blossoms or unusual petal counts. In one special part of my gardens, the tiger lilies bloom with ten to twelve petals instead of the typical five or six. It's important to know that these antique tiger lilies were rescued from the old family farmstead. I dug them up just before the great flood of 1993 hit and left my in-law's farm under twelve feet of water for months. So the magic of these lilies comes from some ancient source and not from a sterile and fairy-unfriendly nursery.

Originally I planted the lilies together in my garden, but after a few years when they expanded I began to thin them out and then transplant them around. The first time I transplanted some lilies, I added a thick row of these plants along the northwest side of my house to fill in a blank spot. As I transplanted them I said a little blessing over the plants and asked the fairies to keep an eye on them, so they would have no problem becoming established in their new home.

I guess they heard me. For the last ten years those "fairy guarded" tiger lilies bloom with double blossoms. When I divided the original bunch of lilies again to spread them around the yard, they retained their petal count. The only ones who "morphed" were the fairy-blessed lilies I planted along the foundation. I have left these double fairy lilies untouched for all these years, out of respect for their special blossoms.

Another hint that the fairies have found their way to your flower and herb gardens is how your garden fares over the winter months. If you have tender herbs and annuals that survive your cold winters and keep getting bigger every year, you should say a little thank-you to the fairies. For surely they are tending your plants even in the coldest and darkest days of winter. Tender herbs like rosemary or thyme that survive cold winters and come back on their own are a wonder in my hardiness zone—especially considering recent hard winters.

A friend of mine who lives in an apartment managed to carve out a little spot for a culinary herb garden. His neighbors love it and it's like a miniature jungle, complete with a Green Man statue to guard over the plants.

This winter when I saw his garden I was shocked. The plants were not only still hanging in there—they were green and thriving. When I jealously demanded to know how these plants stayed alive, he just laughed. I mean, these plants had been through below-zero temperatures, snow, and ice storms, and while they were a little ragged they were still green—in February.

Finally, with a twinkle in his eye he admitted that the fairies and the god of nature, the Green Man, obviously were hard at work. He told me that he and his fiancée had called the fairies in back when the weather started turning.

I guess the Fae were impressed that someone had bothered to plant a garden deep in the city, where no one would suspect it, and was concerned enough about it to ask for their magical blessing. Obviously, as a result the Fae tended the garden well as a reward. Which goes to show that fairy activity is a year-round event, not just for spring and summer. The fairies of autumn and winter are not to be underestimated—they lend beauty, color, and a life force to your herb garden even during the darkest days of the year.

Keeping the Garden Fairies Happy

Keeping the spirits of nature, the elementals, or fairies happy is a simple and enjoyable task. But start with first things first, and care for your gardens and herbs to the best of your abilities. Use your common sense and keep chemical usage to the bare minimum for ornamental herbs. If you can, try your hand at organic gardening for culinary herbs. You'll have more beneficial insects, including pollinators such as bees and butterflies, if you lay off the chemicals. And you'll be protecting the health of old Mother Earth herself. A healthy and natural garden is actually the very best way to encourage the fairies to make their home in your herb garden.

For fun and for additional magical enticement to the Fae and to add an overall sense of enchantment to your herb garden, create a fairy offering plate. You can keep this simple and use a small terra cotta saucer or perhaps you can watch and pick up a small statue of a fairy and add it to your herb garden. I have seen several varieties of inexpensive figurines that feature a fairy holding an upturned flower. This figurine would even be suitable for tucking bird seed in to.

I have a fairy statue in one of my herb gardens that is sitting and holding an open book on her lap. I have often set a rosebud or a colorful leaf on that open book as my way of giving back to the elemental spirits that watch over and help my gardens. Use your imagination and see what you can come up with. If you have any decorative stepping-stones or a birdbath, these could be employed as well as magical enticement.

During the spring months try gathering a small posy of violets, pansies, or miniature daffodils. Tie these together with a small ribbon and set them out on your offering plate. To keep them fresh longer you could slip the stems into a small, water-filled glass.

In the early and middle summer months, look to your blooming ornamental herbs, such as the peony, yarrow, or roses.

A perfect rosebud, peony blossom, or a bright yellow floret of yarrow would be lovely. In the autumn months, set out a colorful leaf or two, or a few blossoms from a bright chrysanthemum. Seasonal berries and rosehips are another option. In the winter, go with a classic evergreen, such as a sprig of pine, holly, and ivy. If you live in a warmer or tropical climate you can use your imagination and work with the flowers and foliage available to you at that time of the year.

You have a variety of other natural offerings available too that will attract fairy folk. Offering a plain cookie or a piece of homemade bread is a traditional gesture of fairy and human friendship. If you don't care for the idea of a special plate or dish for your fairy gifts, then you could consider these options. At night, go to the center of your garden and crumble a cookie or a slice of bread and scatter it in a ring around you. You can also try pouring a small amount of milk or honey in a spot on the garden soil.

No matter what type of offering or gift you leave for the garden fairies, try whispering this little charm as you do so:

Fairies of the herb garden I call you near,

Welcome to my gardens that I hold so dear.

I leave a small gift for you, accept my thanks and love.

May your magic shower my plants, with joy from above.

And know that they will hear you.

Fairy Days and Times

Gardeners tend to be fascinated by the old ways and the old traditions of earth and its magic. Whenever I teach my class at the community college on flower folklore, the whole room perks up when I begin to discuss fairy times and places.

There are traditional days and times to access the fairy realm. In the best-case scenario, you should call on the fairies at an "in between" time—such as at sunrise, noon, sunset, or midnight. These are among the best times you may request their help with your herb garden.

Days that are opportune for fairy assistance would be on any Full Moon, at the Summer and Winter Solstices and the Spring and Autumn Equinoxes, and of course on Beltane Eve (April 30) and Samhain or Halloween (October 31). These last two dates are "in between" times that last for a whole day. On these special days the veil between the worlds is at its thinnest.

Be sure you are polite in your dealings with the fairies at these times, as folklore and legend tell of dire consequences for those who offend the fairies at "in between" times.

Fairy Herbs and Folklore

The following blooming herbs have a great deal of tradition and folklore behind them in fairy magic. Some of these herbs are culinary, and some are strictly ornamental. Several of these herbs—such as the violet, dandelion, and clover—may be lurking unappreciated in your lawn. So look closely. Or you may already be growing a few ornamental varieties in your gardens.

In general, any herb or strongly scented flower will attract the fairies. So make sure you tuck some of those plants into your gardens as well. Peruse the list below and see what plants grab your attention. Maybe you'll want to slip some of these plants into your herbal gardens to add to the enchanting atmosphere— especially for the sake of the fairy folk.

Note: These meanings and associations are based on legend and folklore. Enjoy their magic and history, but remember this is not a medicinal guide by any means.

Angelica: This gorgeous and stately herb encourages inspiration, protection, and healing with the help of the fairies. Sprinkle a bit of dried angelica leaves at the four corners of your property to surround you and your loved ones with protection and love.

Basil: This culinary and fairy herb brings love and devotion. In your garden, basil brings prosperity and happiness.

Betony (lamb's ears): Lamb's ears are a protective plant and a favored herb for children's gardens because of its soft fuzzy and silver leaves.

Catnip: This herb brings energies of knowledge, mystery, and playfulness. Grow a little patch for your kitty; she will adore you. Cats are fairy creatures, so you hit both bases with catnip.

Chamomile: This plant soothes the spirit and can be a magnet for gentle nature spirits. It attracts prosperity and love, and the tiny flowers are enjoyed by flower fairies.

Clover: Traditionally, this is a favorite plant of fairies. It brings good luck and the blessings of "the little people." Holding clover in your hand is thought to gain you "fairy sight" (the ability to see the fairies).

Dandelion: This is the bane of many suburban lawns. However, this bright yellow flower is the favorite of children and the fairies. Some fairy texts suggest plucking a dandelion puffball on the night of the Full Moon. Then you can make an unselfish wish and blow the seeds to the wind. This way the air-element fairies, or sylphs, are sure to answer your request.

Foxglove: Foxglove is a toxic plant and should be kept out of reach of small children. I waited until my children were older before adding this plant to my gardens. Foxglove has many enchanting folk names. The name foxglove is thought to come from a corruption of the term "folks' gloves"—as the fairies, or folks, were thought to use the bell-shaped blossoms for hats and gloves.

Honeysuckle: This is a wonderfully scented plant that encourages love and prosperity. Its scent perks you up and attracts bees, butterflies, and the fairies. Slipping a blooming branch into a vase and bringing it indoors will promote wealth in the home.

Iris: The iris was named after the Greek goddess of the rainbow. A gorgeous fairy plant that is available in all the colors of the rainbow, it brings wisdom, knowledge, and eloquence.

Jasmine: This is a night-blooming fairy vine that encourages the magic of the evening—mystery, love, psychic dreams, and enchantment.

Lavender: Growing lavender in the garden brings good luck and is protective and healing. It is long believed to be a fairy favorite due to its incredible scent.

Marjoram: This fairy herb is incorporated into charms and spells to draw love and fertility. It is also rumored to help keep a married couple happily together.

Meadowsweet: Also known as "bridal wort," this sweetly scented fairy flower was used as a strewing herb and was popular in bridal bouquets. Its uses include love, joy, a beautiful wedding day, and a happy marriage.

Mint: Mint attracts money and health. Grow mint in containers to help keep its size under control. The fairies seem to have blessed mint with aggressive qualities.

Pansy: The sweet sunny faces of pansies are popular with fairies. The pansy can be incorporated into charms for healing, bringing about a sunny disposition, mending a broken heart after a breakup, or calming feuding friends.

Peony: The peony is considered an herb. Surprise! This gorgeous shrub produces amazingly fragrant flowers in the spring. A popular fairy plant, tuck a peony blossom or two in a vase and set it in the bedroom to ward off bad dreams. Wearing a peony blossom on your blouse or in your hair protects you from bad luck and negativity.

Rose: The rose is an herbal symbol for love and devotion. A popular fairy flower, roses are magical no matter what color they are. But in regard to attracting fairies, the stronger the scent of the rose the more attention the garden will receive. Use rose petals in charm bags or herbal spells to help "speed things up."

Rosemary: Rosemary is for remembrance. This piney-scented edible herb is sacred to the fairies and elves and is a wonderful plant to add to any herb garden. Its texture, form, beauty, and scent are magical. An old name for rosemary was "elf-leaf."

Sage: Sage, as you would expect, brings wisdom. It is also another culinary herb that will winter over nicely in your garden. Clip back the blossoms to help the plant produce more leaves. It is a fairy herb of cleansing and protection.

St. John's wort: This protective herb blooms once a year, typically right around June 20—just in time for the Summer Solstice or Midsummer. It is also known as the "leaf of the blessed." Keeping this herb in your garden will protect you from fairy trickery. Carrying a few stems of the foliage was an old way to avoid being "fairy-led," or lost and confused while wandering through the local enchanted forest.

Thyme: This culinary herb is wonderful to grow in your garden as it attracts the fairies and encourages health, love, and courage. According to legend, any place where thyme grows wild is a spot that has been blessed by the fairies.

Valerian: This is a gorgeous plant with ferny foliage that is topped off by tall, scented flowers in summer. The flowers are used in charm bags or tucked under the pillow to aid in a restful night's sleep. Valerian encourages love, protection, and sleep.

Violet: This is traditionally the fairy flower. Violets guard against Fae mischief and are a sweet and protective little blossom. Transplanting violets around your home is a clever and inexpensive way to use a bit of fairy magic to protect your home, property, and family.

Yarrow: This is an all-purpose, wisewoman's herb. Once upon a time, fairies were thought to whisper healing charms and recipes to the wise folks. Save a spot in your sunny gardens for blooming yarrow. The blossoms are easy to dry, maintain their color well, and may be used for all sorts of positive spells and enchantments.

Closing Thoughts

The fairies of the herb garden will make their presence known to you in subtle ways. If you truly wish to work with the nature spirits, then the most important thing you'll need is an open mind and a loving heart. By working together with this elemental energy in the creation and care of an herb garden, you will assist all of the plants that grow there.

Remember you are more than just an herb gardener. You are a caretaker and a steward of the land. Pass down this folklore and any plant tips you know to new gardeners and to the children in your life.

Open your mind up to the possibilities of the nature spirits and fairies. Then you can reap the benefits in your herb garden and in your life.

For Further Study

Andrews, Ted. *Enchantment of the Faerie Realm.* St. Paul, Minn.: Llewellyn Publications, 2000.

Cunningham, Scott. *Cunningham's Encyclopedia of Magical Herbs.* St. Paul, Minn.: Llewellyn Publications, 1996.

Dugan, Ellen. *Garden Witchery: Magick from the Ground Up.* St. Paul, Minn.: Llewellyn Publications, 2003.

Knight, Sirona. *Faery Magick: Spells, Potions, and Lore from the Earth Spirits.* Franklin Lakes, N.J.: New Page Books, 2003.

Traditional English Gardens

❧ by Chandra Moira Beal ❧

The English are well known for their passionate affair with gardening. From the friendly cottage garden overflowing with a medley of colorful flowers, herbs, and vines, to expansive royal estates surrounded by trim hedges and linear pathways, the English have made gardening their own art form.

The development of the English garden follows the history of Britain itself: from the simple, functional monastic gardens of medieval times, to the pageantry of the Tudor period, from the elaborate elements of the Baroque and the broad landscapes of the Georgian era, to utilitarian vegetable gardens during the world wars and the common suburban garden now.

Flowers played little or no part in the earliest gardens, which were heavily influenced by the formal gardens of Europe. Indeed, Henry VIII modeled the gardens at Hampton Court on the gardens of the French king. With its square lawns, heraldic beasts on poles, and wondrous topiary, this was Britain's prototype garden on a grand scale. The British remained obsessed by European garden design, and they widely emulate the vast rectangular ponds, spectacular fountains, and elaborate parterres (ornamental gardens with paths and beds arranged in a pattern) of France.

Everything changed dramatically in the mid-eighteenth century with the arrival of Lancelot Brown, who was nicknamed "Capability" Brown because of his talent for enhancing the "capabilities of nature." Brown swept away the geometric formality of gardens modeled on Versailles and grassed over huge areas to create natural-looking landscapes with majestic lakes, vistas, and carefully placed clumps of trees. By this time, gardening had become an aristocratic obsession. Whole villages were flattened if they spoiled the view from the house, and classical temples and other symbolic features were placed at strategic points.

By the end of the nineteenth century, quantities of new plants imported from abroad—especially from America and Southeast Asia—were having a widespread impact. This era also saw the brilliant partnership of architect Edwin Lutyens and botanist Gertrude Jekyll, who advocated a new appreciation of plant forms and colors contained within a strong architectural framework.

Britain's focus has turned to conservation in the new millennium. England's Millennium Seed Bank sets out to safeguard the seeds of 24,000 plants worldwide against extinction. Modern Britain has also seen the addition of two stunning new botanical gardens dedicated to preserving plants from around the globe: the Eden Project and the National Botanic Garden of Wales, which includes the largest single-span glasshouse in the world.

An English garden can be easily emulated at home in North America with a little planning and forethought about the design and the plants you want to incorporate. Whether you prefer the rambling look of the cottage garden or the formality of a stately landscape, the sky's the limit on what you can do.

Before You Begin

Before you break ground, measure your available space and make a drawing of it on graph paper to create a working design. Whether you decide to go with a friendly cottage garden style or plan a more formal design, combine perennial and annual herbs with flowers and small shrubs for year-round color and foliage.

If you incorporate herbs into your design, plant varieties that reflect your tastes and that you will actually use. Plant herbs in an area of the garden where they'll get at least half a day of sunlight. Plan your planting in sections that follow the garden's basic shape. Space perennials around a cottage bed like the hours on a clock, but put them at the center or rear of each section in a formal design. Fill spaces between perennials and border shrubbery with annual herbs and flowers. Give the garden a focal point, such as a sundial, bird feeding station, wire obelisk, tall sculpture, or trellis at the center, so that even when plants die back there will be visual interest in the garden.

To create cottage garden ambiance, plan for herbs to overflow their borders and mingle with flowers. Place a few potted herbs in the garden bed to control fast growers like mint. Use any shape (circles and ellipses are popular) for a cottage style bed, and define it with a path that circles and bisects the bed for easy maintenance. Incorporating paths is essential in an English garden, both for style and easy access to the plants. Use paving stones, flagstones, or gravel to define your walkways. Make the paths wide enough to get a wheelbarrow through, and add as many paths as necessary to reach into the bed comfortably for picking and grooming.

Consider a more formal garden style to make the most of small spaces or to complement classical architecture. Sketch a rectangle, square, or perfect circle in quadrants to be bordered entirely by small shrubs and crossed by paths to separate it into equal planting areas. Remember that classic knot garden designs require nearly constant pruning; factor in their maintenance before designing your dream garden.

Not all plants that thrive in the damp and cool climate of Great Britain will do well in North America. Get information about specific plant varieties for your area from your county agricultural agent and local nurseries so you can design for their size and habits.

Medieval Gardens

After the fall of the Roman Empire, the philosophies of Islamic culture spread westward, encouraging learning, gardening, craftsmanship, and the arts. The gardens of Persia were considered representations of heavenly paradise, and Greek and Roman botanical works were translated into Arabic, updating and expanding upon the horticultural wisdom of the ancient Christian and classical world.

Through the Arab conquests of the Mediterranean and Spain, Arabic horticultural influences found their way into Western Europe. Moorish Spain in particular became a center of horticultural expertise. Botanical gardens were established as early as during the tenth century, and Alphonso X of Castile (1252–1284) had Arabic horticultural works translated. Meanwhile, his sister Eleanor, who was a keen gardener, married Edward I of England and imported gardeners from Spain to recreate the gardens of her homeland.

Christianity also played a part in medieval gardening. Religious orders were important landowners and were known for creating gardens for culinary and healing purposes. Herbs were usually grown as part of the infirmary garden. Cloister gardens were often found in monasteries. A direct descendent of the Roman courtyard, where a colonnaded walkway surrounded an area of rectangular lawn, cloisters were used by monks and nuns for walking, reading, and as places of quiet contemplation. The symbolism of plants was important in medieval times. Everything in the garden was a reflection of God, and many plants symbolized Christian ideals or stories in the Bible.

Medieval Garden Design Elements

Flowery Mead

"Mead" here refers not to the fermented honey drink, but to a colorful meadow. Create a formal lawn divided into quarters with pathways. Plant the grassy squares with ornamental flowers and bulbs to create an "enameled mead" or "jewelled lawn." Use brightly colored species such as tulips, crocuses, lilies, dianthus, and viola. Unlike a wild meadow, plunge the plants in the grass and remove them at the end of the summer to make way for a display of autumn-flowering bulbs.

Scented Arbor

An arbor is a lovely place to sit in the shade and enjoy the garden or to use as a rendezvous for a romantic tryst. Build an arched wooden or metal trellis to frame a bench, and plant it with scented climbing roses, honeysuckle, and jasmine.

Turf Seats

A place for quiet contemplation, these grass-covered benches can be planted with scented herbs, such as chamomile, creeping thyme, or mint, that release their scent as you sit on them.

Topiary

Evergreen shrubs can be clipped into simple shapes and used as hedges or to frame entrances. Plant conical-shaped trees to outline a geometric pattern. Also use evergreen shrubs or germander along paths and borders to create a low-growing hedge.

Pebble Pathways

In the gardens of the Alhambra in Spain, the pathways featured geometric patterns created with black and white pebbles. The patterns can be shaped in chevron, square, or diamond patterns—it's up to you.

Fountains

"De Vegetabilis et Plantis," a medieval guide to gardening published in 1260, reads: "If possible, a clean fountain of water in a stone basin should be in the midst." Create a formal pond, preferably circular or square, with a carved stone edge and a single simple fountain.

What to Plant in a Medieval Garden

Roses: White roses were associated with the Virgin Mary, but red ones were linked with the blood of Christ or the Christian martyrs. Several native roses available in medieval times included *Rosa gallica* (the apothecary's rose) and *Rosa alba* (the white rose of York).

Lilies: A symbol of purity associated with the annunciation.

Carnations, dianthus: Introduced from Spain in the 1470s, carnations are said to represent the incarnation.

Columbine: The shape of the flower was seen as a visual representation of the Holy Spirit.

Snowdrops, galanthus: These are also known as "Mary's tapers," because the flowering period of early February is traditionally the time of the religious holiday of Imbolc.

Iris: The royal blue coloring was the traditional color associated with the Virgin Mary.

Violets, viola: Represented the humility of the Virgin.

Lily of the valley: The flowers were often called "Our Lady's Tears," because they flower in May, the month associated with the Virgin Mary.

Tudor Gardens

During the Tudor period, gardens became more about pleasure rather than simply being utilitarian vegetable or herb gardens. Royal gardens were used for exercise, sport, and entertainment. They showed off the riches of the landowner and included tennis courts and bowling greens.

Owning land was a status symbol. Sumptuous gardens boasting heraldic beasts and sundials were designed to compete with the gardens of French royalty. The deer park became the living larder and hunting reserve of the Tudor monarchs and leading landowners, many of whom gained new territory following Henry VIII's dissolution of the monasteries.

Recreational buildings within parks became popular, and the design of large houses and parks became more integrated. Features such as banqueting houses and mounts were designed to look out into the park. A view became a thing to be admired.

Brightly colored heraldic "beastes" were distinctively English and peculiar to royal gardens. Richard II adopted the white hart as his emblem, and Henry VII devised the "Tudor Rose," which combined the red rose of Lancaster and the white rose of York to symbolize unity.

Gardens were laid out in symmetrical geometric designs close to the main house. Knot gardens were highly fashionable. New orchards were established to meet the fashionable demand for fruit. Plants were still enjoyed for their beauty and usefulness, just as in medieval times, but their symbolism often related to the virtues of the virgin queen, Elizabeth I, rather than the Virgin Mary.

The most popular plants were roses, lilies, violets, cowslips, marigolds, and primroses.

When Queen Elizabeth I announced her intention to visit the Earl of Leicester, a new garden spanning over an acre was constructed immediately. It included bowers (shady, leafy recesses), scented flowers, and orchards filled with apples, pears, and ripe cherries.

Tudor Garden Design Elements

Knot Garden

Create a square or rectangular pattern with one or more different types of evergreen shrubs. Interlace the lines so they seem to weave in and out of each other. In Tudor times, beds enclosed by these patterns sometimes contained flowers, but often they were grassed or filled with colored sand and gravel to enhance the complexity of the design. Knot-masters were highly regarded craftsmen, and the trend was to have a garden with "knotts so enknotted, it cannot be exprest."

Quincunx

This is a formal garden layout that is divided into quarters with gravel pathways, a fountain in the middle, and knot garden features in the beds.

Heraldic Emblems

Gilded greyhounds, lions, leopards, dragons, and antelopes were brightly painted and topped with gold weather vanes or flags. They were traditionally placed on posts painted green and white around the royal gardens—green for eternity, white for purity.

What to Plant in a Tudor Garden

Apples: Try old fruit varieties, such as the apple variety "Deci" or "melio d'Ezio," named after General Ezio who brought it north from Rome when he fought with Attila the Hun in 450 AD.

Pears: The black Worcester pear became the emblem of Worcestershire after it was spotted by Queen Elizabeth I at Whystone Farm in Worcestershire.

Snowdrops, galanthus, nivalis: Snowdrops come from the eastern Mediterranean. Galanthus means "milk flower," and nivalis means "growing near snow."

Baroque Gardens

The civil war in 1642 turned English society on its head. In 1649, the House of Lords was abolished, and many of the nobility went to live abroad. With the Restoration in 1660, Charles II brought the French style of gardening with him from his exile.

Italian renaissance gardens were big influences. However, unlike the Italian landscape of valleys and hills and terraces, the French countryside was flatter and densely wooded. French gardens in the 1600s took over vast landscapes with great avenues stretching into distant woods. They demonstrated power over nature with the clipping of trees, shrubs, and fruit bushes, tall clipped hedges, and the layout of great parterres.

The French also developed the idea of the ornamental canal, which served a practical purpose of draining marshy ground. The French royalty actively encouraged Italian artists to migrate to France where some were employed to work on a variety of French royal gardens.

When William III and Mary II came to the throne in 1689, they brought the Dutch influence with them. The gardens at Hampton Court went through major development during this period, and most of the Tudor garden traditions were swept away in the face of the new fashion. Canals, clipped evergreens, parterres, and orangeries were added to many gardens.

The relationship of people and plants also changed. Plants were regarded as beautiful in their own right and as subjects for botanical observation, which influenced the change to flower gardening. Plant hunting continued, and more species were imported to Britain, including tulips.

Baroque Garden Design Elements

Parterre de Broderie

The low, neat habit of *Buxus sempervirens* (evergreen shrub) is suited to embroider the parterre with tightly clipped scrolls and arabesques that became the hallmark of French baroque patterns.

Avenue of Trees

A long, straight avenue or line of large forest trees across deer parks is a classic formal feature of baroque gardens, indicating human's control over nature.

While few of us have deer parks, in a larger garden an avenue can be used to accentuate length and mark out an area for walking or for vehicles. On a smaller scale, an avenue of small trees could be used along a pathway leading to a focal point, such as a statue.

Fountains

A hydraulic fountain was the ultimate status symbol for a baroque garden. Statuary in the middle of a still pool, such as gods and goddesses or water animals spouting water, will give the baroque effect.

What to Plant in a Baroque Garden

Buxus sempervirens: Use them for low-growing hedges.

Tulips: The "tulip mania" craze reached its peak in 1624 when fanatical collectors were trading in their houses, businesses, ships, and farms for bulbs. The bubble burst in 1637, causing bankruptcy and ultimately the loss of several Dutch colonies.

Sweet peas: Sweet peas arrived in the UK in 1699.

Angelica archangelica: Introduced by the Tradescants in 1617 and recommended as a remedy against the plague.

Morning glory: Arrived in the UK in 1621 from Mexico.

Lobelia: *Lobelia cardinalis* was brought over from North America in 1626.

Agapanthus: *Agapanthus africanus* came from the Cape of Good Hope in 1629.

Georgian Gardens

This era w´ the birth of the landscape movement. From about 1700 onard, visiting gardens became a national pastime, and formal dens were on the way out. Landscapers advocated a return ature, and the grand tour of Europe became a part of every leman's education. After seeing the ruins of ancient Rom Greece, landowners came home to England hoping to crea assic wilderness in their country estates.

second half of the century, Capability Brown came to ce. His design formula was based on the idea that the should run right up to the walls of the house, which ually be set on high ground to enjoy the best view. A belt broken to open up views of the countryside beyond, led the landscape, and further clumps were planted at points to create vistas to soften or emphasize the vast aces. Man-made lakes were linked by ornamental bridges des, and temples backed by trees made focal points on banks or islands.

wn used beech, oak, Scots pine, and sweet chestnut to scenes that took in the changing seasons and the light. edging would surround flowerbeds filled with bright, con-ng bedding plants. These plants, such as geraniums and lia, were tender or half-hardy and varied from year to year season to season. These gaudy displays were an ideal vehicle to display the owner's financial well-being and the gardener's talents. By 1840, the most popular plants for such displays were chrysanthemums, roses, and dahlias. Each of these was going through a rapid evolution via hybridization—in 1839 there were more than 500 cultivars of dahlias alone.

Georgian Garden Design Elements

Framing Views

Using large plants or trees is an attractive way to frame a structure or emphasize the natural landscape, maximizing views from a house. You could create a similar effect on a smaller scale using trellises, pillars, arches, or gazebos.

Ha-Ha

A ha-ha is a hidden ditch that creates a barrier for shee[p] and deer without interrupting the view. Again, it allows th[e coun]tryside to appear to be part of the garden.

Classical Statues

Statues were added to gardens to add a sense of awe and sple[ndor.]

What to Grow in a Georgian Garden

Yew, *Taxus baccata:* Trees and evergreens such as laurel and yew.

Rhododendron: This was an exotic plant species that was imported from the Near East.

Victorian Gardens

During the Victorian era, there was a reawakened desire for a garden designed for ostentation or novelty rather than harmony in the landscape. Increased communication and the invention of the steam engine epitomized the energy of the time. The Victorian period was celebrated for its progress, invention, new ideas, and new discoveries.

As industry and commerce prospered, a wealthy middle class emerged who wished to live near their source of income but apart from the squalor and overcrowding of the city core. Improved transportation and roads meant that villas could be built on the outskirts of town where there was fresh air. This also meant an opportunity to display newfound wealth.

Wealthy Victorians also created many public spaces and parks, encouraging the use of more broad-leaved trees and plants to relieve the gloom of popular evergreens.

By the mid-Victorian period, the industrial revolution was at its height, and Britain's influence in the world approached its apogee. The Great Exhibition of 1851 also demonstrated the country's enthusiasm for new technologies and designs. Joseph Paxton's innovative Crystal Palace was itself inspirational in glasshouse construction, and affordable forms of these types of buildings became popular for growing special exotics.

At the time of the Golden Jubilee in 1887, the British Empire was being celebrated and reflected in late Victorian gardens. They were seen as status symbols, but also as places for family entertainment and healthy pursuits, such as croquet and tennis. Heated conservatories displayed rare exotics and provided venues for social enjoyment. Fantasy-themed gardens were popular, such as the remarkable copy of the Matterhorn in the garden at Friar Park, Henley.

Victorian Garden Design Elements

Artificial Stone

The manufacture of artificial stone during this time enabled many people to add fountains, statues, vases, and rockeries to their gardens. In the 1840s, a new cement was invented that could be poured over rocks to form vast boulders. These were then fashioned into naturalistic rock formations.

Arboretums

Discoveries of impressive trees from abroad prompted people to enhance their properties with an arboretum.

Italian Terraces

An Italian terrace was considered a suitable platform for both a noble and a middle-class house. These terraces were usually balustraded and decorated with urns and vases, grandiose flights of steps, and parterres, and they linked the garden to the house.

Japanese Gardens

Japanese gardens with bridges and teahouses were fashionable.

Woodland Gardens

Woodland gardens were a new innovation and used the new rhododendrons and azalea varieties coming from China.

What to Plant in a Victorian Garden

Auriculas, *Primula auricular*: Brightly colored primulas were collected by many Victorians and aroused great excitement at spring flower shows. Auriculas reached a peak in the late nineteenth century, when lucrative cash prizes led to fierce competition between exhibitors.

Ferns: Ferns became an extremely popular genus of plant to collect. Victorians would keep them in specially designed glasshouses known as ferneries.

Roses: In Victorian times, the fashion was to keep a separate formal rose garden within the boundaries of the main garden. In the early twentieth century, the designer Gertrude Jekyll introduced a relaxed method of using roses in mixed borders and as climbers and ramblers.

Fruit: Exotic fruits, such as figs and dessert grapes, became popular in greenhouses, as well as hardy fruit trees trained to grow in patterns, such as espaliers, cordons, and fans, that would adorn the sides of a walled garden.

Evergreens: Because they were cheaper to maintain than bedding and had good resistance to pollution, many evergreen plants—such as the Portuguese laurel, *Prunus lusitanica*, spotted laurel, and *Aucuba japonica*—became popular in Victorian gardens.

Bedding plants: Bedding plants organized in intricate patterns became fashionable in both private gardens and public parks in the 1830s. Tender flowering plants from South America—such as heliotropes, salvias, lobelias, and cannas—added bright splashes of color to gardens.

Twentieth-Century Gardens

The twentieth century provided a wealth of new approaches to gardening. More plants became commercially available to gardeners, so now there were thousands of plant varieties in Britain, compared to just 250 in medieval times. Labor-saving inventions and new scientific discoveries fueled creative gardening. As a result, horticulturists created new garden designs.

This was an accomplishment, especially after the troubled start to the century. In the aftermath of World War I, with millions of lives lost and Britain in financial tatters, extravagant gardens were now untenable. No one could justify such opulence. Gardens therefore became lower in maintenance.

World War II delivered a second blow to the horticultural world. The labor force, already half of what it had been before World War I, became stressed again. All available land, including the royal parks, was turned over for growing food. After the war, modernist gardens blended the urban public places and housing estate style with the older naturalistic form of gardening and employed concrete planters, abstract layouts, bold architecture, and colorful mixed plantings. Bedding systems were banished, and Brits returned to using native species and local materials to create informal, wild, woodland gardens.

Low maintenance was the new gardening mantra, although many suburbanites of the new middle classes embraced the Gardenesque style in their villas, using ornamental shrubberies and bedding and other exotics with a formal design, so that gardens could be seen as works of art. New import laws enabled live plant transportation. The newly invented gas-powered lawnmower helped create manicured lawns. Overall, the style was eclectic, varying from Chinese to Italianate.

The garden gnome made its debut, as did carpet bedding, rhododendrons, ferns, and alpines. In the kitchen garden, hot beds nurtured exotic pineapples and melons. Japan became a model for inspiration and increased demand for flowering cherries, peonies, and chrysanthemums.

Modern Garden Design Elements

Woodland Gardens

Woodland gardens were popular after the war as they were inexpensive to maintain. After World War I, 200-plus new varieties of rhododendron were introduced, causing a boom in rhododendron breeding that gave us the hybrids known today.

Garden Rooms

Large gardens would be divided up into individual rooms, creating different moods when plants flowered in succession.

Suburban Gardening

As London and other major towns expanded, small private back and front gardens with tended lawns, rose gardens, and cottage garden plants became fashionable in the suburbs.

Materials

Recycled architecture and materials were used, including modern materials such as steel, plastic, and concrete.

What to Plant in a Modern Garden:

Dahlias, chrysanthemums, and asters: These brightly colored plants became popular as gardening spread as a leisure activity. Nurseries now specialized in certain plants, and breeding developed new varieties.

Vegetables: During and after the world wars, vegetable growing became a necessity for many people to supplement meager food rations. Vegetables were grown among ornamental plants in flowerbeds.

Herbal Pot Luck

by Elizabeth Barrette

A container garden offers many advantages over an ordinary full-sized garden. First, there is the matter of size. Not everyone has the space for a large garden. However, you can put a container garden on a patio, balcony, or even a windowsill. You can choose small or large pots; you can fill one or a few or dozens.

Potted plants also enjoy mobility. You can move houseplants outdoors in the summer, tender perennials indoors in the winter. Shift them around to catch more sunlight or more shade; move them to a sheltered place in stormy weather. You can shuffle containers so blooming plants will be front and center, or you can move suitable herbs to your altar for your current needs. You can even rearrange your herbal garden when you get bored.

Consider also the matter of flexibility. Different herbs have contradictory needs. Some require light soil, others heavy. Some form mats of shallow roots and need room to spread in broad containers. Others have taproots that belong in deep, narrow pots. In a container garden, you can give each plant exactly what it needs without harming its neighbors.

Attractive pots of various colors and shapes also help call attention to focal points in your house or yard. You may cluster them to create an indoor jungle in a bay window or add a homey touch to the kitchen. Potted plants can frame a path, statue, or fountain. They soften the edges of patios and balconies, pointing people toward benches or doors. A particularly splendid container, such as a cauldron overflowing with witchy herbs, can become a focal point itself!

Choosing Containers

The choice of plant containers is nearly limitless. Their material and shape may suggest possible uses or plants. Combine different sizes and styles for variety, or repeat just one for a more formal effect. You can even find or make containers with distinctive magical or Pagan motifs, such as cauldrons or Green Man urns. Below are some common options.

Barrels and tubs made of wood create a rustic mood. They can be filled with soil or water, but last longer with a plastic liner. Their large size makes them suitable for herbs requiring lots of room.

Bathroom fixtures, such as sinks, bathtubs, and toilets add a touch of whimsy to the garden. Seal the drain to make an ideal container for herbs that need constant moisture, such as cattail or marsh mallow.

Boots and shoes are a rustic tradition, usually planted with houseleek. They also work for strawberries, thyme, and other small creeping herbs. And you can reuse your footwear instead of sending it to the landfill.

Ceramic pots come in all shapes and sizes, making them suitable for every herb. Colored glazes reduce water loss from evaporation. Watch for magical or mythical imagery. Move them inside before frost or they may fracture.

Concrete urns and troughs are large and durable and lend a stately solidity to the garden. Put a wheeled tray underneath if you expect to move them. Fill them with plants that need lots of room.

Fiberglass mimics the appearance of concrete, ceramic, or wood but is much cheaper and lighter. It's also less durable. Use where less weight is a necessity.

Glass has limited but spectacular uses. A clear terrarium indoors allows you to grow tropical herbs. You can also fill colored bottles with water and use them to root cuttings.

Hanging baskets may be plastic, wood, or wire, lined with sphagnum moss. They require lots of watering and shelter from wind. Fill them with low plants like creeping thyme or prostrate rosemary.

Metal containers are heavy but dramatic. They are fairly durable, although iron rust can cause problems. Copper and brass stabilize with a patina.

Plastic is cheap and versatile, available in all colors and sizes, and suitable for any herb. It's also fragile and doesn't last long, though.

Stone stands second to none for stability. Although it is heavy and expensive, it lasts forever. Use it to anchor your design or enhance earth energy. Many Mediterranean herbs intensify their flavor when grown in a rock garden.

Terra-cotta is a kind of unglazed ceramic. Left plain, it has an earthy and natural appearance. Its porous walls allow air circulation and excellent drainage. Use for herbs that don't like wet feet.

Tree stump and **log** gardens make use of otherwise unsightly features. Rotten wood is rich in nutrients and holds water well. Fill with woodland herbs like angelica, lady's mantle, or sweet woodruff.

Urns and **other upright containers** provide space for taproots. Here you can grow bay laurel or comfrey. Be sure to support them so they won't tip over.

Window boxes are convenient for kitchen use or in small homes. Their wide, shallow shape makes them good for sprawling herbs such as prostrate rosemary, or for those that tolerate pruning, like English thyme.

Decorating Containers

Although containers come in many colorful options, you don't have to settle for what you can find at the store. You can buy plain ones and decorate them according to your own tastes. This way, you can give your herb garden a specific magical or spiritual theme.

Bamboo makes an excellent decorative covering for pots. Its natural tan color blends into rustic settings. It is especially appropriate for Eastern-style gardens. Bamboo also holds dye beautifully. You can find colored bamboo at most craft stores. Cut the canes to match the size of your container and glue them to the sides, completely covering the underlying material. You can use small, straight twigs from trees or bushes in a similar fashion.

Baskets provide a quick cover for other containers. Most baskets are made of wood or rattan, but some are metal.

Decoupage is the art of covering rigid objects with pieces of glass or other materials, using a special adhesive to attach the pieces and fill the cracks between them. Use appropriately colored glass, mirror shards, or found objects, such as buttons, to cover a plain container. You can add runes, zodiac signs, or other magical emblems to the patterns.

Paint is the most versatile choice for decorating containers. Terra-cotta and concrete take paint especially well. You can buy outdoor paints and clear sealants designed for garden use. Paint your favorite deity, totem, or elemental sign on your pots. You can even apply paint to leaves and press them against the container to leave a lacy imprint.

Seashells are a traditional decoration for potted plants. Small shells may be applied in the decoupage style. Medium ones make lovely accents. Glue a few to the sides of the pot, or place a row of them around the upper rim. Enormous specimens, such as conch shells, can be used as pots themselves.

Potting Media and Fertilizers

Containers require special filling, not just ordinary garden soil. You can buy ready-made potting mix in a variety of compositions to suit the needs of different plants. Alternatively, you can mix your own, using ingredients purchased at a garden store.

Potting mix needs a balanced texture that will not clump or crust over, holding some water without getting soggy. Vermiculite is a porous material made from expanded mica. It allows airflow and retains water. Perlite is lightweight, crushed rock that doesn't absorb water but creates air pockets. Sand aids aeration, drainage, and weight, which is useful in keeping tall containers from tipping over. Especially useful are polymer crystals, or hydrogels, which absorb many times their weight in water and release it slowly.

Organic materials add body and nutrients to the mix. Peat moss is very light, and excellent for both aeration and water management. Sawdust is heavier and holds more water. Bark chips absorb little water but create air pockets. Compost is rarely used in potting media because it can introduce pests or diseases.

Mulch makes a container garden look tidier, keeps potting mixes from blowing away, retards weeds, and reduces water loss from evaporation. Apply one to two inches of mulch depending on the size of the pot, and keep it a little away from the plant's stem. Sphagnum moss can work as a mulch but may blow away in windy areas. Bark is excellent, stays put, and breaks down gradually over time, and it gives a rustic character. Gravel looks a bit more formal and does not break down. Marbles come in bright colors and are especially eye-catching in a sunny garden.

Another important unique feature of container gardens is that potted plants require fertilization. They cannot draw on a large body of soil for nutrients, so you must add the proper amount. The three main elements are nitrogen, phosphorus, and potassium—listed in that order on the fertilizer label. Fertilizer comes in various forms. You can buy potting mix with fertilizer already added, in which case you needn't worry about adding more for some weeks. Time-release granules or pellets are ideal for container gardens because they feed slowly over a long period. Insertable sticks are tidy, but concentrate the nutrients in one part of the pot. Water-soluble fertilizer is convenient, but leaches out in the rain. Unless it is designed for foliage feeding, you must be careful not to splash it on the plants themselves, because it can burn their leaves.

Suitable Herbs

Most herbs grow well in pots, making them ideal plants for a container garden. Also, those herbs useful for magical, spiritual, or medicinal purposes come from all around the world, so their differing needs are often easier to meet with them in separate containers. Pots also keep the more vigorous species from inundating the tender ones. Some herbs especially good for container gardening are listed below.

The type of container should be chosen based on the size and habit of the intended plant, or you can decide on a container and look for suitable herbs to fill it. The following herbs grow well in small pots: basil, chamomile, chives, marjoram, summer savory, English or lemon thyme, sweet woodruff.

For medium pots, consider: artemesia, calendula, catnip, dill, horehound, lady's mantle, lavender, lemon balm, mugwort, parsley, rue, stevia, tarragon, yarrow, and winter savory.

These herbs need large pots: angelica, bay laurel, comfrey, lemon verbena, mother of thyme, rose, sage, and sunflower.

Plants well suited to hanging baskets include: creeping pennyroyal, creeping thyme, mint, oregano, prostrate rosemary, and prostrate sage.

Angelica, with its lush leaves and towering growth, creates a tropical mood and is especially dramatic when grown in a large urn. It loves moisture. Use to repel evil.

Artemesia balances the garden with its delicate, silvery foliage. Sacred to all lunar deities, it makes a nice altar offering. Dry it to repel moths.

Basil comes in many forms, some with vivid purple leaves. Grow for fragrance or color. It is an essential cooking herb, too. Magically, basil attracts money and love.

Bay laurel is a large bush or small tree and is sacred to Apollo. Dry the leaves for cooking. It aids digestion.

Calendula produces cheery yellow or orange flowers that are used by Hindus to decorate altars. Dry the petals to add color to potpourri or to foods like rice or soup.

Catnip entices cats, but also makes a good offering for feline deities. Its soft leaves release a musky scent and make a tea high in vitamin C. Pots keep the plant from roaming.

Chamomile has two main varieties: German and Roman. The German is preferred in herbalism. Its tiny yellow and white flowers brighten the garden. Dried, they make a good bedtime tea; also good for stomach complaints.

Chives come in plain or garlic form, the latter with a stronger odor. Chop the fresh leaves for use in soups or salads. This herb also repels evil.

Comfrey, with its downy leaves and drooping blue flowers, creates a woodland mood—especially when in wooden containers. Use the leaves to make a skin salve.

Dill lightens the garden with its airy sprays. This protective herb also strengthens other types of magic. Use the seeds in pickling and cooking.

Horehound is known in Egyptian tradition as the "seed of Horus." It likes dry, alkaline soil. Horehound makes excellent cough syrup and sore throat lozenges.

Lady's mantle is famous for the way its leaves catch silvery drops of dew or rain. This water holds potent magic. It looks at home in log gardens and woodsy settings. The leaves and stems make a tea beneficial to pregnant women.

Lavender purifies and blesses. Dry the flowers for craft projects. Lavender oil soothes insect bites and minor scrapes. In troughs, the plant makes an attractive low hedge.

Lemon balm is sacred to Diana. Its citrus scent relieves depression and attracts pollinating bees. Pots near walkways allow visitors to touch the plant, releasing its fragrance. Use the leaves in potpourri or in a tea to soothe colds.

Lemon verbena is a half-hardy shrub that, with winter protection, can grow rather large. Its dried leaves retain a scent for several years, which is useful in potpourri. For massage oil, combine it with rosemary or lavender.

Marjoram disinfects and preserves. According to legend, Aphrodite created it as a symbol of happiness.

Mint uplifts the spirit. Its many varieties include spearmint and peppermint, as well as exotics like ginger and chocolate mint. Crystallize the leaves for use in tea or decoration. In the garden, keep mint in easy reach for nibbling.

Mugwort appears in protection charms and also enhances psychic powers. In late summer, its cream-colored flowers yield a heavy sweet fragrance. Move the pot forward to enjoy this—otherwise, use mugwort's height as a backdrop.

Oregano is green with striking gold highlights. Its name means "joy of the mountain." It brings happiness and health.

Parsley is not just a garnish, but has been used to decorate tombs. There are curly and flat-leaved varieties. Grow parsley in large containers alongside roses to improve their health and fragrance.

Pennyroyal repels insects, especially fleas. It likes a lot of water, making it good for bog gardens. Choose the creeping form for hanging baskets.

Rose has numerous varieties, but the best for magical use are "old garden" roses. Use flowers in love spells, hips for tea, candied petals as confectionary. Roses may be clipped for a formal look or allowed to ramble over a log garden.

Rosemary enhances memory and symbolizes fidelity. It makes fragrant topiary in formal gardens, especially when grown in urns or troughs. Prostrate rosemary dangles from hanging baskets. Dry the stems for barbecue skewers or incense. Add leaves to meat or potatoes.

Rue is a potent insect repellent and banishing herb. Its bluish leaves add visual interest.

Sage magically conveys longevity and stability. In food, its leaves aid digestion. Choose prostrate sage for hanging baskets. Upright sage comes in green, golden, purple, or variegated types. Its dignity suits classical containers.

Stevia is new to the herbal scene, as a sugar substitute. Dried leaves lend intense sweetness to foods. Use for friendship or love spells. Keep container in easy reach for picking leaves when needed.

Summer savory has a spicy flavor and is good with beans. It's an aphrodisiac and an antiseptic. This tender annual is vulnerable to cold weather. Bring its pot inside in autumn, and you can enjoy its fresh leaves longer.

Sunflower produces seeds for people and birds. The spectacular blooms are sacred to all solar deities. Grow in sturdy containers made of concrete, and provide stem support in windy areas.

Sweet woodruff is essential for May wine and Beltane decorations. It is sacred to forest deities and a perfect groundcover for log gardens. Dried leaves deter insects and freshen potpourri.

Tarragon is the "dragon herb" and can bestow courage and ferocity. When chewed, it sweetens the breath but dulls the sense of taste, which is useful before swallowing bitter medicine. Use sprigs to flavor bottles of vinegar.

Thyme has a rich, musky flavor. It bestows vigor and courage. Woolly thyme or mother of thyme look good in hanging baskets. English thyme makes a fine hedge in a formal garden. Lemon thyme is dramatic with its yellow leaves and potent lemon tang and is good with fish.

Winter savory is a perennial with a peppery flavor and is excellent for salt-free diets. Use it to flavor sausage or salami. The creeping form is ideal for rock gardens.

Yarrow promotes health in plants and people alike. Its leaves speed composting, and its flowers add warm colors to the garden. Dry the stems for I Ching divination.

Magical Themes

Containers can make thematic gardening more flexible and more cohesive. For a fairy garden, you might buy pots that have Little People on them. You can move some plants from one thematic garden to another to adjust for different magical purposes. Here are some possible themes for magical gardens.

Fairy folk: Plant herbs associated with the Little People, such as Corsican mint, elfin thyme, lady's mantle, rose, and yarrow. Log or stump gardens create a woodland sanctuary. For a whimsical touch, use boots or tea tins as containers. Add pinwheels or wind chimes for motion.

Fragrance: Choose herbs with scented flowers or leaves, such as catnip, lavender, lemon balm, mint, rose, rosemary, and scented geranium. Containers should not distract from the odors—terra-cotta, ceramic, and barrels work well. Plants should be within easy reach for touching and sniffing.

Healing: A medicinal garden can include herbs like calendula, catnip, chamomile, comfrey, horehound, lemon balm, mint, and yarrow. Aim for a soothing atmosphere, using smooth rounded containers. Wood, terra-cotta, and gentle shades of green will promote healing.

Kitchen Witch: Collect popular cooking herbs, such as basil, chives, dill, mint, parsley, rosemary, sage, and thyme. Grow them indoors in a window box or just outside your door. Choose pots decorated with homey or kitchen motifs, or consider old bowls or pitchers as containers.

Moon goddess: Honor her with artemesia, lady's mantle, moonflower, rosemary, viola, white rose, and white-flowering thyme. Silvery foliage and white or blue flowers are magical in moonlight. White bathtubs, unpainted concrete, silver-toned metal, and white or blue ceramic add to the effect—especially if decorated with celestial motifs.

Petting zoo: Many herbs, such as catnip, horehound, lady's mantle, lamb's ear, rosemary, and woolly thyme, delight the fingertips. Troughs and urns bring these within easy reach.

Protection: Create a safe space with warding herbs, such as angelica, cactus, houseleek, mugwort, sage, and rue. Troughs or rows of pots create a strong border. Urns or pots decorated with gargoyles make excellent sentries, as do hanging baskets bracketing a door.

Sun god: Honor him with bay laurel, chamomile, chives, lemon thyme, marigold, and sunflower. Iron, brass, wood, and ceramic in shades of red and yellow make excellent containers. It is easy to find pots decorated with solar images. Put this garden in a sunny place.

Go Plant Your Garden

No matter where you live, container gardens offer an opportunity to garden with herbs. You can move the pots around to take advantage of changing weather or personal tastes. Each plant gets exactly what it needs without annoying its neighbors. Best of all, the materials and decorations of the pots themselves add to the magical energy and signature of your garden.

And none of this has to be expensive. Use your ingenuity to make found objects into containers. Recycling is magic too!

Autumn in the Herb Garden

⤞ by James Kambos ⤝

To the herbalist, autumn brings a feeling of achievement and a sense of fulfillment. Thyme spill over garden paths, and the artemesias' silvery foliage illuminates starry autumn nights. Most of the competing brilliant-hued blooms of high summer have faded now, but the textures, colors, and shapes of the foliage stand out and take center stage. The amber glow of autumn mornings, the brilliant blue afternoon skies, and the lingering light of the fall Full Moons all seem to enhance the appearance of the herb garden.

As beautiful as the herb garden can be in autumn, it is also a bittersweet time of year. The amount of daylight dwindles, light autumn frosts begin to blacken the annual flowers, and golden leaves begin to fall. If you garden in a northern region, you must face the fact that it is now time to put your herb garden to bed for the season.

Learn First Before You Act

Before you begin preparing the herb garden for its winter rest, take time to learn about the herbs you grow. Most perennial herbs don't need too much pampering to make it through the rigors of winter. And most trees and shrubs that may be included in the herb border usually also don't require any special protection. However, this is a good time to do any shaping or pruning if needed.

Depending on what herbs you grow and which plant hardiness zone you live in, some herbs could be left alone—at least until hard frost. Naturally, annual herbs, such as dill or basil, should be harvested before any frost. And you must also consider if there are any annual herbs or tender perennial herbs—such as rosemary—that you might want to move indoors for the winter.

Deciding which herbs to winter indoors should take place in August or September before any frost damage can occur. These herbs should be planted in proper containers and given sunny locations indoors where temperatures stay in the 50–70 degree (Fahrenheit) range.

Besides rosemary, other tender herbs that make good houseplants during winter can include, but are not limited to, basil, scented geraniums, pineapple sage, and the tender lavender varieties, such as French and fernleaf lavender.

Tips on Winterizing Your Herb Garden

If you ask five different gardeners how to ready the herb garden for winter, you'll likely get five very different answers—all of which may work. Gardeners tend to have different opinions on subjects, such as cutting back herb plants—if you should and, if so, when to do it. Other subjects, such as mulching and fertilizing, can also bring different responses, depending.

The advice I'll give you here comes from hands-on experience gained while raising herbs these past twenty years. Some of my advice comes from simple trial and error, while other tips come from some of the finest herbalists I know.

Perennials

The question most herb gardeners ask when facing their first autumn and winter seasons is whether or not they should cut back the hardy perennial herbs or leave them standing. There are two theories on this subject. Some gardeners believe if the dead stems are allowed to stand through the winter, the plants will be better protected and have less chance of having their roots exposed during winter's freezing/thawing cycles. In this case, the plants will need to be cut back in the spring and all dead plant material will then need to be cleared out of the border and composted. This method is fine, if your herb garden is small, but if your garden is large, this will require a lot of extra work in the spring—a time when there are many other garden chores.

To ease the burden of spring cleanup in the herb garden, I let most of my nonwoody perennial herbs experience a couple of frosts. After this I begin the process of cutting back the dead growth, leaving two to four inches of stem intact.

This method is good for two reasons: First, it allows the herbs to die back naturally, which gives the plants' nutrients a chance to travel from the foliage to the root system where the life force will be stored for next spring's growth. Secondly, cutting back in the fall will keep the herb garden tidy and lets you see the garden in its "bare bones" form, giving you a chance to envision design ideas for the following year. Even so, I must stress that cutting back your herbs to within a couple of inches from the ground is crucial. This will allow the old stems to catch and hold the snow, which will give extra protection from winter's freezing and thawing cycles.

Since most herbs can be harvested two, perhaps three times a season, this will minimize the amount of growth you'll need to cut back in the fall. By summer's end, however, certain herbs, such as cat mints (*nepeta*), tend to look a bit shaggy. In cases such as this, I usually cut them back severely in August. This will give them time to send out a flush of new growth that may be left in place and allowed to die back naturally after a killing frost.

The new growth will serve as nature's own mulch and will protect the plant until next spring. Other herbs, such as lemon balm and hardy geranium (cranesbill), can also be treated in a similar manner.

Culinary and Other Herbs

Certain culinary herbs, such as thyme, needn't be cut back until spring. In my zone six garden, thyme can frequently be harvested until Christmas. Parsley, usually considered an annual, can normally tough it out well into winter, if planted in a protected spot.

Some herbs, like artemesia, don't reach their peak until late summer. This would include the wormwoods and southern-woods. Their silvery beauty can especially be enjoyed in late autumn; for this reason, I delay cutting them back until spring.

The nonwoody, or herbaceous, perennials—such as betony, mints, monarda, oregano, rue, tansy and yarrow—can be cut back freely, two to four inches from the ground after a killing frost. Woody perennial herbs, lavender for example, should not be cut back at all, as doing so could be fatal to the plant. Lavenders are shrubby and bloom on old wood. In spring you can then shear off any dead growth or remove dead branches.

As I cut back the plants in my herb garden, all plant material is turned into my compost pile so it may return to mother earth. If any plant appears to be diseased, do not compost it. This could spread the disease throughout the garden next spring. Instead, bag the diseased plant and dispose of it in the trash.

Mulching

Depending on the severity of your winter climate you may choose to mulch your herb garden or at least mulch around certain tender plants. The most important rule to remember about mulching is to wait until a couple of hard frosts have occurred, freezing the soil to a depth of one or two inches before applying any mulch.

Mulching too early, before the soil has frozen, can invite a variety of problems. If the ground hasn't frozen, plants may continue to grow beneath the mulch. When the cold does finally freeze the soil, new plant growth could be killed. Mulching before the ground has frozen can also attract mice and other pests that could seek protection beneath the mulch, leading to severe plant damage. Waiting for a good freeze will assure you that the herb plants are dormant, the ground is frozen, and that your plants are ready for their "winter blanket" of mulch.

Note: The purpose of mulch is not to keep the plants warm. Instead, mulch is used to keep the soil frozen, which in turn helps the plants remain dormant during the winter. Also remember—do not remove your fall mulch until spring weather has truly arrived in the following growing season. Removing mulch too early the next year could expose the roots to the drying winds of early spring, which can sometimes be more harmful than cold temperatures. A layer of mulch put down in the fall will also give you the added bonus of inhibiting weed growth as the weather warms in the spring.

You can use any good organic matter as mulching material. This includes compost, peat moss, fine bark mulch, salt hay, shredded leaves, or evergreen branches. You may also use a combination of these.

It's always a fun challenge to attempt growing herbs that aren't considered hardy for your area. If you've planted any of these herbs that are considered tender perennials and may not be completely hardy in your agricultural zone, applying a thicker multilayered covering of mulch can help these misplaced herbs winter over.

For example, if you choose to grow an herb that is intended for a climate milder than yours, you can protect it like this—

place a layer of chopped leaves around the plant's base and, over this, add a layer of evergreen branches. Mulching in this manner adds an extra growing zone of protection to your herb plants that may keep it alive in the cold months.

Autumn Planting in the Herb Garden

In many ways autumn is also an excellent time to plant. Warm days, cool nights, and autumn rains can enable the herb gardener to gain a growing season and get a head start on spring planting. After fall cleanup is under way, you may notice some empty spaces in the herb border. If you wish, plant a few herbs now— such as butterfly flower (*asclepias*), coneflower (*echinacea*), foxglove (*digitalis*), geranium (*cranesbill*), and yarrow (*achillea*). Any crowded or overgrown clumps of herbs can also be successfully lifted, divided, and replanted before autumn frosts occur.

Spring-blooming bulbs may also be added to the herb garden during autumn. Good choices include chionodoxa, crocus, miniature daffodils, and snowdrops. These flower bulbs are good companion plants for herbs. They require little care and, as they're small, it's easy to tuck them here and there, in groups of ten or twelve along the edge of the herb bed.

Bulb plants also add early-season color, brightening the herb garden during the transitional period between winter and spring. Since these bulbs are small and bloom early, their foliage will die back quickly so they won't interfere with garden chores as you begin spring cleanup. And, as your herb plants break dormancy in the spring, their vigorous new growth will fill in any bare spaces left when these early spring flowers begin to fade.

Fertilizing

Autumn is the perfect time to fertilize new and established herb plants. A sprinkling of any good organic fertilizer around the base of the plants, followed by gently working the fertilizer into the soil, is all it takes.

There are several good fertilizers you can use. Rotted dry manure or well-aged material from your own compost pile are fine. Another excellent option is to purchase bags of planting mix made for planting trees and shrubs. These mixes usually contain nothing but organic materials—manure, tree bark, peat moss, and top soil. Read the labels to be sure the contents are 100 percent natural.

Planting mixes are usually sold in forty-pound bags at any good garden or farm supply store. When used as a top dressing, planting mixes can be applied autumn or spring. When fertilizing, keep in mind that some herbs, like oregano and thyme, don't require much fertilizing and may do well in lean soil.

The Herb Gardener's Checklist for Autumn

There is no need to rush getting the herb garden ready for fall and winter. The process can easily take two to three months. What follows is a list of chores that can gradually be accomplished any time from late summer to late autumn.

Not all of these tasks may apply to your situation; this is just a guideline. Working in the herb garden at this time of year will help you enjoy the crisp autumn weather. You may even find that getting the herb garden ready for its season of rest can be quite pleasurable.

Late Summer and Early Autumn

Harvest all annual herbs for culinary use and preserve them according to your favorite methods.

Harvest and begin drying herbs you wish to use for decorative purposes.

Decide which herbs you wish to winter indoors. Pot them and begin to get them acclimated to their winter home.

Deadhead all herbs that tend to become weedy, to prevent reseeding.

Take photographs of your herb garden from all angles. This will help you decide what you'd like to do next year or if you want to make any changes. As winter passes, it's easy to forget just how big the lavender grew or how far that thyme plant spread.

Make this the year you begin an herb gardener's journal. You may simply use a plain notebook or purchase an attractive blank gardener's journal sold at bookstores. In your journal make notes concerning any plant or color combinations you especially enjoyed. Place garden photos in your journal also. And don't forget to record any failures too, as these should be used as learning experiences.

Lift and divide any overgrown plants. This way you'll gain a growing season. Do this early, so plants develop a root system before the first frost.

Remove any diseased plants and place them in the trash; don't compost them.

Mid-Autumn

Begin cutting back nonwoody herbs after frosts have occurred.

Begin raking leaves out of herb beds.

Begin fertilizing with any good organic matter.

Plant spring-blooming bulbs.

Prepare new planting areas for next year and keep them weeded.

Continue cutting and drying herbs for decorative use.

Remove annual herbs that have been killed by frost.

Set out bird feeders; the birds these will draw add activity and interest to the herb garden during this quiet time of the year.

Late Autumn

Drain hoses and put them away.

Remove fragile garden ornaments; clean and store gazing balls, statuary, flowerpots, and the like.

Do a final weeding—you'll thank yourself come spring.

Apply mulch, if the ground has frozen.

Add notes to your gardener's journal; highlight ideas you have for next year.

Place markers in the garden near herbs that break dormancy late, so you don't accidentally remove them early next spring.

Clean potting shed; oil tools to prevent rust.

From now through winter, weather permitting, walk around your herb garden and check for potential problems. If you see a plant heaved above the soil, tap it back into the ground with your foot, and add extra mulch.

Hang up your hoe and take a bow; you and your herb garden deserve a rest!

Into Winter

As I write this it is a brilliant late August afternoon. The spring and summer bustle in the herb garden is over. From my patio, I can see the signs that the wheel of the year is about to make its final turn. The dogwood tree that shades my north herb bed is covered with scarlet berries. In the center of the border, my statue of Pan, the ancient Greek nature god, is almost concealed by the gold oregano that I divided just last year. It is not autumn yet, but there is the feeling of autumn. And I am ready.

In many ways the herb garden grows best in autumn—on paper and in our minds. The gardening books and magazines I've accumulated over the summer, but haven't had a chance to read yet, are stacked by my favorite chair near the woodstove. Basil and dill hang in bunches, perfuming the kitchen with their scents.

Soon enough, the herb garden, as seen from the small-paned window in my den, will glow with autumn colors of amber and gold. In another month, frosts will sear the garden with coppery tones, revealing the simple but beautiful contours of the herb border. The hummingbirds will leave, and the monarch butterflies prepare for their long flights south. The silence comes.

Above all in autumn I will take pleasure in the most precious gifts the season brings to the herb gardener—a time to dream, and a time to nurture ideas for next year.

Culinary
Herbs

Sage:
The Wise Herb

❧ by Magenta Griffith ❧

S age, a shrubby perennial herb of the mint family, is native to the Mediterranean region. Sage can be grown in most climates or anywhere in a pot on a windowsill, and it is now found all over the world. The plants grow to a height of about two feet and generally do not bloom until the second season.

Sage grows well in many parts of the United States and is grown to a limited extent for commercial markets as well. Sage leaves are silver- or gray-green with a fuzzy texture, but there are newer varieties that come in different colors. They have a slightly bitter flavor and a distinctive aroma.

The botanical name for sage is *Salvia officinalis*.

Culinary sage is related to various ornamental salvia varieties, such as

scarlet sage, *Salvia splendens*. There are hundreds of species of salvia, but only a handful are used in cooking. Most varieties are ornamental. Culinary varieties include golden garden sage (*Salvia officinalis icterina*), which has green and gold irregularly variegated leaves. Purple garden sage (*Salvia officinalis purpurea*) has dark-purple new leaves that turn a soft green with age. Tricolor sage (*Salvia officinalis tricolor*) is cream, green, and pink. Dwarf garden sage (*Salvia officinalis minum*) grows well in a container. All of these have basically the same flavor as garden sage. The golden and the tricolor sages can be less winter-hardy than the common garden sage.

A sweeter variety, pineapple sage (*Salvia elegans*, also called honey melon sage), has a more delicate flavor and can't stand up to long cooking at high temperatures. Add to salads or to cutup fruit to serve as an appetizer. Pineapple sage has oils that are released at very low temperatures, and it will lose its flavor if cooked for a long time or at sustained high temperatures.

By the way, prairie sage, used by Native Americans as a purifying smudge, is a different species of plant, *artemisia ludoviciana*. The smell is very similar to European sage, so early settlers assumed it was a related plant. It is actually more closely related to wormwood (*Artemisia absinthium*), mugwort (*Artemisia vulgaris*), and tarragon (*Artemisia dracunculus*). Prairie sage is not suitable for cooking, as its flavor is bitter.

Growing Sage

Sage can be grown from seeds, stem cuttings, or by dividing an existing plant. Sow the seed indoors six to eight weeks before the last spring frost, and transplant the young plants when they are two to three inches high. Sage starts from seed fairly easily; however, plants grown from seed are generally of mixed types. For this reason, cuttings made from desirable plants are often preferred. Sage needs to receive at least six hours of sunlight each day to develop its full flavor.

Sage needs well-drained soil to discourage slugs and rot. If your soil drains poorly, add organic materials like compost. Mulching can also help the soil. The mulch should be about three inches deep and pulled slightly away from the stem of the plant. Sage can attract both spider mites and aphids. Usually, beneficial insects will counteract the problem, although it is unfortunate that first the pesky bug must establish itself for the helpful bug to arrive.

Spraying with water should be the first method of insect control. Hose off the plants several times each week. If you need stronger measures, use a horticultural soap and follow directions on the label precisely. Encourage good air circulation to prevent mildew and heat problems. If your soil is healthy, you probably won't need to worry about how acid or alkaline it is. If your soil is very acidic, a little lime will help sage grow well.

A few plants set in a corner of the garden or in a perennial flower or herb bed will furnish sufficient leaves for ordinary family use. Six to eight inches of the top growth can be cut from the plant about twice during the season. Never cut further down the stem than where there are leaves. Harvest before late fall since late harvesting can cause the plant to die over the winter.

Using Sage

For drying large amounts of sage leaves, cut the flowers before they bloom, and wait until the plants have grown back. Otherwise, the leaves could be harvested before the plant blooms. If possible, wash the plants in the garden with a fine spray of water the night before. Cut in the morning, as soon as the dew has dried. You can pick the individual leaves and spread them on screens to dry in a well-ventilated room away from direct sunlight.

When they are completely dry, pack them in an airtight container. If you cut whole stems, cut them as long as possible without cutting into old wood. Hang these in bunches of three or four in a dark, dry area. As soon as they are dry and crisp, strip the leaves whole, if possible, and seal them in an airtight container. The flavor should remain potent for three or four months.

Freshly picked sage can be woven into wreaths. Once dried, these can be hung in a room to keep the air fresh and smelling sweet. The individual leaves can be plucked off and used, as long as you keep the wreath clean and away from contamination. If you hang a sage wreath too near a stove, cooking grease can condense on it.

Sage is sold as fresh sprigs or dried leaves. Store fresh sage in the refrigerator, wrapped in paper towels and enclosed in a plastic bag. Fresh sage leaves should be aromatic, with no soft spots or dry edges. Wrap the leaves in paper towels and store them in a plastic bag in the refrigerator. Use them within five days. Fresh leaves may also be covered in olive oil and stored in the refrigerator up to two months. Use the flavored oil for sautéing or in salad dressing. To freeze fresh sage leaves, wash and dry them, removing leaves from the stems. Pack them loosely in freezer bags. These will keep for up to one year. Freezing will intensify the flavor of the herb so adjust recipes accordingly.

Dried sage can be found with other seasonings in most supermarkets. As with all dried herbs, store closed containers in a cool, dry place away from light. It will keep for up to one year.

Dried sage is preferred by most cooks and comes in whole leaf, rubbed, and ground form. Rubbed sage has a light, velvety texture; ground sage is a powder. Crush dried sage leaves in the palm of the hand to release their flavor. Use ground sage sparingly, as foods absorb its flavor more quickly than leaf sage. Chopped leaves can be used to flavor salads, pickles, and cheese. It is one of the most popular herbs in the United States.

The country that most often uses sage is Italy, where the most common use is to flavor meat and poultry dishes. Veal, which is sometimes thought bland, can profit a lot from this herb. Saltimbocca alla Romana is probably the most famous sage dish. Very thin veal steaks are fried together with raw salt-cured ham (prociutto crudo) and fresh sage leaves and then deglazed with red or white wine.

Sage leaves fried in butter until the butter turns brown make an easy and interesting, but not exactly light, sauce to be eaten with Italian pasta or gnocchi, a form of tiny dumpling.

Sage is a very powerful flavor and tends to dominate. Its slightly bitter taste is complex and strong and not appreciated by everyone. Use sage cautiously, as it can easily overpower other flavors. Because of its strong taste, sage does not combine well with weakly aromatic or delicate herbs. Sage is the primary herb in poultry seasoning. It is sometimes combined with other strong flavors, such as garlic and green pepper, for seasoning barbecued or fried meat.

Besides the traditional use in stuffing, sage is good with pork, sausage, other meats, and cheese. It is often combined with thyme and used with beans and in soups. Use sage with fruit in vinegars. The bluish-purple flowers of garden sage make an attractive garnish in salads, butters, and soft cheeses. You can also freeze sage leaves in ice cubes for an attractive garnish to add to fruit drinks.

Hamburgers can be seasoned with a blend of freshly chopped or dried sage, mint, rosemary, oregano, and basil. Sage can be used to flavor pâté, eggs, pasta, sauces, soups, beef stews, and vegetables. It holds up well for long cooking, such as a turkey or a soup. It adds depth to the flavor.

When you add fresh sage to dishes, such as soup or beans, you can put in a whole sage branch, then remove it when the dish has finished cooking. The leaves cook off; you can pull the branch out with tongs or a slotted spoon.

Sage is a wonderful flavor enhancer for seafood, vegetables, bread sticks, corn breads, muffins, and other savory breads. Rub sage, cracked pepper, and garlic into pork tenderloin or chops before cooking. Use the leaves sparingly with onion for stuffing pork, ducks, or geese. Crush fresh leaves to blend with cottage or cream cheese. Potatoes can also be boiled with a bit of sage.

Here are a few recipes that use sage.

Sage Stuffing For Turkey

3 Tbls. oil

2 onions, finely chopped

4 stalks celery, finely chopped

1 apple, peeled, cored, and finely chopped

1 tsp. dried thyme

1 Tbl. dried sage

1 tsp. black pepper

1 tsp. salt or celery salt

6 cups cubed dried bread

In a large frying pan, sauté the onions in the oil until transparent. Add the celery and sauté until no longer crisp. Add the apple and herbs, and sauté another minute. Turn off the heat, and add the bread. Mix thoroughly. This should stuff a 15-pound turkey.

Wild Rice Poultry Stuffing

1 cup wild rice, uncooked

2 Tbls. butter

1 large onion, chopped

3–4 stalks celery, finely chopped

½ lb. mushrooms, chopped

1–2 tsps. dried sage

1 tsp. thyme

Salt and pepper to taste

Soak the wild rice in 2 cups of water for 1 hour. Drain, add 2 cups of water, and simmer until done, about 30–45 minutes. In a large frying pan, melt the butter. Add the onions, sauté about 5 minutes, then add celery and mushrooms and sauté another 5 minutes. Drain rice and add to vegetable mixture. This will stuff a 12-pound turkey.

Crock Pot Pork Roast

3–4 lb. pork loin roast

1 onion, cut into eighths

1 apple, peeled, cored, and chopped

4 large potatoes, peeled and cut into quarters

2 carrots, each cut into 2 or 3 large pieces

1 cup cider

1 tsp. dried sage

1 tsp. dried thyme

¼ tsp. pepper

1 tsp. salt

Place pork roast in a Crock Pot. Surround it with onion and apple pieces, then potatoes and carrots. Pour cider in, and add sage, thyme, and pepper. Cook on high setting about 6 hours. Check for doneness; pork should not have any pink in the middle. Serve it on a platter surrounded by potatoes and carrots. You can serve the cooking broth as is, or make gravy from it.

Homemade Breakfast Sausage

1 lb. ground pork

2 tsps. rubbed fresh sage

½ tsp. salt

½ tsp. poultry seasoning

½ tsp. pepper

1 pinch ground allspice

Thoroughly combine all ingredients and shape into 6 patties. Chill at least 1 hour. Fry for 3–4 minutes per side or until the sausage patties are browned and no longer at all pink in the center.

Easy Onion & Herb Focaccia

1   loaf frozen bread dough, thawed

1   Tbl. olive oil

1   Tbl. chopped onion

2   tsps. chopped fresh sage, or 1 tsp. dried sage leaves

2   tsps. chopped fresh rosemary, or ½ tsp. dried rosemary

Heat oven to 425 degrees. Grease a cookie sheet or 12-inch pizza pan. Roll out dough and place it on the pan. Press down dough into a circle moving from center to edge. Brush with oil. Sprinkle with remaining ingredients. Bake 10 to 12 minutes or until golden brown. Serve warm or cool, cut into wedges.

Savory Corn Bread

1   cup cornmeal

1   cup flour

4   tsps. baking powder

¼   tsp. salt

1   tsp. dried sage

1   egg

1   cup milk

1   cup oil

Mix the dry ingredients, then add the egg, milk, and oil, and stir just enough to mix. Bake in a greased 8 x 8 pan for 20–25 minutes at 350° F or until slightly browned on top.

Sage Beauty

Sage has also been used as a beauty aid. Early Greeks drank, applied, or bathed in sage tea. Turkish women said sage was a wonderful hair dye, and it is still recommended today for use in dark hair. Put a handful of the leaves in a cup of cold water, boil it for fifteen minutes; cool, strain, and use the tea as a rinse to darken faded or graying hair.

Sage was a sacred ceremonial herb of the Romans and was associated with immortality or, at least, longevity. It was also said to increase mental capacity. The Greek Theophrastus classified sage as a "coronary Herbe," because it flushed disease from the body, easing any undue strain on the heart. The genus name, *Salvia*, comes from the Latin for "salvation."

Charlemagne had it grown in his royal gardens. There is an old Arabic belief that if your sage grows well you will live a long time. The early Dutch ate a handful of the leaves every day as a snack, a salad, or one course of a meal, because of its nutritive value. During the fourteenth century, three leaves a day were to be eaten to avoid the "evil aire" all day long. As far as medicinal uses, herbalists used sage for just about every complaint there was. Mrs. Leyel, a British herbalist, thought that it was particularly good for the lungs and brain.

In the Middle Ages, people drank sage in tea and used sage to treat colds, fevers, liver trouble, epilepsy, memory loss, and eye problems. It has also been used for aches, seasickness, sterility, nerves, coughs, hemorrhoids, snakebites, worms, palsy, ulcers, fever, hypertension, hoarseness, lethargy, measles, diabetes, cramps, and insomnia. Sage is considered useful in alleviating hot flashes associated with menopause.

Throughout French history, sage was a major medical herb, primarily because of its antibacterial properties. Sage was held to be a preventative medication, because its disinfectant properties cleansed the inner body of germs and diseases. Early in the eighteenth century, the strong smelling herb was used to disguise the rancid flavor of putrefying meat when there was no other way of keeping meat fresh. Lewis Spence reported that sage was a favorite of Hungarian gypsies; they believed that it attracted good and dispelled evil.

The Chinese value sage for its healing properties. Sage tea was and still is primarily used as a gargle for sore throat and as an aid to digestion. A sage tea can be made by steeping one tea-spoon of dried sage in one cup of hot water for about ten minutes.

The origin of the word "sage" is itself somewhat unclear. Sage most likely came to Middle English as *sauge*, from Old French, and before that from Latin, *salvia*, or "healthy." Other dictionaries state that salvia means "saved," in allusion to the herb's reputed healing virtues.

No one knows for certain if there is any relationship between the meaning of "sage" as a healthy or saving herb and the meaning of sage as "wise."

No matter what the origin of the word, sage is a very useful herb, to be used wisely.

Chocolate

✺ by Sheri Richerson ✺

C hocolate… The word makes our mouth water, but where does chocolate come from? In a world where natural resources struggle to keep up with growing demands of societies, let's take a look at the fascinating tree, *Theobroma cacao*, and its wondrous product: chocolate.

Theobroma, which means "food of the gods," grows wild in the tropical rain forests of the world. The ancient Maya of Central America were the first to discover cacao, or cocoa, pods.

These discoveries led to the creation of a spicy drink by the Aztecs some time between the thirteenth and sixteenth centuries, although there is no documentation recording the event.

Anthropologists believe the Aztecs allowed the seeds to ferment. Once they were fermented, they were allowed

to dry in the sun. The seeds were then roasted, crushed, and the resulting powder was added to water and spices. This drink was considered a luxury item and reserved for warriors and the nobility. Later, the seeds were burned as an incense or given as an offering during rituals and ceremonies. Cocoa pods were even used as money.

By the sixteenth century, chocolate had been discovered by the Spanish. They found it to be bitter, so they added sugar to it and kept it secret for nearly a century before the rest of Europe discovered it.

The first chocolate house was opened in London in 1657, and from there chocolate use spread like wildfire—first as a drink and then, in the late seventeenth and early eighteenth centuries, the Italians began to experiment with it as a food. Everything from soup to liver had chocolate added to it.

During a demonstration at the Field Museum in Chicago for the opening of the Chocolate Exhibit, Wolfgang Puck created what he calls "Mom's Chocolate Cake" for the crowd to taste.

"When I grew up," he said, "chocolate was really special." His mother gave the children two little pieces each day.

During the presentation, Puck gave several tips for cooking with chocolate. He said to always melt the chocolate using a double boiler and try not to put water in it. He recommended using a good quality bittersweet chocolate, saying cheaper chocolate has a lot of cocoa butter in it, but not a lot of particles of chocolate. He also suggested that using parchment paper on the bottom of the pan would help the cake or whatever you are baking come out easier.

A port or cabernet fortified wine goes well with chocolate. For tasting the differences in chocolate, he suggests a port wine.

Some Qualities of Chocolate

Over the years, chocolate has also been rumored to be an aphrodisiac. The scientific evidence behind this suggests that chocolate contains small amounts of a chemical called phenyl ethylamine (PEA) that is a mild mood elevator. It is in fact, the same chemical that our brains produce when we are happy or "in love."

Chocolate has often been considered bad for your health; however, this is another myth that needs to be discarded. Throughout history, chocolate has been used as food and medicine. Cocoa contains antibacterial agents that fight tooth decay, and chocolate has a positive effect on cholesterol levels. Chocolate contains stearic acid, which does not raise bad cholesterol; however, cocoa butter, which is in chocolate, contains oleic acid, which may actually raise good cholesterol. Furthermore, despite common belief, chocolate has been proven not to affect skin conditions.

Here is another interesting health fact about chocolate. A 1.5-ounce milk chocolate bar contains three grams of protein, 15 percent of the daily value of riboflavin, 9 percent of the daily value of calcium, and 7 percent of the daily value of iron. Besides being an extremely popular natural resource, chocolate has a rich and diverse history and is beneficial to your health because of the natural vitamins and minerals found in the cocoa bean.

The Basics: Making Chocolate from Scratch

To make chocolate from scratch, scoop the ripe cocoa seeds out of the pods.

Place the seeds in baskets or under banana leaves for approximately one week, allowing them to ferment.

Once they are fermented, clean the seeds and lay them in the Sun to dry.

This process may take several days.

Once dry, the seeds need to be roasted over an open fire. Roasting the seeds will give them more flavor.

Remove the shells and crush the meaty seed on a stone surface until you get a soft paste.

Add desired sweetener and milk.

In today's fast-paced world, many people are looking for healthier ways to eat—seeking out foods that are low in carbs and high in nutritional benefit.

Below are two recipes that are indeed low carb, while still containing delicious chocolate.

Chilled Chocolate Soup

This recipe serves four.

1 pint low-fat chocolate milk
½ cup granulated sugar
6 ounces bittersweet chocolate chips
½ cup hazelnut liquor

Combine the low-fat chocolate milk and sugar in a heavy-duty saucepan. Whisk continually until the mixture boils and the sugar is dissolved. Pour the mixture over the chocolate chips and whisk until the chips melt. Add the liquor and chill. Serve topped with whipped cream dusted with cocoa powder and a side of fresh, ripe fruit and nuts.

Chocolate Banana Salad

1 tsp. stevia
1½ Tbls. flour
1 egg, beaten
½ cup lemon juice
2 cups boiling hot chocolate
1–2 bananas
Pecans

Combine stevia and flour in a heavy saucepan. Add the beaten egg and mix well. Add lemon juice and hot chocolate while continuing to mix. Cook over low heat until slightly thickened. Chill, then add sliced bananas and pecans and stir to coat.

Chocolate Chex Party Mix

Appetizers have not gone out of style. Here is a great recipe for one.

9   cups Chex cereal

2   cups shredded coconut

1   cup pecans, chopped

1   cup light brown sugar

½   cup butter

½   cup Karo light corn syrup

1   tsp. vanilla extract

½   tsp. baking soda

12 ounces semisweet chocolate chips

    Raisins

Preheat the oven to 250 degrees F. Combine the cereal, coconut, and pecans in a shallow pan. In a small saucepan, bring the brown sugar, butter, and corn syrup to boiling while constantly stirring. Stop stirring and allow the mixture to boil for 5 minutes. Stir in vanilla and baking soda. Pour over the cereal mixture and stir until evenly coated. Bake for approximately 1 hour, stirring every 15 minutes. Stir in chocolate chips and raisins.

Chocolate Beef Ribs

Meat is great when it is combined with chocolate. While this may sound like something fresh out of a cartoon, try these meat recipes and see what you think. You will be pleasantly surprised.

3   pounds beef ribs

4   Tbls. butter

½   cup vinegar

1   cup tomato juice

1   clove garlic

2   Tbls. white sugar

1   tsp. seasoning salt

2   Tbls. Worcestershire sauce

½   cup catsup

1   tsp. cocoa powder

½   cup water

1   tsp. paprika

½   tsp. chili powder

½   tsp. cayenne pepper

1   Tbl. butter

1   Tbl. A-1 steak sauce

Brown the ribs in the butter, then remove and place in a roasting pan. In a saucepan, combine the remaining ingredients and simmer over low heat for 15 minutes, stirring constantly. Pour the mixture over the top of the ribs.

Cover the roasting pan and place in a 350 degree F oven until the meat falls from the bones, approximately 2½ hours, depending on the thickness of the meat.

As the ribs cook, remove the cover every half an hour and baste. Bake uncovered for the last 15 minutes.

Turkey Molé

Poultry was one of the earliest foods to be combined with chocolate. Surprise your guests with this recipe for turkey mole.

1   turkey breast

1½ tsps. salt

2   medium onions, chopped

    Bacon fat

2   garlic cloves

2   Tbls. chili powder

1   small dried, seeded, chopped hot red chili pepper

1   cup ground nuts
1   ounce bitter chocolate

Cut the turkey into small pieces and place them in a large pot. Add enough water to cover and bring to a boil. Add the salt and simmer for 30 minutes.

While the turkey is simmering, brown the onion in the bacon fat. Add this to the pot along with the remainder of the ingredients. Continue to simmer until the turkey is tender and the sauce is well-blended and thick. This is good served with rice or polenta.

Chocolate Scrambled Eggs

Chocolate and eggs might sound like another odd combination, but why not? After all, we do use eggs in baking. Try this delicious recipe and see. The recipe serves two.

5   eggs, beaten
1   cup milk
3   Tbls. cocoa
1   Tbl. black pepper

Preheat the skillet over medium heat. Combine all the ingredients in a medium-sized bowl, and whisk until well blended. Pour the mixture into the skillet and stir continually until the eggs are firm.

Chocolate Cheese Soufflé

Cheese and chocolate, chocolate and cheese...

1   cup chocolate milk
3   Tbls. all-purpose flour
1   Tbl. butter
4   large brown eggs
1   Tbl. cornstarch
1½   cups shredded cheese

In a heavy saucepan, combine the chocolate milk and flour. Bring to a boil, stirring constantly. Continue to cook the mixture at a boil for four minutes, stirring constantly.

Add the butter, stir until melted, and remove the pan from the heat. Separate the egg whites from the egg yolks, setting the whites aside. Add the yolks to the milk mixture, beating well after each addition. Add the cornstarch and shredded cheese to the mixture, and set it aside. Beat the egg whites until stiff peaks form. Fold the egg whites into the milk and cheese mixture. Pour the mixture into a lightly greased soufflé dish.

Bake at 350 degrees F for approximately 40 minutes, making sure not to open the oven door while the soufflé is cooking. Serve immediately with a green salad.

Chocolate Mint Carrots

If you don't like vegetables, try these chocolate mint carrots for a real taste treat. This recipe also works with snow peas.

    2   Tbls. butter
    1   Tbl. chopped chocolate mint
    8   ounces fresh carrots

Steam or boil carrots until tender and drain. Add butter and mint leaves to a saucepan and add carrots. Sauté just until the butter melts. Remove from heat and serve.

Spicy Chocolate Crab Apples

Chocolate and fruit seem a natural fit. The recipe below is great, but of course don't forget an easy way to combine chocolate and fruit is simply to melt chocolate and dip fruit into it.

    2   cups sugar
    1   cup white wine vinegar
    ½   cup water
    1   Tbl. whole cloves
    1   cinnamon stick, broken in pieces

1   Tbl. fresh grated ginger

½   tsp. whole allspice berries

½   tsp. cocoa powder

6   cups crab apples

In a nonreactive saucepan, combine all ingredients except the crab apples. Bring to a rolling boil, stirring continually to dissolve sugar. Reduce heat and simmer for ten minutes. Remove from heat.

Pierce crab apples in numerous places with a fork. Add the crab apples to the hot liquid in the pan. Return the pan to the heat and bring to 180 degrees, using a candy thermometer to check.

Stir apples frequently, continuing to maintain the temperature for approximately ten minutes or until the apples easily pierce with a toothpick or cake tester. Carefully ladle apples and sauce into prepared canning jars, filling to within a quarter of an inch from the top of the jar. Wipe the edges of the jar so that it is clean, and seal with canning lid.

Let the jars stand undisturbed for 24 hours, then check to make sure the lid is sealed. Store in a dark cool place for at least 2 weeks, then enjoy.

Chocolate Nut Salad

Who would have imagined that you could add chocolate to salads? Give this tasty salad a try and see what you think.

1   dozen dates

1   dozen figs

12   ounces English walnuts

1   cup celery, diced

Juice from one orange

½   tsp. cocoa powder

Chop the dates and figs into bite-size pieces. Crush the walnuts and combine with fruit pieces. Mix well. Add the juice from one orange and the cocoa powder, stirring until well mixed. Serve on a lettuce leaf.

Chocolate Taco Seasoning Mix

This recipe for a taco seasoning mix can be used on more than just tacos. Try it on chicken, beef, and more.

8 tsps. lemon pepper

6 tsps. dried red pepper seeds, crushed

4 tsps. cayenne pepper seeds, crushed

4 tsps. chili powder

4 tsps. granulated beef bouillon

4 tsps. cocoa powder

2 tsps. garlic powder

1 tsp. seasoning salt

2 tsps. cornstarch

Combine all ingredients in a large container and mix well. For each pound of ground beef or other meat, add 7½ tsps. of seasoning and ½ cup of water. Bring the mixture to a boil, reduce heat, and simmer for 10 minutes.

Chocolate Zucchini Nut Loaf

Chocolate added to bread is not a new idea; however, add it to your regular zucchini bread and wait for exclamations of surprise.

1 egg, beaten

½ cup ripe zucchini, shredded

⅓ tsp. powdered stevia

½ cup brown sugar

3 Tbls. butter

2 Tbls. hot chocolate

1 cup flour

½ tsp. baking soda

½   tsp. salt (optional)

½   tsp. ground nutmeg

½   tsp. cinnamon

⅛   tsp. ground ginger

½   cup raisins

½   cup chopped walnuts

Combine beaten egg, shredded zucchini, both sugars, butter, and hot chocolate in a medium-sized mixing bowl. Beat until well blended. Combine remaining dry ingredients, except raisins and walnuts, in a small bowl and mix well. Add the dry ingredients to the zucchini mixture. Beat with an electric mixer on a medium speed until well mixed. By hand, stir in raisins and walnuts. Pour batter into a well-greased loaf pan. Bake it at 350 degrees F for approximately 40 minutes or until bread is done. Cool in pan for 10 minutes, then remove and finish cooling on a wire rack. Wrap the cooled loaf in plastic wrap and store overnight in the refrigerator.

Chocolate Spiced Bread Pudding

Desserts are a very natural food to flavor with chocolate. Try this little twist on an old favorite, bread pudding.

6   cups bread cubes

½   cup melted butter

1   cup granulated sugar

½   cup cocoa powder

½   cup cinnamon chips

1½   cups milk

1½   cups cream

8   oz. milk chocolate

2   eggs, beaten

1   cup confectioner's sugar

Place the bread cubes in a large bowl and drizzle with the melted butter, then toss to coat. Mix the sugar and cocoa powder together, sprinkle over the cubes, and toss again. Mix in half of the cinnamon chips. Butter an 8-inch glass baking dish and spread the mixture evenly into the baking dish. In a saucepan, heat the milk and 1 cup of the cream just to the boiling point. Do not boil. Remove the milk from the heat, and whisk in the chocolate until melted and smooth. In a medium bowl, beat the eggs until frothy, then slowly mix the eggs into the chocolate mixture. Pour the milk-egg mixture over the bread cubes and refrigerate for 1 hour. Preheat the oven to 350 degrees and bake the pudding until it is set, approximately 35 minutes. The center will move slightly. While it is baking, prepare the glaze using the rest of the cinnamon chips and ½ cup of the cream. Microwave these two items until the chips are melted, and then mix in the confectioner's sugar until the mixture is smooth. Drizzle this over the warm pudding and serve.

Drink of the Maya

When you think of a chocolate beverage, your first thoughts are likely hot cocoa or chocolate milk. Here is a recipe for an original chocolate drink, influenced by Mayan traditions. To enjoy this drink as it was originally made, you will need to locate a ripe cocoa pod.

First you should scoop the cocoa seeds out of the pods. Place the seeds in baskets or under banana leaves for approximately one week, allowing them to ferment.

Once they are fermented, clean the seeds and lay them in the Sun to dry. This may take several days. Once dry, the seeds need to be roasted over an open fire. Roasting the seeds will give them more flavor.

Remove the shells and crush the meaty seed on a stone surface until you get a soft paste. Scoop this into a vessel or hand shaker and add water, cornmeal, honey, or chili peppers. Pour from one container to another until the drink is frothy, then enjoy.

Chocolate Soft Drink

½ cup chocolate syrup

½ cup cold milk

⅔ cup carbonated water, chilled

Pour the chocolate syrup into a chilled glass and stir in milk. Hold the carbonated water approximately 5 inches from the top of the glass and slowly add until a thick foam comes to the top of the glass. Stir the mixture once, being careful not to cause it to overflow. Drink immediately.

Chocolate Beauty Recipes

More and more beauty products containing the essential oil of *Theobroma cacao* are being brought into the market. After years of being used as beauty products in their native countries, the rest of the world is beginning to catch on. Here are some recipes for homemade beauty products that contain chocolate or, at least, the scent of chocolate.

Chocolate Mint Essential Oil

3 Tbls. chocolate mint leaves

1 pint vegetable oil

1 Tbl. white vinegar

Use a mortar and pestle to crush the veins of the chocolate mint leaves. Place the crushed leaves into a quart container. Fill with one pint of warm vegetable oil. Add one tablespoon of plain white vinegar. Cap the jar and set in a warm sunny window for one week, then strain.

If the scent is strong enough, cap and store in a cool, dark place. If the scent is too weak, begin over, making sure to use the liquid mixture you already have and adding more fresh herbs. Repeat the process as often as you like until your essential oil is a strength of your liking.

Chocolate-Scented Body Lotion

⅓ cup rose water

⅓ cup glycerin

⅓ cup lemon juice

Chocolate-scented oil (see previous recipe)

Mix together the rose water, glycerin, and lemon juice in a container that will seal and can be shaken. Shake ingredients until well mixed. Add in enough chocolate-scented oil to suit your personal scent preferences. Use immediately. This is especially good to use on sun-damaged skin.

Chocolate Mint Astringent

1 cup chocolate mint leaves

1 cup boiling water

Using a mortar and pestle, break the veins in the chocolate mint leaves. Pour the leaves into a large bowl. Cover the leaves with boiling water. Place your head close to the bowl, being careful not to get too close. Place a towel over your head. Breathe deeply for approximately 5 minutes. Remove the towel and allow the mixture to cool. Once the mixture is cool, soak a clean washcloth in the mixture and apply to the face and neck area.

Chocolate Home Product Recipes

If you really love the smell of chocolate, try these household products that will make your home smell like chocolate. One warning here: the intense chocolate smell might just entice you to eat more chocolate!

Chocolate Mint Rug Freshener

⅛ cup chocolate mint leaves

⅛ cup lavender flowers

5 lemon eucalyptus leaves

4   lime balm leaves

1   box of baking soda

4   tsps.ground fennel seeds

1   tsp. ground cinnamon

Combine chocolate mint leaves, lavender flowers, lemon eucalyptus leaves, and lime balm. Place the leaves in an oven on the lowest setting until just dry enough to crush. In a large bowl, combine baking soda, fennel, and cinnamon. Add the leaves to the baking soda mixture. Stir to crush leaves and mix ingredients. Sprinkle on rugs. Wait approximately 10 minutes and vacuum floors.

Chocolate Mint Laundry Freshener

2   lemons

2   oranges

1   cup chocolate mint leaves

White vinegar

Baking soda

Thinly slice ripe lemons and oranges. Place the slices, including any juice, into a clear jar with a lid (such as a canning jar). Using a mortar and pestle, break the veins in the chocolate mint leaves. Add the leaves to the jar with the lemons and oranges. Place a clean rock or other similar item on top of the lemon and orange slices and the mint leaves. Top the jar off with the white vinegar making sure that the orange and lemon slices and the mint leaves are below the vinegar. Cap and set in a sunny window for approximately 1 week.

Strain the contents so that you have a clear liquid. If the scent is not strong enough, restart and work your way back through adding additional lemons, oranges, and mint leaves to the mixture you've already made. When you are ready to use the mixture, use 1 cup of the liquid and 1 teaspoon of baking soda per load of laundry. This should be added to your rinse cycle.

Peanut Butter Carob Chip Doggie Treats

It is a known fact that dogs love chocolate. However, chocolate is toxic to dogs. The solution to the problem is to offer your dog homemade treats that contain carob chips instead.

2   Tbls. corn oil

½   cup peanut butter

1   cup water

1   cup whole wheat flour

2   cups white flour

½   cup carob chips

Preheat oven to 350 degrees F. Cream together the oil, peanut butter, and water. Add flour, alternating between the whole wheat and white varieties, ½ cup at a time. Mix well. Stir in carob chips.

Roll out the dough on wax paper until it is approximately ½-inch thick. Use cookie cutters to cut the dough into shapes. Place the cookies on an ungreased cookie sheet and bake for approximately 20 minutes.

Thyme Enough

by Elizabeth Barrette

T hyme is one of the world's most popular herbs. It appears in kitchen gardens and in monastery gardens. You can find it at the grocery store, always dried and sometimes fresh. Its different varieties offer intriguing diversity. But unbeknownst to many who use it for more ordinary purposes, thyme also holds considerable magic.

The History of Thyme

The scientific name for thyme is *Thymus*, which derives from a Greek word most likely meaning "courage." This name-origin is suitable for this invigorating herb, although another possibility is the word comes from "to fumigate" and refers to the ancient practice of burning the herb as an insect repellent.

Thyme's culinary uses helped speed the spread of the herb. The Sicilian variety *T. herba-barona* was imported to continental Europe for the caraway-like flavor it imparted to beef.

Diverse cultures instilled thyme with symbolism. To the Greeks, it represented style and elegance. During the Middle Ages, it had a wide reputation for chivalry. The French related it to the republican spirit. Because of its usefulness as a strewing herb, many societies associate it with the home.

Over time, people discovered more of its medical properties too. At first, they used thyme to stuff pillows for relieving melancholy. From the fifteenth through seventeenth centuries, it remained a popular remedy against plagues. The essential oil of thyme remained in use as an antiseptic as late as World War I.

Thyme finally reached the Americas with the first European settlers. It now grows wild in some parts of North America, as gardeners and livestock helped scatter the seeds.

Thyme Varieties

There are about two dozen different kinds of thyme. The main division is between wild thyme (*T. serpyllum*) and common thyme (*T. vulgaris*). Wild thyme, also known as creeping thyme, mountain thyme, or mother-of-thyme, has a low, spreading growth habit. Its dense mat makes a perfect ground cover accented with pink-mauve flowers. It reaches about four inches in height. Common thyme, also known as English or culinary thyme, has an upright and bushy form with oval green leaves and white flowers. This tiny shrub can be trimmed into a hedge for knotwork gardens. Untrimmed, it can grow up to fifteen inches high. It's the most popular kind used in cooking. Below are some of the other thymes you may encounter.

Broadleaf thyme (*T. pulegioides*) forms a hardy shrub with mauve flowers. Its leaves are larger and rounder than common thyme and have a more robust flavor.

Camphor thyme (*T. camphoratus*) is compact with dark-green leaves. It grows to a height of up to twelve inches. Although it requires a dry, mild climate, its medicinal scent makes it especially useful for fumigation or purification.

Caraway thyme (*T. herba-barona*) has narrow, shiny, dark green leaves and lavender flowers. Its strong caraway flavor makes it ideal for flavoring soups, meat, and vegetables. It also does well as a ground cover or in rock gardens and hanging baskets. This plant only grows two to five inches high, and its limp stems make it flop over.

The related **nutmeg thyme** (*T. herba-barona "nutmeg"*) has plumper stalks and pink flowers and reaches four inches in height. In addition to its spicy scent, its fast-creeping growth habit makes it worth planting if you can obtain it.

Creeping red thyme (*T. praecox arcticus "coccineus"*) forms a dense, dark-green mat up to four inches in height. In bloom, it becomes a carpet of dark pink, almost red, flowers. This variety is most popular for planting between stepping-stones. Its scent is mild, but it tolerates some foot traffic.

Elfin thyme (*T. serpyllum "elfin"*) forms a flat mat less than half an inch high, with tiny dark-green leaves. It's a must for fairy gardens but also works well in rock gardens.

Fragrant thyme (*T. x citriodorus "fragrantissimus"*) is a giant thyme that reaches fifteen inches in height. It has blue-gray leaves and pale lilac flowers. Its unique fruity, sweet flavor is perfect for mild dishes, including those made with fruit. Another variety sometimes sold as fragrant thyme (*T. odoratissimus*) smells more of citrus blossoms. Its long, loose stems bear unusual pink flowers with a purple calyx.

Golden creeping thyme (*T. praecox arcticus "aureus"*) has a low habit and rosy-purple blooms. It requires full sunlight in order to maintain its vivid yellow color. Choose this if you want a golden plant that has a traditional thyme fragrance and extra-dense leaves.

Lemon thyme (*T. x citriodorus*) has dark-green, glossy leaves, whose antiseptic powers make them a natural preservative.

Wild lemon thyme (*T. serpyllum "lemon curd"*) has wiry, pinkish-brown stems and tiny pink flowers. Its sparse leaves are green and sweet-tart.

Citrus thyme (*T. serpyllum "citriodorus"*) has a more generalized citrus scent, but is a hardy creeper with attractive pink blooms.

The more spectacular **golden lemon thyme** (*T. x citriodorus "aureus" or "Doone Valley"*) features bright yellow leaves as well as potent citrus scent. Its lemony flavor goes well with fish or chicken, and also makes excellent tea.

Note: Any of the lemon thyme varieties can substitute for lemon in a spell, if you can't get real lemon. Golden lemon thyme works well in a solar garden. Most of the lemon varieties grow up to ten inches in height.

Pine-scented thyme (*T. Broussonetii*) has lavender-pink flowers and a shrubby form. It reaches twelve inches in height, and its piney scent makes it a suitable substitute in spells if you can't find actual evergreen sprigs. It's also good for purification.

Another **pine-scented thyme** (*T. caespititius*) forms little mounds, dense with tiny leaf clusters, only a few inches high. This one looks terrific in rock gardens.

Silver thyme (*T. x citriodorus "argenteus" or "silver queen"*) is a striking miniature shrub with gray-green leaves edged in white. It grows to about ten inches high and makes a perfect accent in pots or hanging baskets. This thyme variety is a must for lunar or goddess gardens. Plant silver queen thyme for winter interest; it bears rose-pink terminal leaf buds in winter.

Another choice is *T. vulgaris "silver posy,"* whose variegated leaves have an especially mild flavor. Its pinkish stems dry more easily than other varieties.

White creeping thyme (*T. serpyllum "snowdrift"*) grows low but thick, reaching up to four inches in height. Although faintly scented, it yields a profusion of dense white blossoms over bright green leaves. This display makes it an ideal ground cover or edging plant, and like the red-flowering kind, it tolerates some footprints. You can create a "checkerboard" or "barber pole" pattern by alternating two thyme varieties.

Woolly thyme (*T. pseudolanuginosus*) delights the fingers with its fuzzy green leaves. Rosy flowers later cover the low-growing mat, which reaches up to two inches in height. This variety is good for rock gardens and edgings, and it makes another good natural ground cover for lunar or goddess gardens.

Cultivating Thyme

All varieties of thyme are perennial, although some are tender and may not survive severe winters. The ground cover varieties of wild thyme need plenty of room for their fibrous roots to spread.

The bushy varieties of common thyme need less space, and some can be clipped into attractive miniature hedges. Thyme is native to the western Mediterranean area but has been naturalized in other parts of Europe and North America. Thus it survives hardiness zones 5–9 and prefers full sunlight, although it can tolerate partial shade. Soil should be light, dry, well-drained, and slightly alkaline.

Novice gardeners may wish to begin with common thyme, the easiest to grow. Mother-of-thyme is another good choice.

Intermediate gardeners can experiment with the colorful (golden or silver) or scented (lemon, pine, or caraway) types. Woolly and elfin thyme can be delicate, but they are suitable for fairly experienced gardeners.

To grow thyme from seed, plant it indoors (unless you live in very warm regions) because seeds need a temperature near 70 degrees F to sprout. Preferably, start plants during the waxing Moon. Cluster planting creates a more vigorous crop, so sow about twenty seeds in a small pot filled with a sterile medium, then sprinkle over with sand. Mist daily until seedlings emerge. Then water at the roots only when soil becomes dry. After two weeks, feed with fish emulsion.

Thyme plants should be several inches high (for bushy types) or wide (for mat types) before transplanting. Harden off by setting them outside in the sunlight for several hours a days for a few days before planting them in the garden. Place bushy varieties six inches apart and creeping varieties at least a foot apart. Water thoroughly after planting.

To propagate thyme, choose from two methods. Divide creeping thyme varieties by uprooting the plant and carefully separating it into two or three sections. Then replant and water thoroughly. Do this in spring. Take cuttings from bushy thyme varieties, always clipping from the new shoots and not the old woody stems. Put the cuttings in wet sand and keep moist until new growth appears. They can then be transplanted to individual pots.

In the garden, thyme is gregarious. Companion planting with eggplant, potatoes, or tomatoes strengthens the vegetables. Good companion herbs include Mexican marigold mint, parsley, rosemary, sage, and salad burnet. Thyme also discourages infestations of cabbageworms and whiteflies.

Because of its rich heritage and diverse varieties, thyme belongs in many theme gardens. For a kitchen, medieval, or evergreen garden, use common thyme. For a romantic garden, choose from golden, silver, or lemon thyme. For a fairy garden, plant wild or elfin thyme. For ground cover, use wild or woolly thyme.

Thyme is relatively tough but has some weaknesses. Avoid wetting the leaves, as this reduces fragrance and encourages fungal diseases. In cold climates, protect plants with generous mulch during the winter. Replace kitchen herbs every few years, as they get woody.

Harvesting Thyme

To obtain the best flavor, and to avoid competition from bees, pick thyme just before it blooms. You can also collect the flowers, which have a daintier flavor. Harvest thyme in late morning, after the dew dries but before the Sun grows intense. Take a few sprigs at a time if you want to use them fresh.

For near-fresh flavor in winter, freeze the thyme immediately after picking. Lay tender sprigs on a cookie sheet and freeze for several hours. Then seal in a freezer bag or carton, label, and store. Alternatively, puree the leaves with a little water in a blender, then freeze the paste in ice cube trays. Once solid, pop the herbal cubes into a bag, label, and store.

For drying, trim bushy varieties to about two inches high, or trim creeping varieties back to a small patch. Tie the stems in bunches and hang to dry in a warm, dark place. Alternatively, you can remove the leaves and dry them on screens. Once the thyme is fully dry, crumble it into an airtight jar. Label with the plant's name and the date, and store out of direct sunlight. Dried herbs keep for six to twelve months.

For magical applications, harvest thyme during the Full Moon. Silver or woolly thyme gains extra power from moonlight, while golden or lemon thyme gains power from the Sun— so you may wish to cut those at the appropriate time of night or day. During the growing season, it's best to use fresh herbs in spells, but dried herbs also work. Some Witches cut magical herbs with an athame or bolline; others use consecrated scissors or garden clippers. Say a few words of thanks or leave an offering for the plant whenever you harvest herbs for magic.

You may get several cuttings of thyme through the growing season. However, stop harvesting five or six weeks before the first frost. This allows the plants to harden off and store energy before the freeze.

Culinary Uses of Thyme

Thyme ranks among the most popular herbs for cooking. Common thyme has a complex musky-herbal flavor; wild thyme is a little milder. The many different varieties include other flavors, such as lemon, pine, and caraway. Some even have a fruity aspect to their flavor. Most recipes, however, expect common thyme.

This herb characterizes certain ethnic cuisines. It's a famous ingredient in Cajun and Creole cooking, as well as in mainland French fare. British cooking has employed thyme since the Middle Ages, and American cooking since the time of the first Europeans.

Some cooks use thyme as a garnish. It makes a good topping for soups—just lay a sprig over a swirl of sour cream or yogurt on the surface of the soup. It can also make a bed for serving fish, seafood, or artichoke hearts.

Thyme is an essential ingredient in herbal seasoning blends. Classic examples include *bouquets garnis*, *herbes de Provence*, and *fines herbes*. It combines well with other herbs, especially basil, garlic, and lemon. Arabian cooks used powdered thyme together with sumac.

Long strands of thyme work well in bottles. Benedictine monks used it to flavor their liqueur. Add sprigs to olives, herbed vinegar, or herbed oil. Greek and import shops often carry thyme-flavored honey, but honey from the flowers of thyme is harder to find. Some types of savory preserves also benefit from a sprig of thyme. The dainty leaves even look nice through glass. Herbed mayonnaise or herbed butter in crocks are also delightful with thyme.

The leaves do well as a flavoring for meat dishes, such as beef, fish, goose, lamb, poultry, veal, and wild game. Caraway thyme is especially suited for beef, lemon thyme for seafood or fruit. Use thyme freely in soups, stews, and stocks. This herb holds up particularly well in dishes that require long, slow cooking that more delicate herbs may not withstand. It also aids the digestion of fatty meats.

For vegetables, choose from asparagus, beans, broccoli, carrots, corn, cucumbers, eggplant, leeks, mushrooms, onions, parsnips, peas, potatoes, spinach, sweet peppers, and tomatoes. Thyme also is excellent in stuffing, pâté, and sausage. It combines well with cheese or eggs.

Medicinal Applications

People have used thyme for centuries and, over the years, our knowledge of its curative effects has grown. It can be used by itself, as a "simple," or blended with other herbs. Thyme is antiseptic, antispasmodic, calming, carminative, deodorant, expectorant, germicidal, and rubifacient. It brings a sweat, reduces fever, and combats viral infection. It's especially good for treating melancholic complaints, such as depression or chronic fatigue syndrome.

Wild thyme also has mild sedative properties. The essential oil, distilled from the leaves and flowers, is antiseptic and stimulating. In particular, scientific studies have confirmed that thyme strengthens the immune system.

Tea made from thyme helps with shortness of breath or congested lungs. It can uplift the spirits, relieving depression, but it can also soothe nightmares and makes a flexible treatment for nervous complaints. It also aids digestion, especially for complaints like flatulence, colic, and stomach cramps.

Historically, thyme was boiled in wine for a digestive drink, but contemporary herbalists are less enthusiastic about alcohol. Lemon varieties of thyme make an especially pleasant and effective tea. Wild thyme tea is recommended for cough, hangover, flu, and sore throat. Thyme honey is ideal for sweetening expectorant herb teas.

As a fumigator, thyme relieves asthma, bronchitis, flu, sinusitis, sore throat, and whooping cough. It enhances the immune system and stamina, combating lethargy. It also kills airborne pathogens. Thyme oil diffuses easily in an aromatherapy lamp, mister, or simmering potpourri pot.

For external use, mash the leaves with a little water to form a paste. Apply to sores or inflammations. Thyme honey can be used similarly. A heavier poultice of the leaves, layered in a damp cloth, is useful in treating lung complaints.

The essential oil of thyme is called thymol. It also contains phenol and carvacrol. Use with care, as thymol can prove toxic in large amounts. In small amounts it may still irritate sensitive skin. Thyme oil is a nerve tonic, used externally for treating colds, depression, muscle pain, and respiratory complaints. It's also an ingredient in some acne lotions, aftershave, cologne, mouthwash, and soap. As noted above, it works well for aromatherapy, where it's also less irritating.

Magical Properties of Thyme

Thyme has many correspondences. It is feminine in gender, ruled by the planet Venus and the element water. Its powers include courage, healing, love, psychic enhancement, purification, and sleep.

The ancient Greeks burned thyme in their temples for consecration and purification, but also as an offering to the gods. It is especially sacred to Adephaghia, the Greek goddess of food and good eating. Invoke this goddess with a sumptuous feast and nosegays of thyme and other herbs. The priestesses of Artemis, Aphrodite, and other goddesses were sometimes called *melissae*, which means "honey priestesses." Thyme, which attracts bees and makes excellent honey with its pollen, was often grown around their temples.

Traditional gardeners grow a patch of thyme to provide a home for fairies. It also attracts pollinating insects that are closely associated with fairies. Wear a sprig to see fairies and other discorporeal beings. This herb evokes the magical qualities of nature.

Symbolically, thyme means "join the nature beings." In the old flower language of tussie-mussies, it means "activity." Use the flowers and leaves to signify new beginnings or the start of a new project.

Burn thyme as a smudging herb for good health or to purify your space before a magical ritual. Carry the herb for good health or to develop psychic powers. Wear a sprig in your hair to make yourself irresistible. Take a bath infused with thyme and marjoram to release the troubles of the past. Sniff thyme for courage and invigoration. A pillow stuffed with thyme dispels nightmares and promotes safe, positive dreams.

Miscellaneous Purposes of Thyme

Thyme has other uses around the house. Place sprigs among clothes or linens to dispel musty odors and deter insect pests. The flowers make an especially nice addition to potpourri. Both the leaves and flowers can be used to stuff sachets.

The antiseptic and stimulating qualities of thyme make it useful in cosmetics. It appears in herbal lotions and baths. Herb water for a facial rinse can be made by adding a drop or two of its essential oil to a pint of distilled water. You can also make it with fresh herbs by crushing the leaves, boiling briefly, and then allowing the mixture to cool; strain before using.

Herb vinegar (also used in cooking) makes a more invigorating facial rinse. It uses the Sun's power to instill cider vinegar with active components. Stuff a glass bottle with thyme, fill with vinegar, and seal tightly. Then leave it in a sunny window for several weeks, shaking occasionally.

Bathing with herbs is romantic and refreshing, but takes a little common sense. If you just throw the leaves in, they'll get stuck all over you. Enclose dried or fresh thyme in a muslin bag or a tea ball, and hang it from the spigot while you fill the tub.

For a morning pick-me-up, blend thyme with other stimulating herbs, such as basil, lavender, or rosemary. Thyme flowers yield a more delicate fragrance and combine with most other herb blossoms.

Cooking with Southwestern Herbs

❧ by Chandra Moira Beal ❧

T he idea of Southwestern cooking conjures up all sorts of exciting, exotic flavors—fiery chilies, fragrant spices, smoky peppers, sweet corn, and earthy beans. But it's the regional herbs that bring these dishes to life, adding simple but flavorful aromas and tastes to the meal and flecking the plate with vibrant color. Fresh herbs balance the otherwise hot and spicy cooking with cool, green vegetable flavors. From the refreshing and cooling cilantro to the bitter estafiate, Southwestern cooking is incomplete without the addition of herbs.

Defining the Southwest

The regions of the Southwest include California, Arizona, New Mexico, Colorado, and Texas—although growing seasons, cultures, and cooking customs overlap geographical borders. Many recipes evolved from Native American tribal cooking and from Mexico where the influences of the Mayan, Aztec, and Spanish cultures are prominent. The herbs that grow wild and abundantly in these areas make frequent appearances in the region's recipes, in recipes ranging from kitchen staples to medicinal teas.

The typical Southwest climate is arid and dry with plenty of sunshine and mild winters, but there is a lot of variance. Texas alone has five gardening zones, and Colorado winters are anything but mild.

Southwestern herbs typically don't need overly rich soil, just dirt that is loose and porous and drains well. They tolerate arid conditions and thrive in rocky, sandy limestone terrain. These herbs require at least six hours of sunshine a day, which is why they're ideal for growing in the Southwest. Many will appreciate a few hours of afternoon shade. They do tend to need plenty of water, and mulching can help retain moisture in the intensive summer heat.

Many of these herbs will grow in the northern states if they're given plenty of Sun and protection from the cold during winter. If you live in an area that freezes regularly, container gardens are a great way to enjoy these herbs year round. Just plant them in pots that can be moved indoors as soon as the temperatures drop.

Most Southwestern herbs do well grown from seeds or transplanted from rooted cuttings. These herbs can be grown in window boxes, old wine barrels, clay or wooden containers, pots on patios, and along walkways—making them versatile, easy, and convenient for all.

Using Southwestern Herbs

Cilantro (Coriandrum sativum)

Cilantro is one of the most popular herbs in Southwestern cuisine. Its cool, refreshing leaves balance the fiery chilies that are ubiquitous in many regional recipes. The refreshing, bittersweet pungency of cilantro is what gives it its unique flavor profile. There is no substitute for cilantro's flavor, and it should always be used in its fresh form. Some people have an aversion to the strong aroma and slightly soapy taste of this herb, but most people love it.

Cilantro seeds are known as coriander, and they have a mellow, citrus-like flavor that is not interchangeable with the fresh leaves. Cilantro is to Southwest cooking what parsley is to many American meals. You may see it garnishing an entree, find it floating atop soup, stuffed inside tacos, sprinkled over guacamole, or tossed in a salad. Cilantro is readily available in most supermarkets, typically sold in generous, inexpensive bundles.

Cilantro is an annual that likes loose, rich, well-drained soil and full sunlight. Sow the seeds in the fall about half an inch deep, then spread the seedlings one foot apart. It will tolerate freezing temperatures and frost and thrives in the garden in the cooler months. This herb will grow about two feet high and one and a half feet wide, but the leaves are best used when the plant is about six inches high. The leaves become spindly and lacy as the flowers appear, detracting nutrients and flavor from the robust leaves.

Cilantro's leaves are flat and green, resembling Italian parsley. When rubbed between the fingers, they produce a strong, pungent aroma. Cilantro doesn't dry well and loses its flavor quickly, so always use it fresh. You can store a fresh bunch in the refrigerator with the stems in a jar of water loosely covered with a plastic bag.

Cilantro Seasoned Potatoes

Use a combination of red, white, Yukon gold, and purple potatoes in this dish for a colorful blend of flavors.

This can be served hot as a side dish or at room temperature as an appetizer sprinkled with shredded Parmesan cheese and red chili powder.

2   pounds potatoes, washed and quartered

2   Tbls. butter

3   Tbls. olive oil

4   cloves garlic, crushed or finely diced

4   Tbls. fresh lime juice

2   tsps. coriander seeds, freshly ground

1   bunch green onions with tops, chopped

1   cup fresh cilantro, loosely chopped

1   Tbl. chili powder

    Salt and pepper to taste

½   cup shredded Parmesan cheese

Cover the potatoes with cold, salted water and bring to a boil. Reduce heat and simmer about 12 minutes, but do not over-cook. Meanwhile, melt the butter in a small saucepan with the olive oil, garlic, lime juice, and coriander. Drain the potatoes and toss them gently with the butter, adding the onions, cilantro, chili powder, salt, and pepper.

Serve warm or at room temperature, generously sprinkled with chili powder and Parmesan cheese. If chili powder isn't available, you may use paprika combined with cayenne pepper as a substitute.

Epazote (Chenopodium ambrosioides)

Epazote is a tenacious herb that grows like a weed and is able to withstand less than optimum growing conditions. The name comes from the Nahuatl Indian words *epatl* and *tzotl* meaning "an animal with a rank odor." Some describe epazote's potent aroma as similar to turpentine, but don't let that discourage you from employing it in your cooking. This pungent and minty herb is hugely popular in recipes from Southern and Central Mexico. For centuries, Mexican mothers have steeped it in milk and sugar to rid children of intestinal parasites, but it also helps prevent the socially embarrassing consequences of eating beans, especially black beans. Add a couple sprigs of the fresh herb to the bean pot during the last fifteen minutes to reap its benefits.

Epazote thrives along sunny streambeds with some afternoon shade, but does well in poor soil and full Sun, even growing out of cracks in the sidewalk. The serrated leaves resemble a goose's foot. Sow the seeds in the fall, then thin the seedlings to about one foot apart. Epazote will grow into a shrub about three feet high and two feet wide and will reseed itself once it is established. It can be downright invasive, so pinch the seed heads back in the early fall or it will take over the garden.

Frijoles Negros en Olla

1	pound dried black beans
	Water or broth to cover the beans
3	Tbls. olive oil
1	onion, quartered and studded with 2 whole cloves
4–6	garlic cloves, crushed or diced
½	tsp. cumin
1	bay leaf
1–2	whole ancho chilies
	Salt to taste
1	tsp. dried oregano
3	large sprigs fresh epazote

Wash the beans well, place in a cook pot, and cover with cold water or broth two inches over the beans. Add oil, onion, garlic, cumin, and bay leaf. Bring to a boil. Immediately reduce the heat to a simmer and cover. Add chilies and cook 2½ hours. If necessary, add hot water to prevent the beans from bursting.

When the beans are almost tender and cooked through, add the salt, oregano, and epazote. Uncover and cook another 15 minutes.

Serve with green onions, cilantro, sour cream, lime wedges, or salsa.

Estafiate (Artemisia ludoviciana)

Estafiate is a willowy plant with downy silver foliage belonging to the wormwood family. It has a sharp, bitter taste that acts as a tonic and aperitif.

Estafiate doesn't show up as a central ingredient in recipes very often, but makes a nice medicinal tea traditionally used to treat stomach ailments. Simply steep the leaves in hot water and sip. Add half a teaspoon of the chopped leaves to rich sauces and gravies to deglaze the pan. Estafiate's sharp, bitter flavor contrasts well with sweeter sauces based on lingonberries or currants and served with wild game.

Estafiate is an annual that grows straight and tall. It tolerates dry, arid conditions and, like most herbs, enjoys well-drained soil and a sunny location. The stems have a reddish color that are tipped with blossoms of ten to twelve small red and yellow flowers.

The festive color of estafiate makes it pretty in the garden as background to brighter colored plants and a good choice for dried wreaths. The leaves make an attractive garnish on the plate.

Hoja Santa (Piper auritum)

Hoja santa is a semi-woody shrub with large, velvety heart-shaped leaves. It grows into a multibranching bush shaped like an umbrella. This plant is sometimes called a "root beer plant," because when you rub the leaves they release a musky scent similar to sarsaparilla.

The generously sized leaves make great edible wrappers for shredded pork or a sauté of onions, squash, corn, and tomatoes. You can also tear up the leaves to use in tamale fillings, dried shrimp and fish dishes, and mole sauce. Remove the stems and the center veins before chopping or tearing the leaves with your hands. Hoja santa can be added to black beans toward the end of cooking for a flavorful kick. Use half of a small leaf in the bean pot.

Hoja santa enjoys full Sun with some afternoon shade and rich, well-drained soil. It can be watered daily. When mature, Hoja santa produces long, white, cylindrical flowers in the summer that have a slightly rough texture. Oil glands form gelatinous balls on the undersides of the leaves. Hoja santa spreads like bamboo with underground linear roots. It dies back in freezing weather but new shoots will appear each spring.

Molé Verde with Hoja Santa

2   cups unhulled, raw pumpkin seeds

2   cups chicken or beef broth

6   ounces tomatillos, husks removed, rinsed, and coarsely chopped

6   large sorrel leaves, rinsed, stems removed, and coarsely chopped

4   leaves hoja santa, stems and veins removed, coarsely chopped

8   large sprigs epazote, 5 coarsely chopped, 3 whole

4   jalapeno or 6 Serrano chilies, coarsely chopped

¼   cup vegetable oil for frying

Toast the pumpkin seeds in an ungreased pan, turning them over and shaking the pan from time to time to prevent them from burning. Set the seeds aside to cool and then grind them in a coffee grinder or food processor to a fine powder.

Pour 1½ cups of the broth in a blender, gradually adding the tomatillos, sorrel, hoja santa, chopped epazote, and chilies, blending as smooth as possible.

Heat the oil in a flameproof casserole (in which you are going to serve the molé) and fry the blended ingredients, stirring and scraping the bottom of the pan to prevent sticking; cook for about 25 minutes. Add the rest of the epazote.

Stir ½ cup of the broth into the pumpkin seed powder until you have a smooth consistency, and gradually stir into the cooked ingredients. Continue cooking over low heat, stirring constantly for 10 more minutes. Take care that the pumpkin seed mixture does not form into lumps; if this happens, put the sauce back into the blender and blend until smooth. Add any remaining broth and salt to taste. If the sauce is too thick, add a little water to dilute.

Serve molé sauce over enchiladas, eggs, or any bean and rice dishes.

Mexican Mint Marigold (Tagetes lucida)

Mexican mint marigold grows throughout Central and Southern Mexico and is sometimes known as "hierba de las nubes" or "cloud plant." The Tarahumara Indians of Chihuahua and the Huichol tribes of Jalisco favored this herb and used it in religious rituals. The Aztecs purportedly used ground Mexican mint marigold as a numbing powder. They blew it into the faces of sacrificial victims before their hearts were plucked out.

Mexican mint marigold features strongly anise-scented leaves that enliven salads, fish, and game dishes. It is sometimes called "Texas tarragon" and can be used as a substitute in recipes that call for tarragon. Mexican mint marigold has a less assertive or fiery flavor than true French tarragon, but it has more anise flavor, making it superb in vinaigrettes. Traditional uses also include cooking the herb with boiled green corn or chayote squash. It makes a delicious tea all by itself; steep a large handful in a teapot for six or seven minutes.

Cheerful, bright golden flowers appear on Mexican mint marigold in the fall. A perennial, it likes loose, well-draining soil and full sunlight. Plant cuttings by rooting them first in water, then putting them in the ground in early spring, spaced one foot or more apart.

The shrub will grow one to two feet tall and can be invasive, reseeding itself in the fall. Glossy, lance-shaped leaves with serrated edges give Mexican mint marigold a distinct, striking look in the garden.

Mexican Mint Marigold Vinaigrette

This tangy golden dressing is particularly tasty over leafy green and pasta salads or as a marinade for grilled meats or potato salad.

½   cup Mexican mint marigold vinegar (see below)

White white or apple cider vinegar

1   egg yolk

1   large clove garlic, minced

2½ tsps. Dijon mustard

½   tsp. ground pepper

1   tsp. honey

1   Tbl. chopped Mexican mint marigold

½   cup olive oil

Fill a glass jar half full with fresh Mexican mint marigold, stems removed. Cover with vinegar and allow to steep overnight. Strain and use.

Blend the egg yolk, garlic, mustard, pepper, and honey with a fork. Add the vinegar and chopped fresh herbs. Mix well. Slowly whisk in the oil. Makes about 1 cup.

Mexican Oregano (Poliomintha longiflora)

Mexican oregano has smaller, paler leaves than the common Italian oregano, but packs more aroma and taste with a spicy, peppery flavor, making it a good complement to the spicy foods of the Southwest. Oregano comes from the Greek words *oro* ("mountain") and *ganos* ("joy"). Mexican oregano makes a zesty condiment when steeped in red wine vinegar and used in a marinade. You can also add sprigs to hot coals before grilling steaks, or toss a handful into a pot of beans.

Mexican oregano is an attractive perennial with glossy, highly aromatic leaves protruding from woody branches. The leaves are oval and slightly fuzzy on the underside. Abundant tubular flowers blossom in the spring and summer in a riot of pink and violet. It tolerates arid, dry conditions and is freeze-hardy. This oregano likes loose, sandy, well-drained soil and some shade. When mature it reaches a height of up to twenty-four inches.

Oregano Pesto

4–6	cloves garlic
2	cups loosely packed oregano
1	cup fresh parsley
½	cup pine nuts, lightly toasted
½	cup Parmesan cheese, grated
½	tsp. lime zest
1	tsp. fresh lime juice
1–2	Serrano peppers, seeded and finely chopped
½	cup olive oil

Chop the garlic, oregano, parsley, nuts, and cheese in a food processor or blender. Add the lime zest, juice, and chilies. Slowly add the oil until it forms a thick, green paste.

Serve tossed with pasta, melted over steamed squash, or spread on a baguette. This pesto freezes well, so you can enjoy the fresh taste all winter.

Yerba Buena (Mentha sp.)

Yerba buena, literally the "good herb," has been used by people of the Southwest for centuries as a soothing tea for stomachache, headache, and the pains of childbirth. When brewed with cinnamon, clove, and nutmeg, it's a time-honored cure for *la cruda*, a hangover. Yerba buena is also good in tomato-based soups. Its flavor is similar to spearmint, but the leaves are smaller and darker green.

Yerba buena is a perennial creeper, frequently rooting along the stems and making an attractive ground cover or shady border. Yerba buena grows well in rich, moist but well-drained soil in partial shade. It produces tubular white or lavender flowers from April to August. Plant it somewhere where you will often brush against it, such as on a garden path, to give off a lovely minty fragrance.

Yerba Buena Tea

Add fresh or dried leaves to boiling water and let steep for a deliciously soft, minty tea.

Sage (Salvia officinalis)

Sage comes in dozens of varieties and is the quintessential Southwestern herb. Its grayish-green leaves are highly aromatic. This perennial grows into a three-foot-tall shrub with woody stems. Sage likes full sunlight and loose, sandy, alkaline soil. It does well in a climate with lots of heat and humidity; just don't overwater it as it's prone to root rot.

It is essential to give sage good drainage. Growing a small plant in a clay pot is ideal as the clay will warm in the Sun and help keep the roots dry. Sage also starts well as a transplant or can be grown from root cuttings. If grown in an area with mild winters, sage will bear leaves year round. If it dies back in a freeze, it will perk back up in the spring.

Skillet Corn Bread with Sage and Pepper

1½	cups cornmeal
½	cup white flour
½	tsp. salt
3	tsps. baking powder
½	tsp. chili powder
½	tsp. white pepper
1	tsp. paprika
1½	cups buttermilk
1	egg
2	Tbls. honey or molasses

3   heaping Tbls. fresh sage, chopped

2   Tbls. green onions, chopped

2   Tbls. grated Parmesan cheese

2   slices bacon, optional

½   cup oil

Preheat the oven to 425 degrees F. In a medium-sized bowl, mix the cornmeal, flour, salt, baking powder, chili powder, pepper, and paprika. Blend with a fork. In a separate small bowl, mix the buttermilk, egg, and honey molasses until combined, then mix into the dry ingredients. Add the sage, onions, Parmesan cheese, and bacon. In a skillet, heat the oil to near smoking and pour it into the cornmeal mixture. Immediately pour the whole mixture back into the skillet and bake 20–25 minutes until golden brown.

More Recipes Using Southwestern Herbs

Quesitos (Little Cheese Balls)

Chopped fresh Mexican mint marigold

Mexican mint marigold flower petals

Chopped fresh Mexican oregano

Chopped fresh epazote

Chopped yerba buena

Crushed ancho chilies

1   log of goat cheese

Cut the log into half-inch slices and roll the slices into bite-size balls. Roll the cheese balls in the mixture of herbs. These can be made early in the day and will keep well in the refrigerator. Serve on a tray with bunches of red and green grapes.

Pescado con Hoja Santa

6   redfish or red snapper fillets

6   Tbls. butter

1   Tbl. Spicy Seasoning (see below)

6   large hoja santa leaves

1   orange, thinly sliced

6   sprigs Mexican mint marigold

3   green onions with tops, chopped

Spicy Seasoning

½   tsp. whole black peppercorns

1   tsp. whole coriander seeds

½   tsp. whole allspice berries

½   tsp. whole cloves

½   tsp. cayenne

1   tsp. paprika

½   tsp. cinnamon

1   tsp. thyme

1   tsp. oregano

Grind the whole spices into a powder and mix in the dried herbs.

Creole Sauce

3   Tbls. oil

1   medium onion, chopped

4–6   cloves garlic, minced

2   celery stalks, chopped

3   bay leaves

1   medium green bell pepper, chopped

2   Serrano or jalapeno peppers, chopped

1   Tbl. Spicy Seasoning (see above)

1   tsp. brown sugar

1   cup broth

4   large tomatoes, peeled, seeded, and chopped

Heat the oil in a large skillet and sauté the onion, garlic, and celery for about 5 minutes. Add the bay leaves and peppers. Continue to sauté until vegetables are slightly tender (about 3 minutes). Add the remaining Spicy Seasoning, sugar, and broth. Bring to a boil, then reduce the heat and simmer 5 minutes. Add tomatoes and simmer another 10 minutes. Sauce should be thick. Remove bay leaves. Add salt and pepper to taste.

Preheat the oven to 400 degrees F. Brush both sides of the fish fillets with melted butter and sprinkle with Spicy Seasoning. Place each fillet on a hoja santa leaf, cover with ⅓ cup Creole Sauce, 2 thin orange slices, a sprig of marigold, some chopped green onions, and roll up tightly inside the leaf. Place seam-side down in an oiled baking dish. Bake 15 minutes. Pour remaining sauce over the top and serve with black beans and rice.

Leftover Creole Sauce is good on eggs and in omelets.

Herbs for Health

Red Herbs of Chinese Medicine

by Lynn Smythe

In Chinese medicine, menstrual and menopausal problems are closely associated with liver and kidney energies. The liver is where blood (xue) is stored, so it is linked to the menstrual cycle and irregularities here are often defined in terms of weak or stagnant liver energies.

—Penelope Ody, *The Chinese Herbal Cookbook*

Traditional Chinese medicine, also known as TCM, has a long history. The *Pen-ts'ao*, otherwise known as *Emperor Shen-nung's Herbal*, and the *Huang-ti Nei-ching*, otherwise known as *The Yellow Emperor's Classic of Internal Medicine*, are two ancient Chinese medicinal texts dating from the third century BC.

Both of these texts contain a wealth of healing information. For example, the *Herbal* lists over 300 herbal medicinal preparations that were known in China at this time.

Principles of Traditional Chinese Medicine

Herbs, barks, roots, and berries compose many of the remedies used in traditional Chinese medicine. Chinese medicine incorporates a variety of holistic practices in its treatment methods. This includes exercise, acupuncture, massage, medicinal herbs, and a healthy, balancing diet.

Unlike Western medicine that usually only treats individual symptoms as they occur, traditional Chinese medicine treats the patient as a whole, balanced entity. Practitioners of TCM strive to keep their patients' bodies, minds, and souls in balance at all times. This balance of energies is referred to as yin and yang. If a person's yin and yang are out of balance, this will lead to various diseases and disorders. One of the goals of TCM is to bring the patient's yin and yang back into balance.

Here are correspondences explaining the nature of the yin-yang duality of energies, as understood by traditional Chinese medicine.

Yin-Yang Correspondences

Yin—Female, dark, cold, Moon, wet, water, earth, autumn, winter

Yang—Male, light, hot, Sun, dry, fire, air, spring, summer

Color Correspondences in Traditional Chinese Medicine

Strengthening herbs are also important, they are used to tonify qi, jing, and blood and to correct any deficiencies in these vital substances. Some of these traditional remedies are specific to particular organs, helping to correct any weaknesses, which

may lead to ill health, while others are more general in their use.

—Penelope Ody, *The Chinese Herbal Cookbook*

Colors can positively or adversely affect a person's moods and emotions, and this in turn can affect a person's health. Color therapy uses this sensitivity to color to identify and correct any imbalances in the body's internal energy patterns that might lead to emotional or physical health problems. Color therapists believe that each organ and body system has its own characteristic energy state and that disorders can be healed by using the appropriate color to bring the whole body back into balance.

For example, the color red is used to bring more fire and warmth to a cold and stagnant personality. Red is seen as the color of strength, power, motivation, sexuality, and vitality. The color red can be used to help treat a myriad of health problems, including anemia, bronchitis, colds, constipation, lethargy, low blood pressure, poor blood circulation, pneumonia, and tuberculosis.

The color red should be used with caution as an excess of this hue can lead to anger, exhaustion, fever, hostility, and violence along with aggravating or causing high blood pressure. The color green will help to bring an excess of red energy back into balance. Green, which is complementary to the color red, represents the color of balance and is known to be a wonderfully healing and harmonizing color.

The main concept of traditional Chinese medicine is to bring the five elements in a person into balance with one another. See below for the correspondences associated with the five elements of Chinese medicine.

Jing—Essence

Jin-Ye—Body fluids

Qi—Energy, vitality

Shen—Spirit

Xue—Blood

This article focuses on some of the red herbs used in traditional Chinese medicine, which can be helpful for their various healing properties. Many of these herbs will help to bring more of the fire element back into a person's disposition.

Elemental Correspondences in Traditional Chinese Medicine

Element	Climate	Season	Color	Direction
Wood	Wind	Spring	Green	East
Fire	Hot	Summer	Red	South
Earth	Dampness	Late Summer	Yellow	Center
Metal	Dryness	Autumn	White	West
Water	Cold	Winter	Black	North

Element	Emotion	Yin Organ	Yang Organ
Wood	Anger	Liver	Gallbladder
Fire	Joy	Heart	Small Intestine
Earth	Worry	Spleen	Stomach
Metal	Sadness	Lung	Large Intestine
Water	Fear	Kidney	Bladder

Element	Sense Organ	Taste
Wood	Eyes	Sour
Fire	Tongue	Bitter
Earth	Mouth	Sweet
Metal	Nose	Acrid
Water	Ears	Salty

The Meridians

In traditional Chinese medicine the body is divided into twelve meridians. The meridians are invisible pathways by which qi circulates throughout the body. The twelve meridians of Chinese medicine are the lungs, large intestine, stomach, spleen, heart, small intestine, bladder, kidney, pericardium, *san jiao*, gallbladder, and the liver. San jiao, also known as triple heater, maintains a person's temperature while giving strength to one's emotional health.

Each of these twelve meridians is thought to control a function of one's personality. Disease manifests itself in a person due to an over- or under-abundance in one or more of the meridians. Using the appropriate herb can help to restore balance to whichever meridians are out of balance in a person.

Red Herbs

A certain relationship can be seen to exist between the color of an herb and the healing properties that the herb exhibits. Color correspondences are often used in TCM to help balance an excess of any one quality. This article lists and describes ten red herbs commonly used in traditional Chinese medicine. The herbs are listed first by their Chinese name, followed by their Latin scientific name, followed by their common English names.

While this list is far from comprehensive it is a start for anyone wishing to conduct further studies in Chinese medicine. This article is for information purposes only, not for treatment. Please consult a trained medical practitioner before taking these or any other herbal medicines.

Dan Shen

(*Salvia miltiorhiza*): Red rooted sage, Chinese sage, or red ginseng. This is a perennial herb that is hardy in USDA zones 5–8. It can grow to be twelve to thirty inches tall and nine to twelve inches wide. The roots of this plant are harvested in the late fall through early spring.

Properties: Bitter, cool

Meridians: Heart, liver, pericardium

The red roots of this plant are used in Chinese medicine for a variety of problems, including acne, eczema, hepatitis, menstrual problems, and psoriasis. Dan shen is also used to invigorate blood, clear heat, pacify irritability, and soothe stomach pains. It can also be used to support thyroid gland functionality and is helpful to persons suffering from chronic fatigue syndrome. Dan shen stimulates estrogen production, so the long-term use of this herb should be avoided especially when treating women's disorders, such as fibroids and menstrual problems. A regimen of three to four weeks of taking this herb should be followed by a resting period of three to four weeks of not taking the herb.

Da Huang

(*Rheum palmatum*): Chinese rhubarb or Turkey rhubarb. This is a perennial herb that is hardy in USDA zones 5–8. This is a very large plant that can grow to be up to eight feet in height and six feet wide. The rhizomes of six- to ten-year-old plants can be harvested in the fall after the leaves have begun to turn yellow. The entire plant—including the stems, leaves, flowers, and fruit—is tinted red, but it is the rhizomes, which are known as da huang, that are used in Chinese medicine. The leaves of this plant are poisonous and should be avoided.

Properties: Bitter, cool

Meridians: Heart, large intestine, liver, stomach

Depending upon the dosage and the way it is administered, da huang can be used to help treat both diarrhea and constipation. It can also be used to help relieve dyspepsia, gastritis, and hemorrhoids. Internally this herb is used to clear heat from the blood, invigorate the blood, and drain heat and dampness. Du huang can also be used externally for boils, burns, canker sores, and to help cool hot skin.

Di Huang

(*Rehmannia glutinosa*): Chinese foxglove. This perennial herb is hardy in USDA zones 8–10 and can grow to be six to twelve inches tall and twelve inches wide. The undersides of the leaves of this plant have a reddish coloration, and the flowers are yellow, streaked with reddish-brown and reddish-purple. It is the orange-colored roots of this plant that are used in Chinese medicine.

Properties: Sweet, cool

Meridians: Heart, kidney

This plant is utilized as a general tonic that helps strengthen the blood, heart, and kidneys. It is also a very helpful herb for women to use after giving birth, as it will serve to check excessive bleeding. Di huang can also be used to help lower blood pressure and blood cholesterol levels, and it treats cases of constipation, dry mouth, eczema, hepatitis, insomnia, irritability, and throat infections.

Fo Ti

(*Fallopia multiflora*): Chinese cornbind, flowery knotweed. This is a perennial herb that can be grown in USDA zones 9–11. Fo ti is a vining plant that can grow to twenty feet or more in height. Three- to four-year-old roots of this plant can be harvested in the fall for medicinal purposes. The stems of this plant are red when young. The roots of this herb are used as a general tonic in Chinese medicine. Care should be taken when using this herb as it can cause skin rash, diarrhea, and numbness of the extremities when used in excess.

Properties: Bitter, sweet, astringent, warm

Meridians: Kidney, liver

Fo ti has a myriad of uses, including helping to relieve menstrual problems, lowering blood sugar and cholesterol levels, and helping to prevent swollen lymph glands. I have even seen fo ti mentioned as an aid for preventing hair loss and preventing hair from turning gray. Fo ti can be used as a general tonic for a sluggish thyroid and in cases of blood deficiency that manifests itself with symptoms of dizziness, numbness, and weakness.

Qu Mai

(*Dianthus chinensis*): Chinese pink, rainbow pink, or Indian pink. This flowering plant is a short-lived perennial that is hardy in zones 4–7. It is often grown as an annual. Chinese pink will grow to twelve to eighteen inches tall and six to nine inches wide. Harvest this plant just as the flowers are beginning to form. This herb also makes a wonderful ornamental plant with its red and pink flowers with fringed edges. The whole plant is used in Chinese medicine. Chinese pink is often combined with red ginseng to help induce menstruation.

Properties: Bitter, cold

Meridians: Bladder, heart, small intestine

This herb is used as a diuretic and will help drain damp heat from the bladder. Qu mai has antibacterial properties, and so it is often used to help treat urinary tract infections. Qu mai also helps to lower blood pressure and fevers.

Qian Cao Gen

(*Rubia cordifolia*): Indian madder. This is a perennial, climbing plant that can grow to be twenty feet tall and is hardy to USDA zones 6 and above. This plant has red roots, red-brown flowers, and black fruit that produce a red-colored juice. It is the roots, which are specifically known as qian cao gen, that are used in Chinese medicine. Using too much of this herb internally has been known to cause an unhealthy red color in urine, milk, and bones.

Properties: Bitter, sweet, cold

Meridians: Heart, liver

This herb is used internally to help stop bleeding, nosebleeds, and uterine bleeding. It also relieves chest and joint pain. Qian cao gen can be used externally to help clear up eczema. Qian cao gen has antibacterial, diuretic, and expectorant properties that are often exploited in traditional Chinese medicine.

Rou Gui

(*Cinnamomum cassia*): Chinese cinnamon or cassia bark. This plant is a large evergreen tree that is native to China. Rou gui can grow to be forty to one hundred feet tall and fifteen to forty feet wide. The inner brownish-red bark of this plant, known as rou gui in Chinese medicine, is used by herbalists. The leafy twigs of this plant, known as *gou zhi*, are also used in TCM to help lower fever and increase perspiration.

Properties: Pungent, sweet, hot

Meridians: Heart, kidney, liver, spleen

This herb is used generally as an antispasmodic, a carminative, and an appetite stimulant, and it is also used to treat cases of diarrhea, various menstrual problems, and influenza.

Shan Zha

(*Crataegus pinnatifida*): Hedge thorn or Chinese haw. This is a small, deciduous tree that is hardy in zones 4–7. Shan zha can grow to be twenty feet high and wide. It is the red fruits of this tree that are used in Chinese medicine.

Properties: Sweet, sour, warm

Meridians: Liver, spleen, stomach

The raw fruit of this plant is used to treat congestive heart failure, hypertension, and menstrual problems. The baked fruit is used internally to help treat indigestion, bloating, irritable bowel syndrome, and gallbladder problems. This herb can also be used to help lower blood pressure and blood cholesterol levels.

Shi Di

(*Diospyros kaki*): Chinese persimmon, Japanese persimmon. This perennial evergreen tree can be grown in USDA zones 6–9. Chinese persimmon trees can grow to be thirty to fifty feet high and twenty-two feet wide. The calyces of this plant, which are specifically known as shi di, are used to help control internal bleeding. The juice of the reddish-orange fruit is also used in Chinese medicine.

Properties: Bitter, astringent, neutral

Meridians: Large intestine, lung, stomach

Belching and hiccups are two of the symptoms that can be treated with this herb. Constipation can be helped by eating the raw, ripe fruit, while diarrhea can be treated with the cooked, ripe fruit. Some other medicinal uses of this plant include bronchitis, coughs, expectorant, reducing fever and sore throat, and lowering high blood pressure.

Zi Cao

(*Lithospermum erythrorhizon*): Red-rooted gromwell or stone seed. This is a perennial herb that is hardy in USDA zones 8–9. Zi cao can grow to be sixteen to twenty-eight inches tall by twelve inches wide. The roots of this plant turn a reddish-purple color after they are dried.

Properties: Sweet, cold

Meridians: Heart, liver

This herb is used both internally and externally in a variety of traditional Chinese medicine treatments. Internally zi cao can be used to help alleviate constipation, hepatitis, and skin cancer, and externally it can be used for diaper rash, itching skin, and herpes.

In Conclusion

Practitioners of traditional Chinese medicine most often mix customized herbal medicines based on the needs of each of their individual patients, rather than prescribing them a generic drug formula. Generalized herbal formulas are rarely used in Chinese medicine. It is more common for the Chinese medical practitioner to combine four or more herbs in order to make a comprehensive herbal formula.

The main herb or herbs are chosen to help treat the primary symptom of the disease being experienced by the practitioner's patient. The secondary herbs are chosen for a variety of purposes, such as:

To enhance the effects of the main herb being used.

To prevent side effects that could occur when taking the main herb by itself.

To treat any secondary problems that the patient may be experiencing.

To act as an overall general tonic to help strengthen the

patient's body, mind, and spirit connection.

Most of the herbs mentioned in this article should be available in tincture or capsule form at your local health food store. Chinese medicinal herbs are also available in their whole, dried form from a variety of sources.

In traditional Chinese medicine the part of the herb that is used to heal is often made into a nutritious and healing soup or stew. See Penelope Ody's book, *The Chinese Herbal Cookbook: Healing Foods for Inner Balance* (Weatherhill, 2001), for a number of recipes that include Chinese medicinal herbs as part of their ingredients.

Herbs for Insomnia

※ by Leeda Alleyn Pacotti ※

E very animal on our mother planet requires sleep in response to the circadian rhythm of night and day. Sleep revitalizes the body and revivifies the mind, extending life and preserving mental balance. With such benefits from restful sleep, it's amazing so many people disregard and flout this subdued natural state—but disregard they do. Very conservative estimates show that one-third of Americans suffer some form of insomnia.

Sleep deprivation is not isolated to the United States. The World Health Organization reports that one in four adults worldwide experience curtailed sleep. Considering the intricate social structure and highly technical professions in America, the sleepiness and diffused attention levels resulting from insomnia result in lowered productivity, lost creativity, and improper emotional responses in interpersonal contexts. While these consequences are perhaps easily rectified, long-term insomnia has terrible effects. The National Institute of Mental Health finds emotional turbulence among insomniacs often precedes development of depressive disorders. In the workplace, persons performing repetitive tasks experience decreased productivity or reduced ability to remember numbers after just two hours of sleep missed each night. Analytical skills for crucial decisions drop sharply. In conclusive findings about the Exxon Valdez oil spill of 1989, the third mate's sleep deprivation received some of the blame. The National Highway Traffic Safety Administration estimates drivers asleep at the wheel cause more than 200,000 crashes annually.

Insomniacs suffer poorer health than those enjoying a full night's sleep. The natural killer T-cells of the immune system, which attack foreign invasions into the body, are least active in insomniacs, according to a 1995 study.

What Insomnia Is and Is Not

As a general definition, insomnia is a disturbed or noncontinuous sleep state, producing insufficient rest by shortening an individual's necessary duration of slumber and curtailing physical restoration by precluding slower brain wave activity. Although insomnia produces a sensation of tiredness, it is not fatigue, which is usually a symptom of serious illnesses, such as heart problems or cancer. Nor is it simply daytime drowsiness, when sleepy feelings can be attributed to biological conditions, such as sleep apnea or narcolepsy.

Many people erroneously believe insomnia is a profound wakeful period, lasting for days, during which sleep never occurs. Such protracted, unbearable insomnia is rare. Insomnia usually involves sleep that is foreshortened, physically restless, interrupted periods of wakefulness, or delayed to the early morning hours. In more simple terms, any sleep pattern that does not provide an individual's necessary quota of nightly rest is insomnia.

The Three Patterns of Insomnia

Clinical observations of sleep describe three primary patterns of insomnia: Occasional or infrequent, short-term, and chronic.

Occasional or infrequent insomnia extends for one or two nights of bad sleep. Usually, a person has mismanaged biological needs by working or playing into the normal sleep period. Occasional insomnia is rectified by retiring for bed earlier on the next night and resuming the regular bedtime thereafter.

Short-term insomnia lasts between one to three weeks, usually centering around a life-altering event or some kind of approaching deadline. Chronic insomnia is an established conscious expectation or a habit of sleeplessness, lasting more than one month. Experienced by 30–60 million Americans, this chronic phase is the most common and problematic form of insomnia. Chronic insomnia is often treated with sleeping pills, either prescribed or purchased over the counter.

Causes and Precursors of Insomnia

Determining cause is the key to ending the injurious insomniac pattern. This can be problematic, especially when the root is an instilled habituation. Any one of different types of stress, illnesses, psychological disturbance, overwork, life events and transitions, medications, or diet can start insomnia. When any single factor goes unrecognized or unremedied, it often compounds with another to intensify and instill the chronic pattern.

Stress management is crucial in maintaining sleep. Stress induces displays of emotion that often mask fear. People experiencing these displays, either as actor or observer, see them as lapses of self-control. However, the individual reacting to stress has reached the core of personal survival. Without a proper or healthy release, she or he becomes caught in an ingrained flight-or-fight response. This perpetual response is unwarranted, but continual alertness prevents entry into sleep, drains the immune system, and rocks the equilibrium of mental health.

Another type of stress is performance anxiety, created from magnified fearful thoughts about one's ability to accomplish future work projects and employment chores. In terms of insomnia, pondering chores or problems relentlessly delays the onset of sleep, foreshortens it, or intrudes immediately when the person awakens in the middle of the night.

Boredom from inactivity is an insidious stress inducer. When muscles of the body and mind are not sufficiently exhausted from daily activity, sleep becomes elusive. As mentioned before, life events and transitions induce stress that can lead to insomnia. Depending on the life event, the initial emotional response may be fear, anxiety, grief, or depression. If the person cannot control or alter the event, embarrassment, guilt, or regret can merge with the initial base emotion to prolong the stress. Important life events and transitions include marriage, birth, retirement, illness or death of a loved one or friend, relationship problems, a severe or life-threatening health condition, extraordinary accidents, catastrophes, surviving a personal attack, graduating from school, moving to a new home or area of the country, major employment changes, loss of employment or business, financial complications and crises, legal entanglements and disputes, and readjustment to society after imprisonment. Although a typical response to life alterations is short-term insomnia, a chronic stage can arise from persisting ensnarement, as the tired individual mismanages new actions and behaviors to alter daily living.

Illnesses and organic disturbances disrupt restful or continuous sleep. Bothersome symptoms that create multiple awakenings include pain, nausea, coughing, breathing difficulties, urination, and diarrhea. Certain health conditions, too, create sleep problems, often resulting in chronic insomnia. Angina prolongs the time to fall asleep, with chest pain rousing the sleeper. Heartburn, caused by regurgitation of excess stomach acid into the throat, produces both chest pain and an acid taste. Ulcers, too, produce heartburn symptoms during sleep. Hypertension and insomnia interact harmfully. Nonrestorative sleep from insomnia produces increased blood pressure, while pharmaceuticals for hypertension alter sleep rhythms. When diuretics for hypertension are prescribed, increased urination forces the sleeper out of bed. Increased urination during the night develops from bladder infections, incontinence, and prostrate problems.

Migraine headaches are not isolated to the day. Research has discovered migraines occur frequently during REM sleep periods, or dreams. The ensuing sleep disruptions confound adequate rest, making migraine sufferers less able to cope with headaches at any time of the day or night. Joint pain from osteoarthritis usually prevents a person from entering sleep and staying asleep. Periodic leg movement disorder, in which leg muscles jump or startle during sleep, and restless legs syndrome, which makes a person feel crawling sensations while sitting or lying down, produce a physical restlessness, exhibited as extreme tiredness the following day. Pulmonary disease produces spasms at night, waking the sleeper repeatedly. Snoring, resulting from obstructed nasal passages, arouses the sleeper. Thyroid imbalances, hyperactive and hypoactive, affect sleep states. With hypothyroidism, a person sleeps but remains drowsy throughout the day, unable to perform regular activities well. Hyperthyroidism, however, brings on insomnia, keeping the sleeper wakeful.

Other hormonal changes, occurring from adolescence, pregnancy, and menopause, produce organic irregularities that alter sleep patterns. Any emergence of insomnia deserves immediate attention to prevent a chronic pattern that can easily establish during these long-term physiological changes. Persons suffering Seasonal Affective Disorder, a sensitivity to decreased daylight hours, either sleep more often or longer, or are unable to fall asleep or sleep less.

Unfortunately, many medications disrupt or suppress sleep, preventing the natural restoration the body needs to overcome an illness or condition. Among these are antihistamines, birth control pills, beta-blockers, bronchodilators, calcium blockers, cold remedies, decongestants, depressants, dilantin, sleeping pills, steroids (particularly prednisone and cortisone), and thyroid hormones. During a period of stress or illness, a person can develop negative associations about his or her ability to sleep or stay asleep. Consequently, she or he can adopt behaviors that prolong insomnia. Some common poor habits include an irregular sleeping and waking schedule, frequently working or playing into the regular sleep period, sleeping longer or more often on the weekend, watching television late at night, taking long or frequent naps during the day, lying in bed and thinking of work problems, avoiding exercise from feeling too tired, or ingesting caffeine drinks or foods late in the evening.

Some work routines also produce insomnia. Individuals who work night shifts or rotating shifts challenge the body's natural biological wakefulness. Business travel through time zones disrupts sleep with jet lag, which lasts for up to one week.

Remedying Insomnia

Although insomnia is not recognized as an illness, sleep deprivation represents a serious upset to the natural physical order. A variety of remedies and remedial activities can turn an insomniac back into a restful sleeper.

Diet

First attention should go to the daily diet. The diet for the habitual insomniac is the same as that for persons with chronic illnesses, such as cancer, diabetes, or hypertension: beans, fruits, vegetables, whole grains, and portions of lean protein from chicken and fish. Until the body adjusts to this eating pattern, take a multimineral and multivitamin complex after breakfast.

By carefully structuring the daily menu, blood sugar levels remain even throughout the day. Therefore, timing determines a return to a person's natural sleep pattern. Proteins should be eaten at breakfast and lunch, with lunch as the largest meal of the day. At dinner, which should be about three to five hours before bedtime, food choices are limited to vegetables and whole grains.

In good food combinations during evening meals, the naturally occurring amino acid tryptophan, which induces serotonin production and the consequent release of melatonin, is easily obtained. Foods high in tryptophan include bananas, warm cheese and milk, cottage cheese, dates, eggs, figs, nut butters, whole oats, peanut butter, pineapples, rice, turkey, tuna fish and other fish, walnuts, whole wheat crackers and toast, and yogurt. However, tryptophan requires a releasing agent from carbohydrates. Good carbohydrate-rich foods that are good to mix with tryptophan include apples, bran muffin, bread, carob brownies, carrot cake, cheese and crackers, fruit yogurt, rice pudding, undressed tortellini salad, and a turkey sandwich.

One should have finished drinking the daily complement of water by 3:00 pm, and should not drink liquids containing caffeine or alcohol after this time. Alcohol acts as a delayed stimulant during early hours of sleep.

Natural Melatonin

Critical to achieving the full night's rest is melatonin, secreted throughout the night and produced during the day. Although melatonin is available in supplemental form, these frequently have the same additives as sleeping pills. Further, melatonin supplementation should not be used when a person suffers severe allergies, uses antidepressants, has an autoimmune disease such as rheumatoid arthritis, or has conditions of depression, diabetes, epilepsy, eye diseases such as retinitis pigmentosa, immune system cancers such as leukemia and lymphoma, or migraines. Pregnant women and nursing mothers must not take melatonin. Because these supplements produce drowsiness, heavy equipment operators, truck drivers, and pilots need to abstain.

Despite supplements, the earth and human body act in concert to manufacture melatonin. After waking, exposing eyes to sunlight or a strong artificial light neurally signals the brain to start the melatonin cycle. To encourage adequate production, light enters the eyes for about fifteen minutes while the person stands, walks, or exercises. Morning exposure works well for anyone wanting to reestablish the normal sleeping and waking cycle. A person who becomes drowsy in the early evening can delay light exposure to the eyes to the afternoon.

Herbal Remedies

As a general guide to herbal remedies, the preferred effect on the body is calmative, nervine, sedative, or antispasmodic. Although one particular herb can produce excellent results, rotation among several herbs prevents any physical dependence or resistance to an herbal action. One cup of tea, taken thirty minutes before retiring, produces drowsiness. If an herb causes neural jitteriness, it should be excluded from the remedy complement.

Calmative herbs are soothing sedatives that have a mild action on the nervous system. Appropriate for chronic insomnia, calmatives have few, if any, contraindications for preexisting health conditions. Calmative herbs are chamomile, dill, peppermint, and seneca snakeroot.

Nervine herbs, almost all of which have a gentle sedative effect, strengthen the nervous system by relieving stress and tension in muscles. These herbs work well for occasional insomnia, although they should not be used by persons experiencing neurasthenia. Liver congestion and constipation inhibit the sedative qualities of nervines. The nervine herbs include blue vervain, california poppy, kotu kola, hops, hydrangea, lemon verbena, lettuce, lotus plumule, rosemary, thuja, wood betony, and zizyphus.

Sedative herbs tranquilize by lowering organic activity. Because most sedatives are minerals, continuous use produces toxicity. Therefore, they are limited as a single dose for occasional or short-term insomnia. Sedative herbs include amber, ashwagandha, cinnabar, comfrey root, dragon bone, dragon teeth, fluorite, linden flowers, lotus seed, magnetite, oyster shell, rehmannia, schizandra, tiger lily, and wheat chaff.

Antispasmodic herbs relieve muscle spasms and reduce continual neural messaging from muscles to the brain. Antispasmodics are helpful for insomnia arising from prolonged emotional states, such as life crises or transitions. For insomnia, they can be combined with a calmative, nervine, and sedative herb to decrease overwhelming effects. Pregnant women must refrain from using these herbs alone or in combination. Recommended antispasmodic herbs are catnip, henbane, kava kava, lady's slipper, lavender, lemon balm, lime flowers, nutmeg, passionflower, peony root, pulsatilla, sage, scullcap, and valerian.

Herbs to Avoid

Digestant herbs increase organic functions that disturb sleep. These herbs also increase hypertension. Digestants must never be used during pregnancy or lactation or in the presence of any internal inflammation or ulceration. Digestant herbs are asafoetida, black pepper, cayenne pepper, celery seeds, garlic, dry ginger, horseradish, mustard, and prickly ash.

Homeopathic Remedies

You can remedy the problem of a mind unreceptive to sleep with a dosage of four tablets of the appropriate homeopathic remedy in a 30x potency, followed by an immediate return to bed. If sleep does not return in fifteen minutes, the insomnia is acute and the same dosage is then repeated. If sleep is not attained in thirty minutes, the chosen remedy is probably incorrect. The following homeopathic remedies help the mind adjust from stress patterns, such as worry and recurrent thoughts.

Arsenicum album—Sleepless from anxiety or worry

Chamomila—Sleepless from excitement or worry; need to be lulled to sleep, which does not last

Coffea cruda—Sleepless from excitement or joy, the mind racing; remaining awake from tension or too much coffee

Cocculus—Unable to sleep after late or night shift work period; unable to return to sleep after getting up during mid-sleep

Gelsemium sepervirens—Sleepless from anticipation or dread

Ignatia amarata—Sleepless from grief

Lycopodium—Sleepless from worry about the day's events

Nux vomica—Sleepless after mental strain or long hours of study; sleepless from rich foods or excessive stimulants; sleepless after waking between 2:00 am and 3:00 am

Passiflora—Sleepless from restless thinking or inability to stop thinking

Pulsatilla—Sleepless from recurring or repetitive thoughts; sleepless before midnight; sleepless after waking during mid-sleep and needing a snack

Nonmedicinal Health Therapeutics

Most often, an insomniac fails to honor the need for dormant sensory activity. Some simple techniques retrain the body to expect, enter, and remain asleep.

Environmental Reconditioning

Your sleeping environment should be comfortable and free of sensory intrusions. The bedroom needs to be in a quiet, cool, and dark part of the home. If outside noises continually enter the room, heavy floor-length drapes block most sounds. If outside lights are a problem, a dark window shade creates a den-like feeling.

Sensory stimulations in the bedroom awaken the sleeper or prolong sleeplessness. An alarm clock is for waking in the morning, not for monitoring time awake. Avoid using the snooze button. Bedding must be inviting, with a comfortable mattress size and firmness. Pillows are available in various firmnesses, depending on the preferred sleeping position. Additional pillows to support the body are advisable for individuals with back or arthritic pains. Fresh sheets and blankets alert the mind to enter sleep, but the weight of too many blankets or comforters causes overheating and restlessness.

Loose sleeping apparel permits movement during the night and creates tactile comfort for the skin. Purchasing special garments is well worth the expenditure, considering the enhanced quality of slumber and improved performance during the day.

Lifestyle Reconditioning

Your bedroom should have few uses—dressing, sleeping, and sexual activity. Many insomniacs use the bedroom for activities that stimulate wakefulness, such as reading, working, watching television, eating, or talking on the phone. Removing bedroom bookcases, television, telephone, refrigerator, and coffeemaker makes the bedroom a more restful place.

The reptilian or ancient part of the brain responds very well to routine, and this applies to signals to prepare for sleep. Some specific rituals before bed produce yawns in a hurry. Worrying can be relegated to a specific period earlier in the day. Locking doors, taking a warm bath, slipping on special sleepwear, brushing hair and teeth, setting the alarm, and turning off lights can be the brain's signals to be drowsy. Upon lying down, recalling pleasant memories or simply pronouncing mentally, "I am going to sleep," lulls the mind into relaxation and quiet slumber.

To discover the necessary sleep period for rejuvenating rest, retire at a regular time on weekend nights and wake without an alarm. By the way, there is no truth that an older person needs less sleep. In fact, less sleep makes the body get older.

Activities to Interrupt Insomnia

Insomnia can be persistent. However, some simple procedures can put the mind back into a restful mode.

Awakening Therapy

Upon awakening at night and remaining alert for ten minutes, the insomniac gets out of bed and leaves the bedroom. Remaining awake in bed instills the notion that wakefulness in bed is acceptable. Outside the bedroom, he or she engages in nonstimulating or boring mental tasks, such as memorizing foreign words, listening to quiet music, doing needlework, or playing solitaire. He or she returns to bed when sleepy. This method is repeated for all prolonged awakenings throughout the night. However, the insomniac must arise with the alarm and not oversleep, so that the body tires naturally from the next day's activity.

The Chinese Clock

In Chinese medicine, organs and body systems are assigned to different hours of the day, which reflect activity of meridians running through the body. When prematurely awakening, rubbing specific areas of the body facilitates a return to sleep.

Time of Wakefulness	Meridian	Area to Stimulate
9:00 pm–11:00 pm	Triple warmer	Behind ears
11:00 pm–1:00 am	Gallbladder	Above ears
1:00 am–3:00 am	Liver	Area over liver
3:00 am–5:00 am	Lung	Between ribs and shoulders
5:00 am–7:00 am	Large intestine	Between thumb and forefinger
7:00 am–9:00 am	Stomach	Under eyes (lightly tap)
9:00 am–11:00 am	Spleen	Over spleen under left ribs
11:00 am–1:00 pm	Heart	Armpit of left arm
1:00 pm–3:00 pm	Small intestine	Base of little fingers
3:00 pm–5:00 pm	Bladder	Bridge of nose
5:00 pm–7:00 pm	Kidney	Centers of soles behind balls of big toes
7:00 pm–9:00 pm	Pericardium	Middle fingers

Exercise

And finally, to gain restful sleep you should simply exercise for fifteen to thirty minutes at least three to five times per week. This is best performed in the late afternoon, when the mind is ready to release stresses and thoughts. In general, the most beneficial exercise is a brisk thirty-minute walk.

Rudraksha: India's Power Bead

☙ by S. Y. Zenith ☙

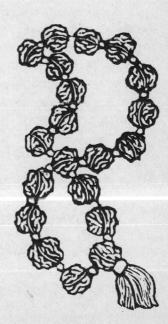

Rudraksha beads are worn in modern times by the who's who of India's political echelons—descendants of Indian royalty, nobility, highly placed officials, Bollywood's top producers, actors, actresses, songbirds, Hyderabad's wealthy Internet moguls, executives, miscellaneous business chiefs—as well as by India's fast-growing middle classes. As they were thought to be sacred in days of yore, rudraksha beads are still revered widely. The mere mention of them in many Indian communities around the world produces excitement, enthusiasm, and eagerness to wear the "holy bead of mother India and the Himalayas" in necklace, bracelet, choker, belly-chain or armlet.

As a rudraksha *sadhaka* (practitioner), it is a great honor, pleasure, and comfort in religious and spiritual work to be able to spread the word about genuine rudraksha to diverse Indian and Hindu communities in Australia, where I live. However, it is ironic that many people living in India, Sri Lanka, Nepal, and Tibet have no access to the genuine item.

Common Misconceptions

As the subject of rudraksha is a vast science in its own right and continues to be researched by scientific, ayurvedic, eastern and western medical and metaphysical teams in and outside India, this brief article can only serve as a mere introduction to rudraksha and its herbal, religious, mystical, and arcane applications. It is hoped that this simple introduction will also diffuse many superstitious and unfounded misconceptions about rudraksha. Such notions that rudraksha can only be worn by holy men like *sadhus*, *nagababas* (Lord Shiva incarnates), ascetics, religous recluses, renunciates, yogis, and those of high religious stature are false.

Another common misconception is that women and Indians of lower castes cannot wear rudraksha. All these are untrue as can be referenced from Sanskrit texts that contain no mention of women being prohibited from wearing or touching rudraksha. In fact, the three mukhi (three-faced or three-faceted) rudraksha representing Lord Agni (the Hindu fire god) is prescribed for women prone to premenstrual tension and blood disorders.

What Is Rudraksha

The phenomenon of rudraksha is one that has existed since the beginning of Indian civilization and was documented in ancient Sanskrit scriptures and various other holy texts. Rudraksha beads are actually seeds of a species of *Elaeocarpaceae* (*tiliaceae* family), a large evergreen tree with broad leaves. This tree is also generally classified into six genus.

E. floribundus Blume, found in the eastern parts of the Himalayas and the Indian state of Assam, has bark and leaves that are used as a mouthwash or gargle for inflamed gums. *E. ganitrus Roxb.* has fruit that is applied as an herbal or ayurvedic medicine for mental disorders, epileptic fits, and as heating or stimulating agents. In Sanskrit, Tamil, Telegu, and Malayalam languages, *Elaeocarpus ganitrus Roxb.* is known as rudraksha. In Hindi, it is called *rudraki* and in Bengali, *rudrakya*. It is the beads of this particular genus that contains the greatest electromagnetic property, and so it is used for making rosaries or wearing as pendants. The beads are used singly or in synergistic combinations of different rudraksha *mukhis* (faces or facets) strung together to form a personal *mala* (garland or necklace). *E. ganitrus Roxb.* is found in Nepal and India (Bihar, Bengal, Assam, Madhya Pradesh, and a few locations in Maharasthra). It also exists in a few parts of Myanmar (Burma), Malaysia, and Indonesia.

E. obiongus Gaertn has fruit that is used for treating rheumatism, arthritis, ulcers, leprosy, dropsy, and piles. In Malayalam, it is called *malankara*. In Marathi, it is known as *khas*. In Tamil, it is *bikki*. *Petiolatus wall* has leaves with juice that makes a medicine for sunstroke. A concoction made from the roots of this tree is used for fevers. *E. serratus Linn* is known in Bengal as *jalpai*, in Tamil as *ulanga-kerei*, in Kannada as *perinkara*, and in Malayalam as *avil*. The leaves from this genus are commonly prescribed for rheumatic ailments and as an antidote to poison. *E. tuberculatus Roxb* is called *dandele* in Kannada. In Malayalam it is called *pilahi*, while Tamils call it *rutthracham*. A bark decoction from this species is prescribed for haemetemesis, indigestion, and biliousness. The nuts are applied for rheumatism, typhoid fever, and epilepsy.

General Habitat and Description

Rudraksha trees are perennial, able to survive in tropical and subtropical locales. They grow to heights between fifty feet and two hundred feet. According to the *Shiva Purana*, "the favorite rudraksha trees of Lord Shiva are grown in Gouda Land." (The mythological "Gouda Land" in reality extends from the

Gangetic Plain on the southern borders of Asia to the foothills of the Himalayas—the middle of the Nepali kingdom to Bhutan and Bangladesh.) Rudraksha trees grow in Assam, Bengal, and Bihar. However, they are localized in eastern Nepal due to climatic and soil suitability. Rudraksha trees are also found in Myanmar (Burma), China, Indochina, Sumatra, and Java.

The trees bear white flowers with fringed petals that develop into drupaceous, globose fleshy fruit resembling the olive. Appearing usually from April to May, the flowers are also ovoid, conical, and elongated. The main tree trunk is cylindrical. The bark is greyish-white, rough in texture with small vertical lenticels and narrow horizontal furrows. The branches spread in various directions, and when grown in its natural habitat the crown forms a pyramid shape. Shiny green on top, the leaves are coriaceous below.

Rudraksha fruits ripen between August and October. The core of the fruit (commonly referred to as "bead" or "seed") is hard and tubercled. "Bead" and "seed" are generalized interchangeable terms used for describing the core of the fruit. The actual seeds are within the core when cut open transversally. Cultivating rudraksha is a difficult process that requires immense patience. It can take one or two years before one sees an encouraging tiny sprout, then the tree takes seven years to bear fruit.

Still, when this finally occurs, the fruits harvested contain beads or seeds of different mukhi (faces or facet) rudraksha.

The "Elaecarpus ganitrus berry," as rudraksha is also called, contains a combination of carbon, hydrogen, nitrogen, oxygen, and trace elements.

Ayurvedic physicians, village folk healers, and medicine men and women in India continue today to use the different rudraksha species that are native to their regions. Knowledge of remedial healing methods are passed down family lines or learned from ayurvedic doctors and a handful of ascetics. Below is a list of ailments for which the wearing and worshipping of rudraksha beads is prescribed by many of them. It is believed that rudraksha's natural electromagnetic properties work in much the same way as deriving chi from Reiki, gem or crystal therapy, and pranic healing principles.

By no means is the forthcoming information intended to substitute for western medicine and pharmaceutical drugs if one is afflicted by acute, chronic, or terminal health concerns. Always consult a qualified health-care professional before attempting any alternative healing methods and folk prescriptions.

The levels of healing differ from person to person. In using rudraksha, all outcomes depend on the karmas of one's ancestors, one's own karmas from preceding births, karmas created during this lifetime, and exercise, dietary, and nutritional habits. Although rudraksha is known to provide relief and remedial comfort where sophisticated drugs and western medical measures failed, it still remains an ancient science that has yet to be further examined and researched.

Rudraksha Treatments

Ailments	Recommended Rudraksha Mukhis
Blood pressure and diabetes	3 mukhi, 5 mukhi, 5 mukhi water therapy, 5 mukhi rosary of 108+1 beads
Cardiac complaints	3 mukhi, 5 mukhi, 11 mukhi, 12 mukhi, 1 mukhi rudraksha
Skin problems	4 mukhi, 8 mukhi, 9 mukhi, 14 mukhi
Joint pain and body aches	7 mukhi, 9 mukhi, 1 mukhi, 12 mukhi
Stomach disorders	2 mukhi, 3 mukhi, 9 mukhi, 12 mukhi, 1 mukhi
Paralysis	3 mukhi, 7 mukhi, 11 mukhi, 14 mukhi
Stress, anxiety, and tension	2 mukhi, 4 mukhi, 3 mukhi, 5 mukhi
Memory deficiency	4 mukhi milk therapy for 20 days, repeated after each gap of 20 days

Menstrual disorders	3 mukhi rudraksha
Nervous breakdown and depression	2 mukhi, 3 mukhi, 11 mukhi
Acidity	5 mukhi water therapy
Headaches and migraine	1 mukhi, 4 mukhi

Water Therapy

The most common rudraksha therapy uses water. For cardiac problems and cholesterol, three beads of 5 mukhi rudraksha are placed in a glass or mug filled with spring water. Those who have access to *Ganga jal* (Ganges water) may wish to add a few drops. This is done after sunset and left to soak overnight. The water is for drinking the next morning upon rising from bed and before breakfast. Those who do not particularly fancy the taste of rudraksha herbal water may wish to add a few drops of rose water available from Indian grocers.

If daily schedules are hectic, make the infusion in a large glass container with a screw-top lid and store in the refrigerator. Rudraksha water can be added to fruit juices, tea, coffee, cordials, mead, sauces, casseroles, and just about any cooking method. It will not make food taste weird unless the herbal water is carelessly left to stagnate and collect dust over a long period of time.

Nasal and Skin Problems

For nasal and breathing problems, three beads of 4 mukhi rudraksha are used for water therapy in the manner described above for 5 mukhi rudraksha. As an herbal wash for skin inflammations or allergies, 4 mukhi rudraksha can be combined in a large glass jar with 8 mukhi and 9 mukhi and immersed in water overnight. After bathing the skin or affected body parts in the shower or bath, take a final rinse with this herbal infusion. If the temperature is too cold, pour the mixture into a large container and add warm water before rinsing from head to foot. Again, rose water may be added, but be sure never to add essential oils or synthetic perfume oils to it.

Pets and Rudraksha

Pets can also benefit from rudraksha herbal infusions. Put a few drops into their drinking bowl with drinking water or milk. The 5 mukhi rudraksha water is also beneficial for maintaining the health of pets prone to high blood pressure and kidney and liver disorders. Canines suffering from skin problems and bald patches due to malnutrition, fungus, infected wounds, and allergies can be scrubbed with baby shampoo, then rinsed thoroughly with lukewarm 4 mukhi and 9 mukhi rudraksha water. Most dermatological cases heal within nine days or around nine weeks. Chronic and severe cases take up to ninety days to heal. Treatment for pets with skin concerns requires a bath and rudraksha rinse at least once a week. Wounds and itchy patches are washed daily with rudraksha water prepared from three beads of 4 mukhi and two beads of 9 mukhi rudraksha.

Milk Therapy

This recipe is a beneficial alternative remedy for mental burn-out. Milk boiled with three beads of 4 mukhi rudraksha enhances memory, cognition, and focus. When added to a bath along with some oatmeal, the milk can also double as a "milky skin wash" for relieving dry skin and other dermatological conditions.

In the case of memory deficiency, milk boiled with 4 mukhi rudraksha should be drunk daily for twenty days. Take a break after this period and resume twenty days later. Add the milk to tea, coffee, hot chocolate, and other beverages, or add to ingredients when making crepes or waffles. Use with coconut milk or buttermilk when stirring up curries. Combine with ingredients when baking cakes or preparing desserts. For warming up the body during wintry mornings, add some to oat porridge.

Mukhi Rudraksha Availability

Each faceted rudraksha bead represents a Hindu deity and is governed by one of the nine planets of the Jyotish astrological system. Although in recent market availability, there exists rudraksha of up to 21 facets in the possession of serious and wealthy collectors, only details from 1 mukhi (facet) to 14 mukhis (facets) are given here. Beads above 14 facets are unaffordable for many of us. Let's take the 21 mukhi rudraksha as an extreme example. It is like coveting an incredibly rare champagne that a beer budget can never buy. In any given decade, only a handful of genuine 21 mukhi rudraksha are found during harvests. The 21 mukhi beads are purchased years ahead, with deposits paid in order to secure priority in obtaining one as soon as it becomes available. This is despite the hefty cost of each bead being $9,000 to $20,000 depending on size, weight, density, clarity of facets, color, distinctive markings, and other quality authentication standards. Genuine 21 mukhi rudraksha are rarely sold outside of India.

Most Sanskrit tomes that mention rudraksha note there were beads from round-shaped 1 mukhi up to 38 mukhis. In modern times, this seems a myth and an unsolved mystery, as beads above 23 mukhis are virtually extinct—as are round-shaped 1 mukhi rudraksha. The only 1 mukhi rudraksha that exists today is half-moon shaped.

The details below are derived from translations of relevant Sanskrit texts:

Rudraksha Mukhis	Symbolic Deity	Planetary Ruler
1 mukhi	The Supreme God	Sun
1 mukhi	Ardhanareshwara (Shiva and Parvati)	Moon
3 mukhi	Lord Agni (fire god)	Mars
4 mukhi	Lord Brahma	Mercury
5 mukhi	Lord Shiva	Jupiter

6 mukhi	Kartikeya or Murugan	Venus
7 mukhi	Maha Lakshmi	Saturn
8 mukhi	Ganesha	Rahu
9 mukhi	Durga Shakti	Ketu
10 mukhi	Lord Vishnu	No ruler; pacifies all 9 planets
11 mukhi	Lord Hanuman and the 11 Rudras	No ruler; pacifies all 9 planets
12 mukhi	Lord Surya and the 12 Adityas	Sun
13 mukhi	Lord Kamadeva	Venus
14 mukhi	Deva Mani	Saturn

Rudraksha and Mystical Properties

1 mukhi—Helps improve concentration and focus regarding spiritual matters; detachment from worldly trappings; guides the serious aspirant into high states of meditation. Affects the *sahasrara* (crown) chakra.

2 mukhi—Draws blessings of unity, union, oneness; balances emotions and enhances relationships.

3 mukhi—Purifies the auric field, removes past karmas; useful for those with inferiority complexes who suffer from fear, guilt, depression, and general weakness.

4 mukhi—Enhances creativity, wit, eloquence, and intelligence; effective for scientists, students, researchers, scholars, writers, artists, journalists and performers.

5 mukhi—Blessings from Lord Shiva; affects all chakras; protection from untimely demise; spirituality. Small 5 mukhi rudraksha are abundant and the most common bead for making Hindu rosaries for prayer and wearing.

6 mukhi—Prevents emotional trauma; bestows wisdom,

learning, and knowledge; gives understanding of love, pleasure, music; affects the sacral plexus.

7 mukhi—Release from financial burdens; prosperity and progress in career or business.

8 mukhi—Dispels obstacles; gives success in all undertakings.

9 mukhi—For those with low energy or metabolic levels; fosters dynamism and fearlessness.

10 mukhi—Contains the ten avatars of Lord Vishnu and the ten directions; pacifies all planets; acts as a protective shield surrounding the auric field; eliminates evil forces.

11 mukhi—Blessings of wisdom, devotion, right judgment; enhances meditation.

12 mukhi—Draws the Sun's energies; bestows courage, inner strength, and resources. Useful for ministers, politicians, business-people, administrators, and executives. Affects the fourth chakra at the heart center. Removes fear, worry, and suspicion; increases motivation.

13 mukhi—For attracting riches, love, honor, and for fulfilling earthly desires and comforts.

14 mukhi—Awakens the sixth sense; grants clairvoyance; eradicates worries, burdens, and miseries; protects from ghosts and negative entities. Powerful in placating the planet Saturn.

Seed Mantras for Rudraksha

1 mukhi—*Om Hreem Namah*

2 mukhi—*Om Namah*

3 mukhi—*Om Kleem Namah*

4 mukhi—*Om Hreem Namah*

5 mukhi—*Om Hreem Namah*

6 mukhi—*Om Hreem Hoom Namah*

7 mukhi—*Om Hoom Namah*

8 mukhi—*Om Hoom Namah*

9 mukhi—*Om Hreem Hoom Namah*

10 mukhi—*Om Hreem Namah Namah*

11 mukhi—*Om Hreem Hoom Namah*

12 mukhi—*Om Krom Kshom Rom Namah*

13 mukhi—*Om Hreem Namah*

14 mukhi—*Om Namah*

Genuine Rudraksha and Fakes

It is no laughing matter that the majority of roadside stalls, shops, and peddlers near Hindu temples in India and Nepal sell fake rudraksha of plastic resin or carved from areca and betel nuts. This "tampered" rudraksha, and other rudraksha of inferior grades, will not give the same effect as authentic rudraksha. Serious rudraksha devotees and seasoned collectors are able to authenticate the real thing from a fake. Many a weary traveler has returned home with inferior quality rudraksha, insect-ridden beads, and even ones the size of oranges. These are sold as one mukhi rudraksha with carvings of serpents, a trident, or a Shiva lingam (phallus shape representing the male divinity of Lord Shiva). All these are useless even though exquisitely crafted by Indian artisans.

Indian and Indonesian rudraksha are not of the same quality as Nepali-grown species—as can be seen by taking measure of weight, color, and the electromagnetic properties emitted by rudraksha. Reiki and other energy workers are able to test the vibrations by touch or dowsing methods. In certain parts of Australia, there is a type of tree called quandong. It is generally used as bush food by Aboriginals. Although referred to as Aussie rudraksha by enthusiasts, quandong is not of the same quality and efficacy as rudraksha from Nepal.

However, quandong is not entirely without its positive properties—its effect is of a lesser quality of rudraksha.

Advanced practitioners in spiritual, esoteric, magical, metaphysical, and Pagan communities specializing in divinatory arts and arcane rituals will find the experimentation and use of real rudraksha beads potently beneficial especially when invoked with a mantra.

Bug Off

❧ by Dallas Jennifer Cobb ❧

With the appearance of the West Nile virus in North America, many people are reaching for commercially made insect repellents, many of which contain the carcinogen DEET (N, N-diethyl-m-toluamide) to ward off mosquitos. To me, it seems ludicrous to risk poisoning ourselves and contracting cancer by using a dangerous chemical, while attempting to protect oneself from the risk of a potentially fatal virus. So what can we do?

Understanding how West Nile virus is transmitted, protecting ourselves generally from mosquito bites, and using herb-based mosquito repellents are our best bets to avoid this disease and the effects of a toxic chemical. This article will cover these topics, and give you simple recipes for making your own mosquito repellents from herbs and essential oils. And, in case you aren't fully convinced, there will be some scary information about the adverse effects of DEET on human health, and its relative inefficacy compared to herbal insect repellents.

The West Nile Virus

West Nile virus has been around since 1937, when it was identified in the West Nile province of Uganda. Since then it has been found in other parts of Africa, the Middle East, west and central Asia, Oceania, and Europe. West Nile virus first appeared in the United States in 1999 with encephalitis, an inflammation of the brain, reported in humans and horses. Confirmed bird cases were reported in Canada in 2001 and human cases in 2002. West Nile virus is presently found through much of central and eastern Canada and the United States, where it has been identified in domestic and wild birds, horses, and humans.

Mosquitos that bite infected birds can acquire West Nile virus. It can then be transferred to humans via a mosquito bite. While it can be transmitted by the bite of an infected mosquito, there is no evidence of West Nile virus being transmitted from animal to human or between humans. Still, health departments recommend that we avoid handling dead birds.

Many people who are infected with West Nile virus suffer few or no symptoms or have a mild fever or dull aching of the body. In rare cases, the infection can cause severe and fatal encephalitis. This severe reaction is more often to occur in older people, infants, and those with a compromised immune system.

If you experience extensive swelling or infection at the site of a mosquito bite, it is recommended that you have a health practitioner examine it and test you for exposure to West Nile virus.

A Bit about Mosquitos

Mosquitos start as eggs in the water, and they grow into larvae and pupae. They leave their water source to become flying adults. Soon after mating, the male mosquito dies. The female may live for up to two months more, laying multiple batches of eggs. While adult mosquitos feed primarily on flower nectars, the female mosquito requires a blood meal to obtain protein to lay eggs. A suitable host is found by the mosquito through its ability to sense carbon dioxide exhalation, heat, and visual movement.

In North America, mosquitos are most prevalent in the warmer seasons, but they are present from early spring through late fall. They are especially prolific following a wet spell or season, as the weather creates the ideal habitat for eggs to grow into maturity.

Protecting Yourself

The best way to protect yourself from West Nile virus is to avoid being bitten by mosquitos. When you are outdoors, wear light-colored long-sleeved clothing to deter mosquitos. Use insect repellents, and avoid going out during the times of day when mosquitos are most prevalent—from dusk until dawn. In North America, West Nile virus cases have occurred primarily in the late summer or early fall, so be especially vigilant in these seasons when mosquitos are most plentiful.

While the chance of contracting West Nile virus from a mosquito bite is low, it is practical to limit your exposure to them. The more bites you receive, the higher your chances of contacting the virus.

Around your home, a good protection practice is to limit the number of places where mosquitos can breed by eliminating standing water. Empty birdbaths, children's pools, and buckets of water. If you use a down-spout collector to gather rainwater (for gardening), make sure the barrel has netting over the top to keep mosquitos out. Fill in any depressions on your lawn or property where water pools, and try to drain any areas where stagnant water sits. Eliminating the breeding grounds of mosquitos limits the number of mosquitos close to the immediate environment of your home.

When planning outings, consider the time of day and the locale you are planning to attend. Try to avoid swamps, marshes, and shorelines around rivers and lakes during peak mosquito season. If you are going camping, plan a trip to a dry area to limit the number of mosquitos contacted while spending a lot of time outdoors.

Dangerous DEET

When you do venture outside, choose your mosquito repellents carefully. While it is important to limit the chances of being bitten by mosquitos, many commercially produced insect repellents contain DEET.

While DEET is the most often recommended means to stop the bites of mosquitos, it isn't really safe. For children, pregnant women, and people with compromised immune systems, the use of DEET can be downright dangerous.

As a known carcinogen, DEET causes cancer. Many of DEET's other known side effects and exclusions are not widely publicized. DEET is a known neurotoxin, meaning it poisons our nervous systems. DEET can cause encephalitis in children. DEET is also known to cause birth defects in fetuses of women who were frequent users of the chemical during their pregnancies. Medical data has shown that adults have experienced dangerous reactions, such as seizures, when the use of a DEET-based repellent was combined with some over-the-counter medications.

In case you are skeptical of an herbalist's motives, know too it is not just the herbal advocates who warn us off of DEET. Research done at Duke University Medical Center has shown that DEET's widespread side effects range from rashes and hives to uncontrollable twitching, muscle spasms, dizziness, and even death. With heavy exposure to DEET, humans may experience memory loss, headache, weakness, fatigue, muscle and joint pain, tremors, and shortness of breath.

Extreme caution should be used when using a DEET-based product, and exposure to DEET should be limited. Children are particularly at risk. Chemicals affect their developing nervous systems, and their skin more readily absorbs the chemicals. With immune systems and livers not fully developed, children don't have the same systemic ability to detoxify harmful chemicals as mature adults do. The Center for Disease Control and the American Academy of Pediatrics caution against the use of DEET on children under three years old. Beyond this, even older children are at risk. DEET has caused toxic encephalopathy, a swelling of the brain that can cause disorientation, convulsions, and death in several girls under age nine.

What can you do to protect children from mosquito bites? Keep them inside during prime mosquito hours, and when they have to go out use common sense to protect them. Cover carriages and strollers with netting to protect infants and babies. Dress older children in appropriate light-colored long-sleeved and long-legged clothing. Dress them in jackets or sweatshirts with hoods, and use a non-DEET insect repellent on them.

And, even if you aren't convinced by all this scary research and documentation, remember: DEET causes cancer.

Herbal Insect Repellents

Researchers at Iowa State University found nepetalactone, the essential oil in catnip (*Nepeta cataria*) that gives the plant its characteristic odor, is ten times more effective at repelling mosquitoes than DEET. Researchers reported that treatment by amounts of nepetalactone one-tenth as much as the typical DEET amount had the same repelling effect on mosquitos.

Catnip is a perennial herb from the mint family. It grows wild in most parts of the United States and Canada and is cultivated for commercial use. It is best known for its ability to attract and stimulate cats, but it has historically been used as an herbal remedy to treat fevers, colds, cramps, insomnia, and migraines.

Other herb-based substances that are effective in repelling mosquitos include the oils from citronella (*Cymbopagon nardus*), eucalyptus (*Eucalyptus globulus*), lavender (*Lavendula angustifolia*), rosemary (*Rosemarinus officinalis*), pennyroyal (*Mentha pulegium*), cedarwood (*Juniperus mexicana*), lemongrass (*Cynbopogon citratus*), and tea tree oil (*Melaleuca alternifolia*). Please note that pennyroyal is contraindicated for pregnant women, because it stimulates uterine contractions and can cause miscarriage.

While the herbs listed above are recommended by herbalists for their efficacy in repelling insects, many lack the scientific research to back them up that catnip has enjoyed of late. If you are a practitioner of homemade herbal remedies, you may not need the stamp of approval that university-based research lends to herbal products. But for those who like the reassurances of experts, research validates traditional knowledge and historical practices.

In addition to catnip, Canada's Pest Management Regulatory Agency is currently reevaluating citronella and lavender oils. So there may be more widely publicized research on these two herbal-based essential oils in the future.

While herbal-based repellents are effective for a shorter time span than DEET-based repellents (two hours on average), their safety and lack of side effects make them preferable for many. Because herbal repellents will need to be applied several times a day, it is probably best to have several different herbal repellent mixtures available. Alternate your use of these so you don't develop a sensitivity to any one product.

A variety of prepared herbal-based insect repellents is available at most natural food and health stores, or you can make your own.

Making Herbal Insect Repellents

Insect repellents can be made easily at home by anyone familiar with herbs. Because of their concentration and efficacy, essential oils are often used. Essential oils are concentrates of the natural oils of plant materials extracted by steam distillation. Because they are concentrated, they should be used with care and patch-tested for any skin reaction prior to regular use. Repellents can be made using oil, witch hazel, or alcohol as the carrier.

While it is advisable to have and use a liquid herbal-based insect repellent, in a pinch you can also go directly to the herb garden. Grab a large bunch of catnip, crush it slightly in your hands so that the leaves are bruised, and then rub it vigorously over your clothes and exposed skin. While it lacks the uniform coverage that a liquid insect repellent provides, you will have anointed yourself with the oils and scent that mosquitos dislike.

Catnip, the Conqueror Oil

Catnip essential oil is very expensive. Because of its efficacy, how-ever, even a 1 percent concentration of catnip oil will repel mosquitos. So splurge, and buy some. As per the research done on catnip, a 5- to 10-percent solution is recommended.

10-Percent Solution

5   tsps. catnip essential oil

1   cup carrier oil

5-Percent Solution

2½   tsps. catnip essential oil

1   cup carrier oil

This recipe is most effective in repelling mosquitos and my preferred herbal insect repellent, but I offer other recipes so you have a few variations to try. You will smell differently at times, and you will not develop a sensitivity to any one combination.

Bug Off Broth (Not for pregnant women)

1   tsp. pennyroyal essential oil

1   tsp. citronella essential oil

1   tsp. eucalyptus essential oil

1   tsp. rosemary essential oil

1   tsp. tansy essential oil

1   cup carrier oil

For carrier oil, use olive or almond depending on your preference. These are both liquid at room temperature and can be used in a pump or spray bottle. For people with nut allergies, olive is recommended. While it has a slightly musky scent that doesn't please everyone, it is highly emollient and readily available in the grocery store. Mix all the ingredients together and store in a dark glass jar, away from the light. For regular use put this in a pump spray bottle or a squeezy bottle with a plastic cap. Before going outdoors, rub some on your hands, then apply to clothing and exposed skin. With a spray bottle, spray the mixture evenly over your clothes and body. Please remember that oil can stain clothes. Avoid contact with your eyes. If a rash develops, discontinue use.

Sweet Smeller Repeller

1   tsp. citronella essential oil

1   tsp. lavender essential oil

½   tsp. tea tree essential oil

1   cup carrier oil

If you use coconut oil as the carrier oil, it adds a sweet earthy aroma to this mix, but because coconut oil is almost solid at room temperature it will not work in a spray bottle. Almond oil is very neutral in scent, so you will detect only the lemony lavender mint scent of the essential oils. This combination will provide 30 to 60 minutes of insect-repelling action.

Citronella Repeller

1   tsp. citronella essential oil

½   cup witch hazel

Witch hazel extract has a double action. It is a suitable carrier for the citronella essential oil and is soothing to insect bites, should you be bitten. You can also substitute a carrier oil or rubbing alcohol. Shake well before each use.

Commercial Herbal Insect Repellents

If you don't want to make your own herbal insect repellents, good-quality commercial products are widely available in health and natural food stores. It is also possible to find these products in high-end children's stores. If you live in an area where these are not readily available, do an online search to find mail order sources.

Mentioning the products here is not an endorsement of any specific product but is intended to describe the range and variety of commercial herbal-based insect repellents currently available in stores.

Nature's Herbal Mosquito & Insect Shield contains catnip oil and promises long-lasting natural protection against insects. It claims to be effective for up to eight hours, but realistically you will have to reapply more frequently.

Dschungel Juice Insect Shield is a water-based insect repellent that claims to have been extensively tested and found both effective against mosquitos and safe for all. It boasts a combination of clove, eucalyptus, geranium, orange, palma rosa, rosemary, and sage essential oils in a natural base. Dschungel Juice is free of chemical preservatives, alcohol, and colorings.

Burt's Bees Herbal Insect Repellent is also said to be safe enough to apply with confidence to children and pets for long-lasting natural protection against biting insects. The active ingredients include lemongrass oil, citronella oil, rosemary oil, grape seed oil, and vitamin E.

Buzz Away contains the essential oils of citronella, cedarwood, eucalyptus, lemongrass, and peppermint, and is registered by the Environmental Protection Agency.

In addition to these commercial brand names, you can also search online for sources of catnip essential oil and citronella essential oil to make your own insect repellents. If you can obtain organic oils, which offer better quality and are untainted by solvents commonly used in the extraction process, spend the extra money and protect yourself that much more.

If You Get Bitten

For relief from the itch of insect bites use lemon balm oil, chickweed cream, or witch hazel directly on the bite. If you can avoid scratching the bite, which disperses the toxins, the itching will be reduced.

Keep an eye on the site of the bite and, if you experience extreme swelling or infection, consult a health-care practitioner, and ask to be tested for West Nile virus exposure.

Remember, the chances of contracting West Nile virus are very small. So, rather than cower indoors in fear, do what you can to limit the presence of mosquitos around your home, cover up, apply an herbal-based insect repellent, and get outdoors. A healthy life is one worth living.

Prostate Health

❧ by Leeda Alleyn Pacotti ❧

As most of us are aware, men are notorious for ignoring health matters. After all, consider the male motto "no pain; no gain." Many men think they can exert away or ignore signs of pain, and it will eventually go away. Just need a little Ben-Gay, and you're good to go.

Sadly, responsibility for the good health of men usually falls to those who love them—moms, wives, significants, or offspring. Those who take on this responsibility usually do a pretty fair job of keeping men in good form. Unfortunately, being aware of someone else's body is not the same as living in it. Without knowledge of men's health needs, neither men nor women can understand and intervene when a common problem arises in the male system that is more serious.

Buried within the abdominal cavity, the prostate is a walnut-sized gland shaped like a doughnut that encircles the urethral canal just below the urinary bladder. Immediately behind the prostate lies the rectal colon. As a part of the reproductive organs, the prostate manufactures most of the fluids found in semen, the ejaculatory carrier for sperm.

Once a man reaches adulthood and until his mid- to late-forties, the prostate maintains its small size. However, in middle age, most men experience a secondary growth of the gland that is considered abnormal but noncancerous. Prostatic hyperplasia is a rapid cellular growth in the central portion of the prostate, where the gland encircles the urethra. Because the prostate is small, difficulties with the additional cellular growth frequently aren't apparent until a man is in his sixties or older.

Urinary symptoms or difficulties often signal prostate enlargement, which gradually strangles the urethral canal. Specifically, a man may have a weak urine stream and difficulty with urinating. There may be an involuntarily interruption in the urine flow, a dribble after the flow is completed, or an increased frequency in urination both day and night. He may also feel the bladder is not fully emptied, or he may notice blood flecks in the urine. Unless he is consciously bothered by these symptoms or experiences continually dull or sharp pain, a man usually will not seek out a medical exam or advice.

As men well know, more is involved in examining a prostatic condition than answering some questions or offering some urine for testing. An allopathic doctor must do a digital rectal exam to feel the prostate gland, which is nestled against the rectal wall. While this organic arrangement is helpful in assessing prostatic growth, it also provides some clues about possible origins of the common condition of prostatitis.

As explained, prostatitis is an inflammation of the gland. Located under the urinary bladder and immediately in front of the rectum, the prostate is a likely candidate for toxic accumulations. Some men ignore urges for urination or a bowel movement until they experience urgent pain. However, this habit of waiting for unbearable distress brings an unwanted eventuality.

Because both the urinary bladder and the rectum fill with toxic wastes from foods and cellular breakdown, the prostate can osmotically absorb toxicities if these organs are not regularly evacuated. Any organ, gland, or tissue mass in a toxic condition inflames or acquires a heated condition. To counteract this inflammation, the body naturally tries to subdue it by increasing water volume within and around the affected organic cells.

As with the site of a small burn, water plumps up and swells the inflamed prostate. Although the watery accumulation helps to cool and soothe the organ, the resulting swelling further cinches the urethral canal. This urethral constriction prevents complete urination, leaving toxic urine in the bladder, which can result in a bladder infection, kidney infection and damage, or development of stones from unflushed sediments. To some extent, a severely swollen prostate inhibits the ease of a bowel movement, which becomes unnecessarily painful as compacted waste moves against the prostate alongside the rectal wall. If a man avoids a bowel movement, retained toxicities can result in rectal inflammations. Should he wait too long between movements, the bowel matter dries and moves with great difficulty, increasing the possibilities of internal and external hemorrhoids.

Should the prostatitis be ignored, the gland becomes a breeding ground for bacterial growth and sudden and acute or chronic prostate infections. The usual first sign of an infection is sharp pain between the scrotum and the rectum. Additionally, what urine is passed burns and ejaculation is painful.

Ultimately, prostatitis, whether noninfectious or infectious, can develop into impotence. Should growth from prostatic hyperplasia progress, a man risks cancer of the prostate.

Allopathic Prostate Treatments

Once prostate enlargement is discovered, most allopathic doctors consider prescribing one of four alphablockers to relax the neck muscles of the bladder and increase the urinary flow. The recognized medications are terazosin (Hytrin), doxazosin (Cardura), tamsulosin (Flomax), and alfuzosin (Uroxatral). For the two-thirds of men given prescriptions, these drugs work to increase flow but do not shrink the prostate. Consequently, they must be taken indefinitely. Alphablockers can cause low blood pressure when taken with impotence medications, such as Viagra.

Another possible medication is finasteride (Proscar and Propecia), which shrinks an unusually large prostate. With a possible side effect of impotence, the long-term effects of finasteride are unknown. This drug does not prevent prostatic cancer.

If a man does not want medications, other allopathic therapies are available: heat therapy, introduced up the length of the urethral canal to destroy excess prostatic tissue; microwave therapy, which introduces controlled heat directly into the enlarged prostate; radio-frequency therapy, during which long needles inserted into the prostate heat from radio waves to destroy excess glandular tissue; electroevaporization, in which a metal instrument emits high-frequency electrical current, cutting and vaporizing excess prostatic tissue; or laser therapy, which produces heat in the prostate for cellular destruction. None of these forms of heat therapy provide a biopsy sample of prostatic tissue.

In place of heat therapies, a man can consider a prostatic stent—a tiny metal coil, placed in the urethral canal to widen it and aid urination. Unfortunately, the stent neither addresses or alleviates any condition or symptom of the prostate gland itself.

Previous surgical treatments for prostatic conditions are now reserved for very severe complications involving kidney stones, bladder stones, or cancer. Although surgeries are effective by reducing enlargements, they are ruled out for men with cardiac conditions, cirrhosis of the liver, diabetes, kidney dysfunctions, psychiatric disorders, or respiratory problems. If a man continues to ignore an inflamed, infected, potentially cancerous prostatic enlargement, the testicles can suffer the same excruciating symptoms. At this point, and especially if developing cancer is found, the surgical option is likely to be radical removal of the prostate gland and possible castration.

Seeking an Alternative

Although clinical findings suggest that half of men in their sixties and nearly 90 percent of men past seventy will suffer painful prostatic enlargement, these conclusions do not reflect some critical information. Is prostatitis more or less coincident with certain genetic segments of the population? Do certain types of professions or work habits contribute to enlargement or inflammation? Given that the symptoms of prostatic enlargement and inflammation have been known for over a century, has the medical scientific community adequately investigated a broad enough spectrum of mental, physical, or habitual factors that could, alone or in combination, alter the normal prostate in middle age?

Unusual growth of any kind indicates that an organ or tissue is undernourished and enlarges as a form of self-protection. Fortunately, three nutrients are identified for the prostate—the minerals selenium and zinc and vitamin E. Selenium is easily obtained from kelp, seafood, garlic, mushrooms, and onions. Because vitamin E works synergistically with selenium, the vitamin can be taken with or after ingesting selenium-rich foods. Zinc is also readily available from raw seeds, such as pumpkin, sunflower, sesame, and peanuts or cashews, all of which can be eaten alone as snacks or added to salads and hot cereals. Other excellent sources of zinc are from lean beef, calf liver, or beef liver, taken from cattle that are not given hormones or steroids.

As a matter of general diet, men need to limit beverages after 7 pm to retard nighttime urination. Alcohol especially increases urine and will irritate the bladder. Coffee has been suggested as a contributor to prostatitis.

Among herbal remedies, saw palmetto has been touted as a cure-all for prostate enlargement. Although this herb has some effectiveness, studies are inconclusive. Further, saw palmetto must be taken for at least three months to observe any difference in prostatic symptoms by reducing hormonal stimulation that causes enlargement. If symptoms have not begun to subside in that time, the herb should be discontinued.

Other possible herbs are juniper berry and kelp, which increase urination. Echinacea helps alleviate the symptoms of enlargement and weakness of the prostate. Herbs to avoid are american gensing, cinnamon, cordyceps, ephedra, epimedium, sarsparilla, and siberian gensing. To help prevent urinary infections, drinking unsugared cranberry juice, found in health food stores, alters the pH level in the bladder.

Certain exercises help the prostate. Walking thirty minutes each day helps stimulate the bladder and the rectal colon to evacuate properly. Remaining inactive to avoid pain increases urinary retention, causing the bladder to press on the enlarged prostate.

A man can also perform a prostate massage. While lying on his back on the floor, he draws up his knees as far as possible and clasps the soles of his feet together. While holding his feet in this position, he forcefully lowers his legs repeatedly.

The most common sense exercise for the prostate is regular sexual activity, which reaches the natural conclusion of ejaculation. Unfortunately, when ejaculation is suppressed, prolonged engorgement of the prostate, with its produced fluids, can lead to its functional and possibly structural damage. Sexual abstinence is not recommended.

Because the prostate gland may still enlarge despite diet and exercise, some testing is required to determine its condition. In naturopathy, such tests are accomplished by muscle-testing responses to direct questions, which can reveal whether natural treatment methods are helping the gland.

Ultimately, though, if natural methods provide little continued relief, only the man at question can decide what course to pursue to rectify his health. We who love our men regard them as too precious to forfeit and will remain right by their sides.

Herbs
for
Beauty

Henna Beauty Treatments

☙ by Stephanie Rose Bird ☙

While many people know henna as a gorgeous hair colorant, the cosmetic use of the plant barely scratches the surface of the plant's dynamic story. Once we begin to explore henna for its use of thousands of years, we find that it is truly a miraculous plant.

Henna possesses a complex array of healing possibilities. More than a beautiful dye for the hair, henna is symbolic of blood, the essence of life. This article explores the history and meaning of henna to various cultures and techniques for using it.

The History of Henna

Henna is an herbaceous shrub called *Lawsonia inermis* in botanical Latin, named after the eighteenth century British explorer John Lawson. The

plant thrives in hot, dry climates. The use of the herb for health and beauty is far older than the British discovery. Samples have been carbon-dated back to 3,500 BC, meaning it has been in use by humans for 7,000 years.

Henna is a Persian word for the plant that has many names. In Arabic it is called *khanna*. In India, henna is called by many names depending on the dialect: *menhadi*, *mehendi*, *mehedi*, *mendi*, *hina*, and *mendika*. Ancient hieroglyphs in tombs in the Valley of the Nile refer to it using the Egyptian name *pouquer*. This name refers to the dye created from the plant that is used to color the fingernails of mummies. A lovely perfume created from the henna plant is mentioned in the K'oran as *camphire*. Since the Hindus of India call it *mehndi*, a name synonymous with the henna plant used for temporary tattoos, I will use it here alternately with henna.

Henna tattoo patterns have been found at dig sites of the early civilization Catal Huyuk from around 7000 BC. The Ugaritics, Canaanites, Cycladics, Minoans, Mycenaeans, and Egyptians created early artifacts showing henna patterns.

In early India, henna was applied by dipping palms and soles into a thick paste of crushed fresh leaves, creating a solid red stain without pattern. Middle Eastern henna decoration was done by mixing dried powdered leaves into a paste and applying it with a stick. Henna is still in use in parts of Asia, especially India and in the Middle East and North African countries, where it flourishes; it is catching on in the United States and Europe.

Here's a rough timeline of henna use:

7000 BC—Catal Huyuk

5000 BC—Turkey

3000 BC—Syria, Cycladic Islands

2100 BC—Israel/Palestine, Jordan, Lebanon

1700 BC—Crete, Cypress, Greece, Libya, Nubia

1300 BC—Iraq, Iran

1200 BC—Tunisia, Kuwait, Morocco, Algeria, Mali, Sudan, Yemen

1000 BC—Jewish culture (worldwide)

550 BC—Muslim culture

400 BC—Pakistan and India

First century AD—Christian (Coptic, Armenian)

AD 700–800—Asia (Sri Lanka, Turkistan, Uzbekistan, China, Tibet, Burma, Thailand)

AD 800—Ethiopia, Nigeria

AD 1200—Indonesia

AD 1800—South Africa

The Uses of Henna:
Cool Medicine for Health and Beauty

Below are listed some medicinal uses of henna.

It is antipyretic (a natural coolant), hence its popularity in hot climates.

It is antispasmodic (soothing), antiseptic, astringent (drying), antibacterial, and antifungal.

It contains natural sun-screening chemicals and is effective for soothing sunburn when applied as a paste topically.

It is a natural deodorant and antiperspirant, especially for the feet.

Dyeing the soles of feet is called a step-in design. This insulates the foot from hot desert sands and is a wonderful adornment and a painted substitute for sandals.

In ayurvedic medicine, henna tea is a beverage used to treat headaches, soothe fevers, and stomach pains.

A henna paste can be applied to the skin for dermatitis (skin ailments).

Folk remedies from around the world feature henna as a curative for rheumatism, nervousness, some kinds of tumors, cancer, sexually transmitted diseases, and leprosy.

In aromatherapy, the scent of the fragrant henna flower is used to make *hina* perfume. This perfume is purchased in small bottles (drams) of thick oil from health food stores and specialty Asian suppliers. The oil can be applied to the pulse points, temples, or crown of the head. The oil-based perfume called Hina Mehndi Attar has a spicy, floral, musky scent. This is a calming and balancing scent used by both men and women.

While henna can be applied anywhere and even taken internally (if prepared by an ayurvedic herbalist), it is best known and most widely used as an application to the hair, hands, and feet.

Henna Tattoos

While some folks do not associate henna tattoos with Africa, it has a lengthy history on the continent. It is believed that the sea-faring Canaanites spread the tradition of using henna across the Mediterranean to North Africa between 1700 and 600 BC. Nerfertiti was a famous redhead whose name translates as "the beautiful one comes." It is thought that her hair was made red with henna. Cleopatra used henna and rose water to create an alluring dip for the sails of her boat when she was approaching Mark Anthony.

The Berber and Tuareg people have a distinctive way of ornamenting with henna that incorporates pre-Islamic mythology and symbols. They formulate a deep, almost black color of henna paste, which is applied in large, bold, geometric patterns.

Henna was incorporated into the customs of Muslims in the sixth century AD. Henna traditions were long established in

Arabia. Henna was used by Mohammed's wives to color his beard. The henna flower is considered the favorite of Mohammed. Muslims use the henna plant in various ways. Some of the most complex and elegant henna designs ever created were done between AD 900 to 1700 in Islamic countries.

Patterns

Since henna has been used around the world from the most ancient of times to the present, I could easily dedicate an entire book to the subject; instead, this is a general introduction to its uses and the meaning of its patterns, particularly in Africa.

In ancient Egypt, henna (called Egyptian privet or mignotte) was used to treat ringworm, headaches, sweaty palms, burning feet, and athlete's foot. A healing gargle was made for sore throat. It wa also used for jaundice, enlarged spleens and skin diseases. In the Middle East and northern Africa, particularly Morocco, henna is incorporated into life. If you would like to try it on your own, follow these directions:

1. Bring 1 cup of water to a boil. Add 2 roschip (or hibiscus tea bags) and 1 black tea bag. Cover. Steep overnight.

2. Pour approximately 1 cup of the green henna powder into a nonreactive (stainless steel or glass) bowl.

3. Add the tea to the powder.

4. Stir to form a thick paste. (Add liquid slowly so that the mix doesn't become watery.)

5. Add a few drops of eucalyptus or clove essential oil to enhance the staining power of henna; this is called a mordant. (Use sparingly, as these are skin irritants; avoid altogether if you have allergies). Let this sit for 1 hour so the color can mature.

6. While maturing the henna batch, create a lemon sugar glaze. Squeeze and strain the juice of a ripe lemon. Add 3 tablespoons white sugar. Stir and set aside.

7. Dip fingers or soles of the feet in the henna, or create a pattern. When the henna begins to dry, apply the lemon sugar with a cotton swab. Reapply lemon sugar every 20 minutes until a protective glaze forms.

8. You can use a porcupine quill (purchased from a beading supply shop or craft store) or bamboo skewer to draw more intricate designs. Most henna artisans prefer pastry-decorating tubes with very narrow tips to spread the henna.

9. When a glaze forms on the hennaed design, gently wrap your hands in gauze or toilet paper to protect the designs.

10. Be sure to keep your hands warm. Hold them near a lit fireplace, over a candle flame (far enough away so that you do not burn yourself), or drink hot tea.

11. Keep the henna on your hands or feet as long as possible—at a minimum, four hours; overnight is preferred. Your dreams will be informative.

12. Flake off the henna.

13. Massage with sesame or olive oil.

Hennaed Feet

Another simple form of mehndi is to henna the feet. Henna can be applied individually to the toes, to the top or bottom of the feet, or as a simple step-in design, similar to the fingertip dip. Just as it sounds, with the step-in design you simply step into a bowl or plate of henna, smooth it out, and follow above directions.

Patterns

Once the henna bug takes hold, you will find that you are quickly ready to move from dots and dips to exquisite patterns. Begin with a simple pattern like diamonds, dots, or stars. Explore traditional patterns from the powerful centers of the negasset—Fez, Marrakech, and Casablanca, Morocco. In these cities, intricate lace-like patterns abound, similar to the Islamic architecture that flourishes there.

The patterns are generally abstract and geometric since the Islamic faith that inspired it forbids the use of realistic imagery. Abstract stylized patterns are commonly shaped into symbols. One of the most important is Elain. Elain is a defensive eye shape that appears in ritual and crafts. Triangles, diamonds, circles, dots, lozenges, and crosses are also popular.

Other Moroccan symbols include magic numbers, magic squares, verses of the K'oran, Arabic script, geometric figures (triangles, squares, crosses, eight-point stars), spirals, circles, diamonds, floral and vegetable shapes, and abstract human hands and eyes.

Images of fierce animals are utilized for protective, defensive magic. These include the snake, a prominent image in African art across the continent and in the diaspora. The snake appears realistic or abstract. It is a symbol of male sexuality, virility, and fertility. The dangerous scorpion is used in imagery in Morocco as a protective symbol. Fish are associated with rain, which assures good crops, sustenance, and fertility. Turtles are associated with the highest character of, for example, saints, as well as with protective energy and fertility. Birds are considered messengers in the K'oran, emblems of heaven and earth. The eagle is a symbol of power. Lizards and salamanders soak up the Sun, thus they are symbols of the search of the individual for spiritual enlightenment.

Henna Medicine for Mind, Body, and Spirit

One of the most revered qualities of henna is its ability to cool. It is a good idea to reflect on the cool qualities of the henna herb:

Henna is a cooling plant that aids with numerous medical disorders.

The soothing patterns of mehndi tattoos are considered a calming influence that uplifts depression.

Mehndi requires patience; cultivating patience quells anxiety and alleviates stress.

Henna invites communal activity, as it is difficult to work with alone.

Personal Reflections on Mehndi: Walking the Beauty Way

Hands help us express our being, they help us shape and define our way of being in this world and beyond. We use our hands in greetings, in farewells, to identify things by pointing, in invocation and worship (hands pressed together or outstretched), or as a sign of goodwill (the peace sign). In weddings and handfastings, hands come together sensuously. Raising our hand in the air is our way of saying, "I am here"; "I exist."

I remember when my mother died I reflected on her hands, placed neatly on her belly in the coffin. I had always looked at Ma's hands. When I sat on her lap and she stroked my head as a toddler, I looked to the tender hands; when she and I made meatballs together, I marveled at her crafty hands; when they were polished, I noticed the beauty in the shape of her oval fingernails; when she smoothed her skirt, I saw the finesse in the movement of her fingers. My head is full of images of my parents' hands.

When my father lay in the intensive care unit on life support, his eyes were clamped shut by virtue of a medically induced coma. Deprived of his hazel eyes, the route to his soul, I was left to reflect on his hands. He had strong hands, the hands of a carver, sculptor, fisherman, and laborer. Sadly, these hands that I had come to identify with him were swollen, almost beyond recognition. Each day I would massage his hands with cooling essential oils, in hopes that somehow I was calming his spirit, connecting to our past together as father and daughter through the touching of our hands.

My father died on St. Valentine's Day—the day of love and of the heart. His passing came during the beginning of my witching hour, dusk. The sky lit up in a beautiful show of deep purple, mysterious indigo, and a spread of warm magenta. The geese headed north, probably frightened by the haunting song of his loved ones, directing him home. I held my hands on top of his until all the warmth left his body. Afterwards, I remained cold, wrapped in the dank darkness of mourning for weeks.

When I was ready for warmth, I huddled near my hearth, finding things to cook just so I could be near it. I looked above it to the calendar. It said March, a cold month where I live. On my "Women of the African Ark" calendar, a mother and daughter huddled together wearing the black *bui-bui* that is the dress of orthodox Islamic faith in Kenya. Below the days of the month, there was a small insert of hands being treated to black henna in Lamu, Kenya; I was intrigued.

My heart began to swell with hope. Perhaps the healing traditions of my sisters in Kenya could help me pass through this dark period of mourning. Perhaps help once again was in the palm of my hand through the grace of my friends from nature.

I began to focus on the art created from henna, which I had heard people call *mehndi*. I did some research and found the best mehndi artist, typically called a negasseh, available in my area to have my palms, hands, and wrists tattooed in memory of my parents.

I reached to mehndi because it honors the beauty of our hands. Mehndi would allow further reflection on how my parents' hands shaped my life. Full recognition of ancestry reminds us that we are but mere vessels, pots shaped neatly by the DNA of our ancestors. My hands are a living testament of the lives of my parents and their parents before them who have now passed to the great beyond.

Our hands are sensual instruments, leading us forward in this journey toward the divine. We want our experiences to transcend the present, see the past, and divine the future. In short, we have an endless quest to grasp spirit. Hands are a type of conduit that leads to and from the soul. The hands are also our tools for touching one another—thus they have the potential to heal, acknowledge, protect, and express love.

Our palms hold magical potentiality, called *ashe* in West Africa. Interesting enough, of all the parts of the body, the palm takes henna the best, staining the deepest color.

As a very flat surface, the palms are loaded with design possibilities. Traditionally, palms are decorated with mandalas, paisley, or spiral shapes. Palms are ideal surfaces because of their even temperature, their thickness, lightness of color, the fact that they are hairless, and because of the dazzling effects that can be produced as a combination of these factors. The wrists are also promising palettes. An important joint and home to important veins, our wrists are typically decorated with vines as symbols of growth and renewal.

The negasseh I was fortunate enough to find covered my palms, wrists, fingers, and the backs of my hands with an intricate, lacy pattern, Moroccan style. He chose specific designs to help ease my mourning and those with promise to replenish the spirit after sustaining loss. I'm happy to say it worked!

Soon after painting my palms, hands, and wrists with elaborate patterns in mehndi, I was back dancing with my sisters, doing American tribal-style belly dancing. This is a joyful way to express with the hands what henna can do for the soul. You have probably already seen many dancers with hennaed hands and feet.

Henna art can imbue your life with health and happiness, filling your heart and home with joy. I hope that you will take some time with family or friends to enjoy the healing beauty of henna.

Herbal Sleep Pillows

✦ by Chandra Moira Beal ✦

For centuries, the fragrance of herbs has been captured in pillows and sweet bags to purify and scent the home. These aromatic pillows were used by Old World mothers to lull their babes into tranquil sleep, by those seeking relief from headache or depression, and by the lonely-hearted who yearned to find true love.

Mothers frequently fashioned small pillows of dill to encourage their children to enter sleep. The word *dilla*, from which the herb eventually took its name, is from a Norse word meaning "to lull." Agrimony was also a popular herb to use in pillows since it was believed to be soporific, or sleep inducing. An old English writing tells us that, "If it is leyed under a manns head, he shal sleepyn as he were dead; He shal never drede ne wakyn till fro under his head it be taken."

Making Herbal Pillows

Fragrant herbs were sewn into pillows and placed at the head of the bed or between the linens. During medieval times, herbal pillows and sachets were more of a necessity than decoration, designed to mask the poor sanitary conditions of the time when fresh air was considered potentially dangerous. Sometimes entire mattresses were stuffed with aromatic herbs both to induce a restful sleep and to repel pests that would otherwise feed on mattress materials.

Good sleep is essential to our health and well-being. The aromas in these little pillows can lull you to sleep on those nights when you are tossing and turning, when you want to promote dreams. They can help you wake up rested and refreshed. The small, cloth-covered packages containing dried herbs and other ingredients are meant to be tucked between your bed pillow and the pillowcase or between your sheets.

Remember that sleep blends are very different from potpourri. Do not expect a sleep blend to have the noticeably strong scents of a potpourri blend. Sleep blends are subtle. Their fragrances are released as you move about on the pillow during the night.

Before creating the sleep pillow, decide what you will be using it for: to repel bad dreams, strengthen your prophetic abilities, rest, healing, etc. Choose your herbs and oils according to the pillow's use. They are very easy to make, even if you have few sewing skills.

Herbs to Promote Sleep

Angelica: Prophetic dreams and visions

Anise: To repel nightmares

Basil: Restorative rest

Bay laurel: Inspiration, repel negativity

Bergamot: Soothe the nerves, give relaxing sleep

Cedarwood: Repel bad dreams

Chamomile: Sleep like a baby

Clary sage: Clarity of thoughts

Cloves: Retrieving buried memories

Elderflowers: Ease headaches

Frankincense: Exotic dreams

Hops: Restful sleep and healing

Hyacinth: Stop nightmares

Jasmine: Increase psychic dreams, lift depression, quiet the nerves, calming

Lavender: Cure depression

Lemon balm: Uplifting and energizing

Lemon verbena: Cheering and invigorating

Lilac: Recalling past lives

Marjoram: Relieve depression

Mint: Refreshing thoughts

Mimosa: Prophetic dreams, getting to the truth, making decisions

Mugwort: Visions and prophetic dreams

Myrrh: Tapping into past lives

Mullein: Repel bad dreams

Orange: Happiness

Oregano: Mental stimulation

Pineapple sage: Warding off negative energy

Rose: Calming

Rosemary: To prevent nightmares and headaches, improve memory

Sandalwood: Spiritual cleansing

St. John's wort: Banishes negative spirits

Thyme: For visions during dreamtime

Valerian: Deep rest

Vanilla: Sensual dreams

The number of herbal blends is endless. Making your own herbal sleep pillows not only saves you money, but using essential oils increases their effectiveness and makes reviving them much easier. If your sleep pillow seems to be losing its fragrance, just open a small corner of the pillow and add a few drops of your essential oils onto the herbs and stitch it closed. If you don't want to go to that trouble then just put a few drops of essential oils on the outside of the pillow and let it dry completely before using.

To increase the aromatic properties of your herbal sleep pillow, mix the herbs and oils the day before you begin sewing. Fill a sealable plastic bag with the herbs and spices you have chosen for stuffing and add the oils of your choice. How many drops to use depends on the size of the sleep pillow, how many you are making, and the strength of the herbs and spices you are planning to use. With most herbs and spices, three to four drops of oil should be sufficient; if you are using cotton batting to stuff the pillow, fifteen or twenty drops would be better. Add no more than five drops at a time until you reach a strength to your taste. Remember, what smells nice standing over the bowl may well be too strong when you sleep on the pillow, so use restraint.

Herbal pillows are made by sewing dried herbs into a square of cloth or a bag, but without a fixative, their aroma is short-lived. Many herbs lose much of their original scent when dried. The lovely scent of the rose, for instance, is greatly diminished when dried. Fixatives help to retain and develop the fragrant combination of herbs used for making herbal pillows.

Cellulose chips are a good fixative for essential oils. Orris root can be substituted, but some people are sensitive to it. Traditional animal-based fixatives are ambergris, civet, and musk. Ambergris is a secretion obtained from the sperm whale, civet from the African civet cat, and musk from the male musk deer of Central Asia. These extracts are available in synthetic form, a product more sensitive to the preservation of wildlife.

Orris root and benzoin are suitable plant fixatives and are widely available. Orris root is obtained by sun-drying and peeling the fresh root of an iris. After drying, the root is stored for two years to develop a delicate violet scent. Orris root is usually purchased in ground, powdered form. Benzoin is a gum that comes from a shrub native to Java and Siam. Benzoin is a common ingredient in incense.

Spices add an interesting scent to the herbal mixture and also act as fixatives. Cinnamon is derived from a tree grown in China, India, and the East Indies, and was used during biblical times to make holy oils to anoint priests and altars. The familiar curled sticks, obtained from the inner bark of a young tree, may be ground and added to the herbal mixture.

Sandalwood, native to the Malabar coast, is another enticing additive. Since ancient times, the wood of this tree was used for making fans and musical instruments and to line closets to ward off moths. Sandalwood is also burned at the altar and is an important ingredient in incense burned in synagogues. Sandalwood comes in chips or shavings, but powder is most suitable for herbal pillows.

The bark of myrrh is highly fragrant and was valued as an embalming agent in Egypt and as a perfume by the ancient Hebrews. Native to Arabia and Ethiopia, the bark of this tree produces a bitter-tasting gum once used as a cure for sore throat. It was burned by the Sun worshippers of Heliopolis each day at noon until the mid-1700s. A powder form of myrrh is obtainable.

These are just a sampling of potential fixative ingredients to which you may add endless combinations of herbs and flowers to complete your herbal blend. If you wish to give your sleep pillow some body, shape, or weight, mix your herbs with flax seeds, rice, or buckwheat. Flax seeds especially have a long shelf life and give a fluid feel to the pillows.

To make your sleep pillows, all you need are two pieces of material, any size or shape that you want, and something to fasten them together. Various materials are suitable for pillow coverings, such as velvet, silk, wool, cotton, satin, or chintz. Fabrics should be soft and breathable to allow the herbal aromas to come through. A layer of muslin or cotton can be placed between the outer layers of material to make the pillow soft and help prevent the herbs from bunching into one corner. Another trick to prevent bunching is to knot a few threads through all the layers once the seams have been securely closed by needle and thread or with a sewing machine. Quilt batting is ideal for herbal pillows since the middle layers of cotton are built into the fabric. Some people prefer to make an inner pillow that contains the herbs, placing it inside an outer slipcover that can be washed.

Most sleep pillows take a rectangular shape and can be tucked underneath a pillow, between sheets, or laid over the eyes. If you care to, fasten a ribbon to each end so you can tie the pillow behind your head while it rests over your eyes. Pillows could also be shaped like the letter "B" with the rounded edges fitting just under your eyes on either side of your nose.

Pillows can be decorated with embroidery, buttons, tassels, jewels—anything your imagination desires. Decorating pillows with bits of ribbon or lace adds a personal finishing touch.

To assemble a basic pillow, lay the fabric pieces together with the pattern sides facing each other. Stitch along three sides of the material, then turn it right side out so the pattern is now on the outside, leaving an opening large enough to add your herbs and stuffing. When you have it filled about three-quarters full (don't overstuff the pillow), fold over the ends and stitch closed.

Sleep pillows should be fairly flat. If made with child-safe herbs and careful, small, tight stitches, they should be safe in even a very young child's bed.

To make a sleep pillow with an inner section and outer slip-cover, cut out two pieces of muslin or plain cloth to hold the herbs. Stitch three sides of the fabric together as you would for a simple pillow. Fill with your herbal mixture. Using fancier outer material, cut two more pieces of material at least two inches longer on all sides than the muslin. Stitch them the same as the inner pillow except sew only to a depth of just less than a half-inch. As with the inner pillow, turn it so the seams are on the inside. If you plan to make this cover removable for washing, turn down a small hem on the open end and attach small Velcro disks or snaps to keep it closed.

Sleep Pillow Recipes

For each of the following recipes, mix together herbs, essential oils, fixatives, spices, and filler seeds (flax, rice, etc.) in a glass bowl. Stir with a wooden spoon. Cover and set aside for four or more hours, or place in a plastic bag and seal it overnight. Using a large spoon or a funnel, pour the mixture into the open end of each pillow to loosely fill, and stitch closed. Shake gently to release the herbal scents.

Rosy Remembrance Dreams

This is a good, all-purpose blend for all ages.

1–2 Tbls. dried mint

1–2 Tbls. dried rosemary

1–2 Tbls. dried rose petals

1–2 Tbls. rice or flaxseeds

Hoppy Dreams

Hops help induce sleep.

½ cup dried hops

½ cup dried lemon verbena leaves

½ cup dried lavender buds

2 Tbls. cellulose chips
4 drops lemon essential oil
4 drops lavender essential oil

Lavender Sleep Pillow

A simple blend with spicy, herbal overtones.

1 cup dried hops
1 cup dried lavender
½ cup dried thyme
3 Tbls. cellulose chips
10 drops lavender oil
10 drops bergamot oil

Aromatic Sleep Pillow

½ cup dried hops
½ cup dried catnip leaves
½ cup dried lemon balm or rosemary leaves
½ cup cellulose chips
2 Tbls. dried lavender
6 drops rosemary oil
3 drops lavender oil

Stress Reducing Rest

½ cup of hops
½ cup of mugwort
⅛ cup of sweet marjoram

Rest and Relaxation Pillow

1 cup dried lemon balm leaves
½ cup dried lavender
3 Tbls. cellulose chips

6   drops lemon essential oil

2   drops lavender oil

Pleasant Dreams Blend

1   cup lavender flowers

1   cup white rose petals

1   cup hops

1   cup lemon balm

2   tsps. orris root powder

2   drops lavender oil

Sweet Dreams

1   cup dried hops

½   cup German chamomile blossoms

2   Tbls. cellulose chips

2   drops geranium oil

2   drops ylang ylang oil

Peaceful Sleep Blend

½   cup roses or rose petals

½   cup rosemary

½   cup lavender flowers

½   cup hops

Relaxing Dreams

½   cup of mugwort

½   cup of lavender flowers

Lover's Dream

½   cup of rose petals

½   cup rosemary

½   cup lavender flowers

2　lemon verbena leaves, crushed

1　tsp. mint

4　whole cloves

1　small piece of cinnamon stick, broken up

3　mimosa flowers

Creative Inspiration Blend

½　cup of rose petals

½　cup mugwort

½　cup lavender flower

⅙　cup chopped pine needles, cut ½-inch or shorter

3　dried marigold blossoms

1　½-inch piece of cinnamon stick, broken up

3　whole cloves

2　tsps. mint

Travel Pillow

½　cup mugwort

½　cup rose petals

½　cup lavender flowers

½　cup marjoram

1　Tbl. passionflower, leaves or petals

A Sultry Home Herbal Spa

❧ by Dallas Jennifer Cobb ❧

Welcome, readers, to the steamy home herbal spa. Not just for women, a sultry home herbal spa can be enjoyed by anyone needing relaxation and rejuvenation after a long week of work. I often start with a big pot of water, adding herbs and essential oils that I need. I don't necessarily end up more beautiful, but I come away feeling pampered and ready to take on the world.

Below are recipes and suggestions for creating a comforting and rejuvenating environment in a home herbal spa. Enjoy.

Setting Up a Spa Environment

Your bathroom is the ideal space to transform into a home herbal spa center. Your tub will be the primary location for all-over body treatments, so envision it dimly lit, surrounded in beauty, and equipped with everything you need in easy reach. In addition to your spa tools and supplies, give yourself a big glass of cool water (in a nonbreakable glass), a small towel to dry your face or hands, and one of those inflatable tub pillows to rest your neck at a comfortable angle. Hang your favorite bathrobe on the door hook to put on after you have beautified and replenished, and make ready the plush slippers.

The bathroom sink is the easiest spot for facial and hair care spa activities and can easily be transformed into an altar with the right lighting and some decorations and ritual or power objects. The altar makes a home herbal spa a spiritual practice, not merely a mundane one.

I like using candles to transform the lighting effects. Their flickering illumination provides a calming influence, and somehow I always look better in the mirror in candle light. When using candles, always exercise caution. They should be firmly set in a nonflammable base, preferably a container that surrounds them and contains the flame. They should be out of the area you are working in so you don't accidentally scorch yourself, your hair, or your towel. When you set up your candles, always consider the aftereffects. Dribbled wax can mean lots of hard work to clean up, so don't counteract the relaxing effects of the spa by letting candles dribble unnecessarily. A safe practice is to locate some small enclosed lanterns for candles so they are shielded from contact with anything flammable.

If you don't use candles, consider draping soft gauzy fabrics over the lights and around the mirrors to soften the light and create a comforting and sensual atmosphere.

The use of incense or essential oil diffusers adds the element of scent, engaging the olfactory system in the overall experience. A small daub of essential oil on the outside of your candle or on a lightbulb will act as a diffuser if you don't already own one. As the lightbulb or candle heats up, the essential oil is made more volatile, releasing its scent and essence into the air.

For facials, the best spa location is not the bathroom but the kitchen, with a steamy pot on the stove. Kitchens can be transformed by using candlelight, clearing the counters of clutter, placing fresh flowers nearby, and bringing ritual objects into the area. Clear the space adjacent to your stove and place your spa tools and supplies there. Acquire a small mirror that can stand independently on the counter to save you traipsing to and from the bathroom throughout your facial.

If you are doing manicure or pedicure procedures, choose your favorite comfy chair and footstool. Drape the furniture with fabrics in warm colors, cover your work surface with fluffy towels to protect the furniture's fabric, and gather the overstuffed pillows to prop you up or place your feet on. Think luxury, then create the perfect miniature temple setting for yourself.

Simple Spa Tools

Most of the tools for doing a home herbal spa are everyday items that you probably have around the house. Before you run out to buy new things, consider what you have.

It is good to collect everything that you need before you start, so you can work uninterrupted in your spa environment. Most important to rejuvenation is peace of mind—create it and maintain it throughout your sultry home herbal spa.

Tools for Facials

If you are doing a facial, you will need the following items:

A lidded stainless steel pot larger than the diameter of your face and large enough to provide a wide plume of steam.

A large towel to cover your head and contain the steam treatment around your face.

A scarf or shower cap to keep your hair up and out of the facial treatment area. I prefer using a cloth scarf, as plastic shower caps often become too warm over time, making my head sweat and itch.

Tools for Manicures and Pedicures

For manicures and pedicures I recommend the following tools:

A simple nail-care kit containing emery board or nail file, nail clippers, toenail clippers, and cuticle tool.

A pumice stone.

A large heavy ceramic bowl or basin for soaking hands or feet.

Two small hand towels, one for each foot or hand.

Cotton swabs or balls large enough to separate your toes.

Oil or nail polish for dressing your nails up after the manicure process.

Tools for Hair Treatments

If you choose to do a hair treatment, you will need these items:
A pair of light latex or plastic gloves to protect your hands.
A medium-sized ceramic bowl in which to mix hair potions.
A large-tooth comb or brush for applying potions to hair.
A plastic shower cap to cover head and generate heat.
A dark-colored warm towel to wrap your covered head.
A hairdresser's cape, if you have one, for covering your shoulders.

Home Herbal Steams and Facials

Sultry home herbal facials involve several steps of treatment: facial steaming, massaging, applying a facial mask, rinsing, and moisturizing. Some people like to include a scrub or exfoliation process as well, which fits in before doing the mask.

Facial steaming opens pores, promotes deep cleansing, and stimulates skin regeneration. If your skin has a rash or acne, steaming isn't recommended because it can activate the oil glands and stimulate blood vessels.

Massage your face and neck using smooth upward strokes. Be very gentle with the soft tissue around your eyes. An invigorating massage is quicker and involves more patting and jostling, whereas a relaxing massage is slow, gentle, and soothing. If you are really stressed, you may want to go a little deeper and massage the tense muscles of your face—especially those around your mouth and jaw. Do this carefully, so that you don't cause more pain or distress to the muscles.

A facial mask is made to suit your skin. For dry skin, consider a moisturizing mask containing egg yolk, mashed avocado, or mashed banana. For oily skin, make an astringent mask using egg whites, lemon juice, or rose water. Neutral skin or combination skin can be treated with a mask of yogurt and lavender water. Apply the mask evenly over your face, using a small sponge, brush, or your fingers. Leave the mask on your face for about fifteen minutes or until it dries and feels tight, then rinse thoroughly.

Start the rinse process using warm water. When you have removed all of the mask material, switch to cooler water for a minute or two. This will stimulate the pores to close, protecting the skin. Pat your face dry lightly with a clean towel.

If you want to exfoliate or use a facial scrub, now is the time to do it. Beware, many scrubs are too abrasive and damaging to tender skin. While your face is clean, apply moisturizing cream or oil to face and neck to penetrate the skin with moisture. A good moisturizing cream should also provide protection for your skin from sun, pollutants, and stress. While a facial can take less than half an hour, it can leave you feeling renewed and your skin looking healthy and glowing.

Dry Skin Moisturizing Mask

Mix one raw egg and one tablespoon of honey, or mix half of a mashed avocado and one tablespoon olive oil, or mix one ripe, mashed banana and one tablespoon of honey.

Oily Skin Astringent Masks

Mix two egg whites and one tablespoon of oatmeal, or mix one egg white and one tablespoon of fresh lemon juice, or mix one egg white with one tablespoon of rose water.

Gentle Facial Cleanser

Start with one-half cup of ground oatmeal and add a chamomile infusion to moisten the oatmeal until it makes a runny paste. Scoop a small amount of the paste into the palm of your hand, and work it into a lather, using circular motions as you rub it over your face. Allow it to dry slightly, and rinse.

Herbal Facial Steaming

In a large pot, bring a quart of water to a boil, and then turn it down slightly. To prevent scalding, the water should be steaming generously but not boiling. Place your towel over your head and, when you are ready, sprinkle one cup of dried herbs into the hot water and steam your face and neck for five minutes.

Herbs to use include:

Calendula: Healing, toning, and astringent for the skin.

Chamomile: Cleansing and soothing.

Lavender: Stimulating, toning, and antiseptic.

Mint: Tingling and astringent; stimulates and cleanses pores.

Orange peel: Invigorating; helps skin to retain its elasticity.

Rosemary: Cleansing, stimulating; promotes skin regeneration.

Sultry Home Herbal Hand and Foot Care

The Perfect Pedicure

A good pedicure takes about forty-five minutes but is worth doing every two weeks or so. In the summer months when bare feet are in greater contact with the world, a once-a-week pedicure is a treat.

At your comfy armchair or at the couch, set up your foot basin, towels, nail kit, and a good book. While you soak your feet for twenty minutes in salt water, relax, read your book, daydream. The water should be as hot as you can stand it. It will cool over time.

After soaking, use a pumice stone to gently remove the rough skin on your heals and soles. Don't scrub too hard—it is not supposed to hurt. Trim your nails when they are soft, being careful not to cut them too short. A straight cut will help to prevent ingrown toenails. Gently push the cuticles back with your rounded cuticle tool, and return your feet to the soaking tub. Using a salt rub, massage your feet to invigorate them and increase circulation.

Sultry Salty Skin Scrub

1 cup coarse sea salt

½ cup pure olive oil

10 drops of your favorite essential oil for scent

Mix these together and store in a wide-mouthed container. This scrub can be used on hands and feet to invigorate and polish the skin or on the body for a seasonal exfoliation. Return your feet to the soak and rinse all of the scrub off. Your feet should feel slightly oily and tingling. Apply a good moisturizer to your feet.

Peppermint Foot Fetish

Mix twenty drops of peppermint essential oil and five tablespoons each of olive and almond oil. Store this in a squeeze bottle for easy application.

Peppermint is invigorating and promotes circulation. This foot oil is great after a long day on your feet. It will leave them feeling tingly and alive. Allow your feet to cool after soaking and before using peppermint oil on them. If you want to apply nail polish, it is good to wait about an hour after applying an oil or moisturizer.

My Favorite Manicure

A good manicure should also be done regularly. Our hands do so much for us and are often neglected. Take the time to indulge your hands in some sultry home herbal care.

Remove any old nail polish, and soak your hands in warm water for about ten minutes. After soaking, thoroughly clean under your nails. After rinsing off any materials, massage a generous amount of cuticle cream into your cuticles, and gently push them back.

Cuticle Cream

2   Tbls. coconut oil

2   Tbls. olive oil

1   tsp. lanolin

½   tsp. grated cocoa butter

10   drops jasmine essential oil

In double boiler, slowly warm the coconut oil, lanolin, and cocoa butter until they melt, then add the olive oil. Remove from heat, stir, and add the jasmine essential oil. Pour into a clean wide-mouthed container. Because coconut oil, lanolin, and cocoa butter are solid at room temperature, this oil will be thick.

Massage cuticle cream into your cuticles regularly. It will keep your cuticles moisturized and softened and easier to push back. Never cut cuticle skin, even if it is raggedy. Use your round edged cuticle tool and gently push cuticles back off of the nail.

Renewal Oil

Combine equal amounts of chamomile and lavender flowers. Coarsely chop plant materials and fill clean, dry jars with them, then pour oil over the chopped herbs, filling the jars. Olive and almond or a mix of the two are commonly used as infusion oils. Add four drops each of rose and geranium essential oils to each jar. Seal, label, and store at room temperature for six weeks, then strain the oil using cheese cloth. Label and store at room temperature.

Warm a small amount of oil in your palms and gently massage into your face and neck. Or massage this oil into your feet, legs, or thighs to alleviate aches and uplift your energy after a long day.

Simple Men's Spa

Many men think spa treatments are something for women only. Yet, with a little encouragement, men will quickly see and feel the benefits of these treatments for themselves. Spa treatments are not about beautifying, but about feeling better in your body.

Secrets for a Close Shave

Many men don't know the best way to shave. Lots of guys will shave first, then jump in the shower to rinse off the lather. It is actually better to shower first, allowing the warm water to soften the facial hair and open the hair follicle. Then the process of shaving is more comfortable, and the result is a closer shave. Shave up or against the direction of the hair to achieve a very close shave. Take your time, and use a shape razor to avoid nicking your skin. Choosing a shaving cream with some oil in it also helps by maintaining the natural moisture of the hair and skin.

Scented Shaving Cream

¼ cup stearic acid powder

2 Tbls. extra virgin olive oil

1 cup hot water

1 tsp. borax

2 Tbls. grated glycerin soap

7 drops essential oil

In a pot, on low, melt the stearic acid powder and oil until they make a clear liquid. Patchouli is manly smelling, peppermint provides a tingle, and orange oil maintains skin health. Mix hot water, borax, and grated soap until they are dissolved. Pour soap solution into the blender, and blend on low for a minute. Slowly add the stearic acid mixture, and blend on high until creamy and uniform. Pour into a clean container with a wide mouth. When shaving, use a shaving brush with warm water to lather the cream and apply.

Making Spa Products

Many spa products can be made easily at home.

Sultry Spa Body Butter

¼ cup cocoa butter

1 tsp. light sesame oil

1   tsp. apricot kernel oil

1   tsp. vitamin E oil

15 drops of orange essential oil

In a small saucepan, place all of the ingredient, and heat very gently until they melt. Stir evenly to mix, then pour into a wide-mouth container. When it is cool, this mix will harden to the consistency of butter. It is good for skin pampering and can be applied after a bath or shower, when the heat of your skin will help the oils to melt and soften.

Rapturous Rose Cold Cream

1½ cups fragrantly scented rose petals (fresh is best)

6   Tbls. olive oil

1½ tsps. beeswax, grated

1   tsp. distilled water

Put the olive oil in the top pot of a double boiler. Heat it gently. Stir in as many rose petals as will go into the oil. Remove from the heat and pour into a heavy jar, then infuse for seven days. Strain the oil from the petals by pouring the concoction into a lightweight tea towel and squeezing out as much oil as you can.

Melt the beeswax in a double boiler, and gradually stir in the rose-infused oil. Remove from the heat, and add the water while stirring constantly. When the cream has the consistency you desire, pour it into a wide-mouthed glass jar. A good cold cream is something to be used daily, morning and night, after thoroughly cleaning your face. It can help to protect the skin from airborne pollutants, ultraviolet rays, and the grit and grime of daily living.

Back-to-Life Bubbling Bath

4   cups baking soda

3   cups citric acid

½   cup cornstarch

24   drops lavender essential oil

12   drops ylang ylang essential oil

Mix all the ingredients together and store in a large sealable container. After you have run your bath, scoop about ¾ of a cup of the mixture into the bath just as you are ready to get in. Enjoy the bubbling effervescence of this bath as it brings you back to life.

Caribbean Island Bath Oil

Infuse jasmine flowers and rose petals in coconut oil for six weeks. Strain and discard the flowers. Pour the oil into a clean plastic bottle with a squirt top. Label and decorate.

To use, squeeze two or three generous squirts under the faucet as you run your bath. As you soak in the rich emollient coconut oil, close your eyes and smell the Caribbean surrounding you. Be sure to clean the bathtub thoroughly after using a bath oil to prevent bath mishaps and grime buildup.

Oatmeal and Chamomile Bath

Pour three cups of boiling water over one cup of oatmeal and three tablespoons of chamomile flowers. Allow to steep for ten minutes. Using a piece of cheesecloth or gauze, strain the flowers and oats out of the fluid, and tie the cloth firmly. Pour the fluid into the bath, and add water to make the appropriate amount and temperature to bathe in. Float the oats and chamomile sachet in the bathwater, and squeeze frequently to release more of the infusion.

Herbal Hair Infusions

Herbs are gentle on hair and can restore natural luster and beauty. Place one ounce of herbs in a large jar and fill the jar with boiling water. Put a lid on the jar and allow herbs to infuse. Use this infusion as a rinse, after shampooing, to treat hair.

Chamomile Hair Rinse

Follow recipe above using chamomile. *Note:* Only infuse for thirty minutes. Use infusion to rinse hair after shampooing. Leave rinse on. Chamomile will bring out the blond highlights naturally present in light-colored hair. You can also combine lemon juice in this rinse for added highlighting effects in the summer sun.

Calendula Hair Rinse

Follow recipe above using calendula. Use infusion to rinse hair after shampooing. Leave rinse on. Calendula will bring out the auburn and red highlights of medium-colored hair.

Rosemary Hair Rinse

Follow recipe above using rosemary. Use infusion to rinse hair after shampooing. Leave rinse on. Rosemary will bring out the rich warmth of dark-colored hair. Rosemary is also known for its ability to prevent hair loss and stimulate the scalp.

Nettle Hair Rinse

Follow recipe above using nettle. Use infusion to rinse hair after shampooing. Leave rinse on. Nettle will help to treat and prevent dandruff and stimulate circulation in the scalp.

Spa Time

Now you are ready to slide into the tub, soak and scrub, and feel the sultry effects of self-care seep into your body. Take the simple tips and recipes from this article, and enjoy the process.

African Body Butters

≫ by Stephanie Rose Bird ≪

For thousands of years, Africans have come to depend on butters from indigenous trees and plants to protect their skin from the ravishing effects of the Sun. Today, African natural butters are formulated and sold internationally. This article discusses the benefits and drawbacks of the most popular African body butters: coconut, cocoa, and shea.

The discussion includes an examination of the use of the butters in women's entrepreneurial, fair-trade, and sustainability projects. Each section contains several recipes, and the article concludes with ample resource suggestions for follow-up.

Cocoa Butter

Cocoa (*Theobroma cacao*) comes from the theobroma cacao tree, which grows

in the tropical rain forests of Central America and Africa (particularly Ghana) and makes a significant impact on the local economy. The tree is a remarkable sight. It has dark-brown bark, resembling the color of chocolate. Curiously, white flowers grow directly from the branches and trunk of the tree. The delicate blossoms create a sharp visual contrast against the deeply colored, rough-looking bark. In fact, the cacao tree is one of the more unusual trees one can find. The scent the tree emits is quite subtle, not the rich chocolate aroma you might expect.

Cocoa butter is created from hydraulic pressings of the cocoa nib or cocoa mass from cocoa beans that are further refined through filtering or centrifuge. The scent of cocoa butter is removed using steam or a vacuum. Some herbalists, massage therapists, and aromatherapists prefer the scentless substance called deodorized cocoa butter.

Cocoa butter is a useful ingredient for vegans (those who prefer no animal products, including beeswax) since cocoa butter is a serviceable hardener, thickener, and counterbalance to stickier ingredients like shea butter. An additional gift of cocoa butter is that no solvents are involved in its manufacture. It is an edible ingredient. The edible aspect is appealing to those who desire wholesome, nurturing ingredients in homemade potions, creams, and healing balms. Cocoa butter is widely available, ships well, is reasonably priced, and has a long shelf life.

Cocoa beans are 15 percent fat. Cocoa butter has been traditionally used as a skin softener, emollient, belly rub, and is a soothing substance for burns. It is useful as a superfatting agent in soap. It has a therapeutic effect in soap, since there is less contact with the lye water. To superfat cold processed soap, add one-half teaspoon melted butter per pound of soap. The high stearic composition of cocoa butter increases the hardness in handmade soaps and healing balms. In a pinch, I have substituted it for beeswax with good results. It can also be used as a base oil in soap making, best combined with other oils, such as coconut oil. The addition of coconut, palm, or almond oil helps create a looser healing balm or salve that melts faster. A hard soap, containing large concentrations of cocoa butter, lasts for a longer time. Cocoa butter-enriched soap will also hold intricate patterns of elaborate molds. Most of the popular contemporary soap making books contain cocoa butter soap recipes. I will provide you with one of my favorite soap recipes later.

Cocoa powder and unsweetened baker's chocolate are used to add natural color to soap. Cocoa powder is recommended for melt-and-pour soaps, while both forms are used in cold processed soap. A wide range of earthy colors result from using this colorant, from light tan to deep chocolate—depending on the amount added. For a medium-brown, add one-half ounce baker's chocolate per two pounds soap, melted with base oils.

Using soap molds adds even more fun to your chocolate soap making. Just pour the freshly made soap into chocolate molds, as you would use any other mold. You can also find heavenly scented chocolate fragrance oil that can be used alone or in combination with a variety of oils. Orange, lemon, or cassia essential oils work well also with handmade cocoa butter products. Vanilla or coconut fragrance oils compliment chocolate soap.

Chocolate Soap Recipe

4.5 ounces goat milk

10 ounces distilled water

5 ounces lye

12 ounces vegetable shortening

8 ounces lard

12 ounces coconut oil

2 ounces unsweetened baker's chocolate

Vegetable cooking spray

1 ounce cocoa butter

Measure all ingredients on a scale. Freeze the milk the night before soap making, and thaw it in the morning. Put on goggles, apron, and plastic gloves for protection. Mix milk and water in a quart-sized Pyrex liquid measuring cup. Stir in lye using stainless steel spoon. Set aside. Melt all fats (except cocoa butter) and chocolate in stainless steel stockpot on medium heat. Remove from heat. Use a candy thermometer to check temperatures. (Be sure to clean thermometer after it is used for the oils so it does not contaminate the water/milk mixture.) Spray some soap or candy molds with the spray oil. Set aside. Melt cocoa butter in the microwave, or a stovetop or regular oven. Set aside. When both sets of ingredients equal 120 degrees, slowly stir the milk/water mixture into the oils with the stainless steel spoon. Continue to stir with a figure "8" motion. The soap is ready to pour into molds when you drizzle a portion on top of the batch and it retains its shape. Stir in the melted cocoa butter, then pour it into the molds. Cover immediately with wool blankets, and do not disturb. After twenty-four hours, remove blankets. Soap solidifies after about two to three days. When the soap is solid, remove it from the mold(s). Set on shelves, away from direct heat or sunlight for five to six weeks. Scrape residue off bottom of bar with a sharp knife, and use knife to bevel edges for a very neat look. Wrap in cellophane or put inside decorative boxes.

Black Cocoa Butter

One of my newest enthusiasms is black cocoa butter. Most of you are probably familiar with the eggshell-colored cocoa butter that has been widely available for quite a while. Most of the ordinary cocoa butter that comes from Africa is processed before the seeds are allowed to germinate. With black cocoa butter, the cacao pods are germinated first, which produces a deep, espresso-colored butter that smells like roasted cocoa.

If you want to try something a little different in your skin-softening regimen, consider using black cocoa butter because it is softer and more readily malleable than the cream-colored type. Black cocoa butter is very easily absorbed by the skin and makes a nice addition to soaps, lip balms, and body butters. It is useful as a hot oil treatment to condition the hair.

Black Cocoa Butter Body Bliss Treat

I love this silky treat for achy muscles around the back, shoulders, and wrist joint areas. This treatment is helpful for the type of pain we get from working with computers all day long.

Start by warming up the sore area by applying a hot water bottle, a warm, flax-filled body pillow heated in the microwave, or a warm heating pad to the area. Have your partner or a friend scoop out some of the cocoa butter. They should warm it by pressing it in their hands until the butter is melted. Your partner can then apply the melted cocoa butter directly to the painful area. Ask them to massage it in until your tight muscles release.

Using Cocoa Butter: The Balm

One of my earliest introductions to the botanical world was through cocoa butter. My cousin lived in a primarily African-American city in northern New Jersey. As most teenage girls do, we were experimenting with styling our hair using hot combs and hot curlers. Of course, quick as a wink, I had a burn on my neck. Just as swiftly, my cousin produced a push-up tin of cocoa butter. She gently dabbed it onto the burned area, and it was quite soothing. I became curious about cocoa butter and was shown by other members of my family how it could also be applied directly to keep the skin pliable.

Today, I like to hold a small piece of cocoa butter in my hand as I run hot water in the bathtub. The cocoa butter melts and then acts as a skin softener as I bathe. After the bath, particularly in the fall and winter, I find cocoa butter useful on rough skin areas. I apply it nightly to my heels after a bath. This also works well on calloused hands after gardening, housework, or crafts.

Coconut

Coconut is a major African crop benefiting the economy of Ghana, the Ivory Coast, Kenya, Nigeria, Mozambique, Togo, Somalia, and Tanzania. Copra, the dried coconut endosperm, is an edible cooking oil that is also used cosmetically. Copra is called *mbata* by the Swahili people and *igi agbon* by the Yoruba. Whatever the name, it provides villages with milk used for cooking and beverages and is a base for molasses and oil. The soap works well, forming a thick lather even in salt water—making it popular with seafaring people for hundreds of years.

Coconut oil can be a polarizing substance in the herbal community—some love it, while others despise it. It is said to be drying to the skin, particularly if used as a soap oil base. Many African body butters are thick emollients that might overwhelm normal or combination skin; coconut oil is a welcome alternative. Coconut soaps are very useful for cleansing oily skin as they make a frothy cleansing lather. For those who enjoy a light moisturizer, coconut cream or other coconut products work. Coconut oil can be combined with cocoa butter or shea butter to create a balanced soap that is neither too astringent nor excessively emollient.

Using Coconut Oil

Another type of coconut skin-care treatment is coconut cream. Coconut cream is available from Togo where women villagers hand-press coconut meat to extract a creamy oil. Coconut cream works well as massage therapy oil because of its silky texture. In Africa, coconut cream has been used as hair conditioner, strengthener, and growth aid. The oil is rubbed into the scalp and may also be applied to the ends. Melted oil, cooled slightly and then applied to the scalp, followed by a shampoo, is preferable for those with oily scalp. I find that when applying coconut cream to my face and hands, it disappears within a minute or so without leaving a trace of greasiness on the skin.

The Shea Tree

You have undoubtedly heard a lot about shea. Shea butter is found in shampoo, conditioners, soap, lotions, and creams. The shea tree is a member of the *Sapotaceae* family. Shea trees are found exclusively in the African Sahel, a semiarid region south of the Sahara Desert. The shea tree is native to Benin, Burkina

Faso, Cameroon, Chad, Cote d'Ivoire, Ghana, Guinea, Mali, Niger, Nigeria, Senegal, Sudan, Togo, and Uganda—where it is distributed in parklands, dry savannahs, and forests. Shea trees live to be 150 to 200 years old. The fat content of the nut of the shea tree is nearly 50 percent.

Shea butter is one of numerous non-timber forest products (NTFPs) that make significant contributions to rural African societies. Shea butter, known locally as *karite* in the Dioula language, is also called women's gold because it brings women significant income. Shea butter has been traded as a commodity at least since the fourteenth century. Today shea butter is the third highest export product in Burkina Faso. It is one of few economic commodities under women's control in Sahelian Africa.

Shea trees have been tenderly cared for by women farmers and their children for hundreds of years, yet with the steady rise in popularity of shea butter in international markets, some concerns have arisen. Agroforestry and environmental organizations fear that overharvesting of the shea nut could contribute to land degradation, eventually leading to desertification. This is one of the reasons I also advocate for use of alternative butters, like mango butter, which will be discussed later.

While in the West we utilize shea almost exclusively as a cosmetic additive, in Africa it has diverse uses. For the Mossi people of Burkina Faso, shea butter is the sole source of fat. Groups in Burkina Faso and elsewhere use shea to make soap, healing balms, cosmetics, candles, lamp oil, and waterproofing putty for housing. Shea wood is used for creating tools, flooring, joinery, chairs, utensils, and mortar and pestles. The wood also creates a fierce heat and can be a substitute for kerosene, although its use as fuel is discouraged because of its more prominent medicinal uses and economic contribution to African villages. The root and bark are used medicinally.

Many types of imported chocolates contain shea. Shea butter is exported to Japan and Europe to enhance pastry dough pliability and to enrich chocolate recipes. In Africa and around the world, shea butter is utilized for its ability to soothe and soften rough skin and to protect against sunburn, chapping, irritation, ulcers, and rheumatism.

The Making of Shea Butter

Creating shea butter from nuts is a monumental, labor-intensive task, involving huge amounts of water and wood, as it is made on an open wood fire. West African women almost exclusively run the production of shea butter processing with the assistance of their children. Manufacture takes place during the rainy season, a time when harvesting duties are already intense for women. Preparation takes several days. Nuts are collected, boiled, sun-dried, hand-shelled, roasted, and then crushed with a mortar and pestle. Water is added and a paste is formed. Several women knead and beat the paste in a pot until a skim floats to the surface. The fat is cleansed repeatedly, yielding white foam. The foam is boiled for several hours. The top layer is skimmed once more, and this yields the white shea butter we use.

Golden Shea

Recently, I had the opportunity to try a lovely shea butter with a golden color imported by the African Shea Butter Company. I enjoyed this product immensely because it retained the scent of the open wood fires on which it was created. This is likely to be a sentiment shared by those who are Pagan, Hedge Witches, or Wiccans who work with herbs, because it reminds us of the power of the elements.

Delving into a jar of golden shea can spiritually transport the user back to the African village where the shea was processed. Those of you who seek a more unprocessed product with a lively spirit still intact would be wise to avoid refined shea butter, which is stripped of its contact with its source.

The Socioeconomic Implications of Shea Butter

The socioeconomic benefits of shea are not to be underestimated. So many of us involved with earth-based spirituality want to help make the world a better place. Purchasing raw ingredients like shea butter makes a direct impact on rural African villages as well as the lives of the women and children who process it for us.

Not long ago, UNIFEM, an organization that helps women in developing countries, helped broker a deal between an upscale French natural cosmetic firm, L'Occitane, and a co-op run by African women. L'Occitane buys much of its shea butter directly from Union des groupements Kiswendsida, a large network of over one hundred shea producers. Without middlemen, all of the profit returns to the villages where the shea butter is harvested and manufactured.

The African Shea Butter Company is a woman-owned and operated mail order firm. I interviewed Tammie Umbel, founder and sole proprietor of this company. During our conversation, it was apparent that African Shea Butter Company's main goal is to help African people through trade. Umbel contracts with African soap makers. Her soap line also includes traditionally dyed African fabric and indigenous papers. The African Shea Butter Company sells a variety of high-grade shea butter in bulk suitable for use by the most discerning herbalist. Umbel is now reaching out to other women's cooperatives that harvest and manufacture baobab, black seed oil, and lemon grass and bourbon geranium essential oils. Dealing with natural oils from Africa is her way of contributing to the well-being of not only her clientele but also of African women and families.

The support of UNIFEM, L'Occitane, the African Shea Butter Company, and numerous other governmental and non-governmental organizations enables women's groups to pool their resources and purchase simple presses. This lessens the amount of physical labor they have to exert to produce the end product. West African women are receiving technical training from organizations and are learning to create and market their own natural cosmetics and healing balms. A huge draw to making botanical products and natural cosmetics is the connection to people through plants. Shea butter is a way that all of us can make connections to our sisters in Africa, possibly making a positive impact on certain aspects of village life.

Using Shea Butter

Shea butter gives natural UV protection. This is one of the reasons it is beloved by Africans whose skin and hair is almost constantly exposed to sunny weather conditions.

Shea butter is a superior fatting agent in herbal soaps. The emollient, softening quality of shea butter makes it useful for hand or foot treatments and hair and body care. It is easily and quickly absorbed when applied topically. Shea butter is very dense and may be too heavy for oily, or certain types of combination skin.

Hot Shea Butter Hair Treatment

For most types of hair, shea is a good hot oil treatment. Shea butter is melted, cooled slightly, then applied warm to the ends of hair where splitting occurs and to the scalp. A clean paintbrush is a handy tool for applying warmed oil to the scalp. Part hair in sections as you work. Work quickly, otherwise the shea will solidify. Put on a plastic cap, and sit out in the Sun if possible or under a dryer for thirty minutes. Alternatively, cover your head with a bath towel to retain heat. After a half-hour, shampoo your hair thoroughly and rinse.

Hair Pomade

Africans have been using shea butter as a hairdressing for hundreds of years. This application is recommended for extremely thick, curly, kinky, or dry hair.

Thin, straight hair would become overwhelmed and weighed down by a shea pomade. Dreadlocks may also appear dull or develop a tendency to attract dirt when shea is applied to them.

Scoop out about a teaspoon of shea butter in the palm of your hand. Use less for short hair and more for longer hair. Place your palms together, and rub gently, using your body heat to melt the shea butter. Once shea transforms from solid to liquid, rub it on your hair, then style as usual. This is fine as a weekly hairdressing pomade.

Shea Namaskara Mudra Meditation

One simple, replenishing practice that I have developed was dictated by the shea butter itself. Shea requires body heat (or some other form of heat) to be used. You may find that taking a little time out to reflect, meditate, or pray while melting your shea is a way to combine plants and spirituality.

Sit down in a comfortable position. I enjoy the padma asana, and those of you who practice yoga might find it natural to sit this way as well. Scoop out a quarter-sized pat of shea butter. Place it into your receptive hand, and place your dominant hand on top. Now bring your hands together to your chest, squeezing them together. In the Buddhist faith this is called the gesture of prayer (*namaskara mudra*). Mudras are symbolic hand gestures often shown in Buddha imagery. I like to do the namaskara mudra while warming my shea butter, because it reminds me to be thankful to those who processed the precious healing butter. I also think about the power we hold in our hands as I warm the oil in my palms. I focus on the hope that my hands will make a difference in this world.

To try a shea mudra meditation, close your eyes. Take deep cleansing breaths. Scoop out some shea. Put your hands together, bring them overhead pressed together, and then slowly move them down the path of your center, stopping at your chest. Rub your hands gently together slowly to encourage the butter to melt. Concentrate on your breathing, your hands, and your thoughts. As an affirmation, say: "I am whole, I am sound, I am free to give with these hands to spirit."

Do this type of reflection for about five minutes a day to release anxiety, stress, and insecurity. When you are finished, use the shea as an emollient body treatment on areas that need softening.

Get to Know Your Butters

Many herbs are being made into butter these days. I have seen hemp butter, aloe butter, almond butter, and illipe butter marketed to herbalists and natural product formulators. Here's a word to the wise, however: Check the ingredient list on your butter products. Whereas shea butter, cocoa butter, illipe butter, and coconut oil are natural oils that have a solid consistency at room temperature and that are made solely from the plant indicated, some butters on the market, like aloe butter, are thickened and emulsified using other ingredients, such as coconut oil or other hydrogenated oils. There is nothing inherently wrong with these manufactured butters, although it is often possible to create them from scratch—thus foregoing the high market price.

There are many wonderful natural plant butters becoming increasingly available from other countries outside Africa. Chief among these are mango butter, which is comparable to shea and Indian kokum butter. Both mango and kokum butter have multiple uses, and their use undoubtedly can make a positive impact on the economy of India, as has happened in Africa.

To get to know your butters, keep an herbalist's recipe book. Take notes on the butter qualities, your skin's reaction to them, and the results of any experimental recipes. I like to jot down the weather conditions outdoors as well. Soon you will discover that certain types of formulations do better in particular weather conditions than in others. There are no panaceas but there are plenty of wonderful nut butters to use for your various needs.

Herbal Beauty Garden

❧ by Chandra Moira Beal ❧

People grow herbs for all sorts of purposes: culinary, decorative, aromatic, and medicinal. Herbs and botanicals have also been used for centuries in beauty treatments, providing simple solutions from nature.

Planting a beauty garden is an easy way to have a wealth of herbal ingredients at your fingertips at all times. You can use the herbs to create toners, baths, cleansers, and facial steams. Some herbs are better used freshly harvested, while others can be dried and stored for year-round use. Below are some common cosmetic herbs, along with growing tips and sample recipes to get your imagination started.

Basil (*Ocimum basilicum*)

Basil has restorative, warming, and antibacterial effects on the skin. The leaves can be used for facial and hair care. Basil is a popular, easy-to-grow herb that comes in a variety of scents and colors. Any variety of basil is fine for use in beauty recipes.

Growing Basil

Basil is a tender perennial in most parts of the country. In colder climates it will grow only in the spring and summer. Common sweet basil has glossy, deep-green leaves, but varieties of basil differ widely in habit and color. A leafy shrub will grow one to three feet depending upon the variety.

To get an early start on the season, basil can be started indoors. It grows just as easily outdoors as long as it is planted well after the threat of frost. Choose a sunny location with well-draining soil. Sow the basil seeds evenly to a depth of one-eighth inch. When seedlings emerge with two to three leaves, thin the plants to six to twelve inches apart. Mulch is a good idea for basil, as the plants need consistent moisture levels. Pinch off flower buds as soon as they appear to encourage a bushier, more productive plant. To keep basil producing, cut early and often, snipping about one-half inch above a node.

Stimulating Basil, Eucalyptus, and Peppermint Bath

½   cup dried basil leaves for mental powers

½   cup dried eucalyptus leaves for concentration

½   cup dried peppermint for mental fatigue

Place all the herbs in a muslin bag or a square of cheesecloth, and secure it with twine. Hang the bag from the faucet so water runs through it as it fills the tub, or toss the bag in your bath like a tea bag. Soak in the bath for twenty minutes.

Calendula (*Calendula officinalis*)

Calendula, also known as pot marigold, is highly beneficial for skin and hair and has anti-inflammatory, antibacterial, and anti-fungal properties. The petals can be used fresh or dried and used in bath vinegars and hair rinses, especially to highlight red or blonde hair.

Growing Calendula

Calendula is a bright, cheery plant that blooms all summer from June until the first frost. The flowers are large and come in blends of yellow, orange, apricot, and cream. The plants are easy to grow in the home garden, reaching heights of up to two feet. Calendula are annuals, but reseed themselves readily in the garden. Deadheading will promote a longer bloom time. Calendula plants thrive in full sunlight, fertile soil, and cool weather.

Calendula Eye Soother

2   Tbls. dried calendula blossoms
⅓   cup distilled water

Add the calendula to the water and bring to a boil. Reduce heat and cover, then simmer for about ten minutes. Strain the blossoms from the infusion and allow the liquid to cool to room temperature. Soak squares of gauze, clean cloth, or cotton pads in the infusion. Squeeze out the excess liquid and place on closed eyes. Leave the squares on your eyes for fifteen minutes, then remove and discard. The leftover infusion stores for up to three days and makes a soothing skin or hair rinse.

Catnip (*Nepeta cataria*)

Catnip is a well-known narcotic for felines and a relaxant for humans. Catnip's pleasant aroma makes it a good choice for inclusion in sleep pillows. Make up a batch of massage oil to rub over yourself or your partner just before bed.

Growing Catnip

Seeds should be sown one-eighth inch deep and covered with fine soil. If you grow your seeds indoors, they should germinate in ten to twenty days. If you grow them outdoors, you should plant your seeds in the fall. When the catnip plants are about two inches tall, thin them out to about six inches apart. When you're ready to harvest in the late summer, cut and dry the mature leafy tops and leaves.

Relaxing Massage Oil

1   quart almond oil

1   ounce catnip leaves

Combine catnip and oil in a saucepan and simmer over low heat for twenty minutes. Let cool completely. Strain out the catnip through a double layer of cheesecloth, and pour oil into an airtight, darkly colored bottle. Store in a cool place.

Dill (*Anethum graveolens*)

Dill is commonly used in the kitchen to flavor dishes, and the seeds are a good breath freshener. Simply chew one-half teaspoon of dill seeds, then spit them out. Dill seeds also make an excellent nail strengthener, moisturizing dry, weak nails.

Growing Dill

Dill is a tall, wispy plant with soft yellow flowers that bloom in a sphere. Both the seeds and feathery leaves are cultivated from this versatile plant. Dill does not transplant well and should be planted from seed. Sow them one-half inch deep in moist, acidic soil in a sunny spot. Keep the soil moist during germination and continue to water into maturity. Allow the plant to reach one foot in height before cutting off the leaves for use. Dill weed is best cut before the plant flowers. To harvest seeds, cut the plants at the base of the stem. Tie them into clumps and hang them upside down with a drop bag to catch the seeds as they fall.

Dill Seed Nail Soak

1   cup boiling water

1   Tbl. dried dill seeds

Pour boiling water over seeds and steep until cool. Strain off liquid and use as a nail soak, or swab onto clean nails nightly.

Fennel (*Foeniculum vulgare*)

Like dill, fennel grows tall and feathery in the garden. The leaves have an anise flavor that is wonderful in tea and culinary recipes. The seeds also have anti-inflammatory properties. Making an infusion of the seeds creates a toner that is cleansing and beneficial for dry, sensitive, mature skin.

Growing Fennel

Plant your seeds right after the last frost. Space seeds one to two inches apart in rows two feet apart, and cover with one-quarter inch of fine soil, tamped down. Keep the soil moist for about one to two weeks until the plants emerge. When plants are four inches tall, thin or transplant them one foot apart in the rows. When the plants are half grown, add soil around the plants to protect the bulbs. Pick the seeds when they are ripe.

Fennel Seed Mask

⅓   cup boiling water

2   tsps. crushed fennel seed

1   Tbl. honey

1   Tbl. ground oatmeal

Add the crushed fennel seeds to the boiling water. Let the mixture infuse for fifteen minutes, then strain. Reserve 1 tablespoon of the infusion for the recipe, and store the rest in the fridge for a facial rinse. Mix the infusion with the honey. Add oatmeal and mix well. Smooth the mixture on your face. Leave on 15 minutes, then rinse with cool or tepid water. Pat dry.

German Chamomile (*Matricaria recutita*)

There are two plants known as chamomile: the more popular German chamomile and the Roman or English chamomile

(*Chamaemelum nobile*). Both have been used to calm frayed nerves, treat various digestive disorders, relieve muscle spasms, and soothe a range of skin conditions and mild infections. German chamomile reduces inflammation and muscle spasms and speeds healing. It also is a mild sedative and aids sleep. The fruit-scented flowers of German chamomile are used in infusions for hair and skin care and in herbal teas and fragrant baths. People with ragweed allergies should not use German chamomile.

Growing German Chamomile

German chamomile is a low-growing, lacy perennial with daisy-like flowers. Chamomile grows wild and close to the ground and can be planted at the borders of herb gardens. It can reach three feet and likes full Sun to partial shade. The flowers dry easily, but cover them with cheesecloth to keep insects away.

Chamomile Dusting Powder

1 cup arrowroot powder
½ cup kaolin clay
½ cup baking soda
1 Tbl. ground, sifted German chamomile blossoms
8 drops orange essential oil
4 drops German chamomile essential oil

Mix all ingredients together in a glass bowl or measuring cup. Cover and set aside overnight. Put the finished product in a shaker container or in a plastic tub with a powder puff.

Hops (*Humulus lupulus*)

Although most commonly known for flavoring beer, hops is a sedative and makes a great bath tea.

Growing Hops

The hop plant is an herbaceous perennial producing annual vines. The vines grow rapidly, winding around their supports in a clockwise direction and clinging with strong, hooked hairs. They can reach heights of up to twenty-five feet before the vines begin to grow to the sides and produce flowers. Hops need mild climates and direct sunlight to flower and ample moisture in the spring and summer. A strong support system—such as fences, buildings, or posts—is needed for the plant to climb on.

Winding Down Bath

1 part dried hops
1 part dried chamomile flowers
1 part dried lavender buds
¼ part dried valerian root

Combine all the herbs and add one drop lavender essential oil for each ¾ ounce of total herbs used. Put the herbs in a glass container with a lid, and gently shake to blend. Let the jar sit for at least a week to allow the herbs to blend. Use ¾ ounce of the herb mixture per bath. The herbs can be tied up in a muslin bag that can be dropped into the tub while it's filling with hot water.

Lady's Mantle (*Alchemilla vulgaris*)

Alchemilla has lime-green leaves and dainty star-shaped flowers. The entire plant is covered in very fine hairs that cause dew or soft rain to gather in its leaves. This liquid was known as "celestial water" and used in the ancient art of alchemy. Lady's mantle has been growing in gardens since before the sixteenth century. The herb became known as Lady's mantle because the scalloped shape of the leaves resembled the mantle (cloak) of the Virgin Mary. Its leaves are astringent and used for facial care.

Growing Lady's Mantle

Lady's mantle can be planted from seeds or from pregrown plants. The seed will germinate in the garden, but will take up to two years to flower. The plants can be divided in the spring or fall and will grow from six to eighteen inches. Lady's mantle needs a fertile soil and some moisture, and can be grown in full sunlight to partial shade. It can be invasive if left to seed.

Lady's Mantle Facial Mask

⅔ cup boiling water
1 Tbl. dried Lady's mantle leaves
1 Tbl. brewer's yeast
2 tsps. rose water

Pour the boiling water over the lady's mantle leaves. Let the mixture steep for ten minutes, then strain. Reserve 1 tablespoon of the infusion for the recipe, and store the rest in the fridge for an astringent facial rinse. Mix the brewer's yeast, rose water, and herbal infusion together. Smooth the mixture on your face. Leave on fifteen minutes, then rinse with cool water and pat dry.

Lemon Balm (*Melissa officinalis*)

Lemon balm's citrus-scented leaves are antibacterial and make a good rinse for troubled skin.

Growing Lemon Balm

This herb grows in nearly any condition—from full sunlight to lots of shade—and it can be grown from seeds, cuttings, or divisions. If you begin with seeds, press them down very lightly. Avoid drying out the seeds, which take a fairly long time to germinate. You should place transplanted plants about eighteen inches apart. Shear plants back frequently to contain growth. Lemon balm does prefer frequent waterings and fertile soil.

Lemon Balm Astringent Toner

1 cup water
½ cup vodka
½ cup lemon balm
½ cup witch hazel

Mix the ingredients together, and place in a jar with a tight-fitting lid. Let sit for two weeks, and strain into a clean bottle.

Lemon Verbena (*Aloysia triphylla*)

Lemon verbena is a highly aromatic herb and a lovely addition to the beauty garden. Its astringent leaves are suited to facial care, especially as a toner. The recipe below is an easy and therapeutic way to cleanse your skin. Use this steam once a week for general maintenance, twice a week if your skin is oily.

Growing Lemon Verbena

Lemon verbena is a native of Chile and Peru, where it grows to fifteen feet tall. In the North American climate, it will generally reach a height of just one to two feet. Lemon verbena needs at least six hours of sunlight and will not survive frost. In cold climates it may be brought inside to survive the winter.

Lemon Verbena Facial Steam

3   Tbls. lemon verbena

6   cups boiling water

Tie back your hair and wash your face as you normally do. Place lemon verbena in a large bowl and pour boiling water over the herbs and stir. Lean over the bowl, keeping your face at least twelve inches away from the surface of the water, and use a bath towel to make a tent over your head and the bowl. Close your eyes and steam for fifteen minutes. Rinse your face with warm and then cool water, and pat dry. After a steam your skin is sensitive, so stay indoors for at least an hour to allow your pores to close.

Peppermint (*Mentha piperita*)

Peppermint is mildly antiseptic and frequently used in mouth and body care. Most people overlook its benefits to skin care—it is an ideal cleanser for normal or oily skin. Peppermint toner removes residue, closes pores, and restores balance to skin.

Growing Peppermint

Peppermint likes full sunlight or partial shade and rich, drained loam that will retain water in summer. It spreads through runners and loves to be cut frequently. Mint is a perennial that should come back easily year to year, although if your winters get really cold, a layer of mulch will protect the plant.

Peppermint Toner

2   Tbls. peppermint leaves (dried)

1   cup boiling water

½   cup witch hazel

1   Tbl. lemon juice

Steep the peppermint in the water for 15 minutes, then strain. Add witch hazel and lemon juice. Apply daily after cleaning the face.

Yarrow (*Achillea millifolium*)

The white-flowered variety of yarrow is astringent and anti-inflammatory, great for soothing tired skin exposed to the elements. Use both the leaves and flowers.

Growing Yarrow

Yarrow seeds germinate in two weeks at mild temperatures under lots of light. Divide the plants in spring and cut off old flowers to prolong the blooming period. Yarrow grows in almost any soil.

Soothing Yarrow Bath Soak

½   cup dried linden to soothe frayed nerves

½   cup dried comfrey to heal skin irritations

½   cup dried yarrow to soothe muscles

2   Tbls. oatmeal to soften the water

Place the herbs in a muslin bag and secure with twine. Add the bag to your bath, and squeeze to release herbal properties. Soak for twenty minutes to enjoy the benefits of this bath.

Herb
Crafts

A Remembrance Potpourri

❧ by Laurel Reufner ❧

Memories of those we have loved and lost are always with us. With time, we may smile instead of cry when a particularly poignant memory is triggered. Still, sometimes we intentionally evoke memories with special objects that remind us of those who have passed on.

This special potpourri is one such object. Made from dried flowers from the funeral of a loved one, as well as special herbs and flowers that have ages-old connections to death, bereavement, and funerals, it serves to help one not only remember the deceased, but also to honor their life and ease the grief that comes with such loss.

This project came about as a special way to honor my stepfather. As is often the case, there were plenty of beautiful flower arrangements present at the funeral, including those from us—his immediate family. In some families, like mine, it is acceptable, even expected, that those close to the deceased will remove some of the flowers in the arrangements present at graveside. Some are placed on the graves of other family members in the cemetery and others are taken home and dried as mementos. While not everyone present will engage in such a practice, for some of us it helps with the healing. Other flower arrangements are sent to hospitals, nursing homes, or special places of worship, and what is left goes home with the immediate family.

While plants are easy to deal with, finding something to do with all the beautiful cut flowers presented a little bit of a challenge. These were, understandably, too special to pitch in the compost, and leaving them in a box somewhere seemed to serve no particular purpose either. A special potpourri, tailored to both my stepfather's personality and memory, seemed the obvious answer.

If you aren't lucky enough to have dried flowers from the funeral of the person you wish to honor, it is perfectly acceptable to buy or collect flowers special to that person and dry them just for this purpose. Perhaps you can even find and dry flowers that were particularly loved by the deceased.

Making the Potpourri

Begin with an ivy bowl, available in many craft stores. Any size will work, except for perhaps really large ones. While you are there, pick up a lovely crocheted doily big enough to cover the top of your ivy bowl, as well as some narrow ribbon in a color you think appropriate to the person you are honoring.

Leave the bowl plain, or decorate it as you wish. My parents lived out in the country where there were always flowers, so mine will either be etched with a butterfly, symbol of the soul in many cultures and evocative of open, flowered spaces. Other symbols that would be appropriate include ivy or grape leaves or a symbol of something that makes you think of the departed. You could also paint the bowl or decorate it in dozens of other ways.

After you have your container, the rest is pretty easy. Here are some basic potpourri-making guidelines to get you started. Try to mix your ingredients together in any kind of bowl but a metal one. Most potpourris have a base of rosebuds or petals. Simply using the dried ingredients will yield a subtle scent. If you desire a stronger scent, use a scented oil. To help the scent last even longer, mix about one-half teaspoon of oil with grated or chopped orris root or cellulose fiber fixative.

Now simply mix together the ingredients for your potpourri, perhaps retaining a few of the nicer looking flowers for the top, and place them in the bowl. Lace the ribbon through the edges of the doily, place the doily over the opening of the bowl, and tie it shut with a bow. If you are worried about dust filtering through the doily and into the bowl, place a piece of plastic wrap over the opening first. The doily will hide the plastic wrap, and the plastic wrap will protect the flowers.

It is a pretty simple project, although what you choose to include in the potpourri may involve some difficult decisions. What follows is a list of several herbs, flowers, and other plants that have a connection to death, remembrance, and bereavement. While these plants have some sort of traditional meaning behind them, please feel free to use whatever your heart or intuition indicate. This is a very personal project meant to be of use to you.

Herbs Associated with Death

Acorns are a symbol of life and immortality—quite appropriate for a powerful personality who lived life to its fullest. It is also a very masculine symbol.

Almonds symbolized hope to the Greeks. Medieval Christians viewed it as signifying divine approval. According to the Victorian French, almonds were symbol of a happy marriage.

Amaranth was considered eternal by the Greeks. It was also a symbol of immortality, probably for the same reasons.

Poets later used it as a symbol of constancy and fidelity, as well as, yet again, immortality.

Birch is the first tree to leaf out in the forest in spring. It is associated with driving out evil and symbolizes purity. Celtic dead were covered in birch boughs. If you are lucky, the tree will have already left bits of its beautiful bark for you to find; if not, take only as much as you need, and be gentle in harvesting it from the tree.

Borage makes men merry and so is a fitting memorial to a merry person. It also inspires courage.

Camellias symbolize steadfastness and eternal love. To the Japanese it symbolizes a sudden death.

Carnations, particularly the pink ones, have been associated with motherhood and Mother's Day for nearly a century. Christian legend claims that carnation flowers sprang up from the ground wherever Mary's tears fell as she walked to Calvary. Carnations are also a popular funeral flower, suitable in commemorating either a mother or a young child. **Coltsfoot** has similar meanings.

Chrysanthemum's ray-like petals symbolized the rays of the Sun to those in the Orient. It brings to mind the union of heaven and earth, fullness, completeness, and immortality. It is also a fitting memorial to a person with a bright, shining personality who lived a long, full life. It is the flower of optimism and cheerfulness, as well as rest and ease after long travails.

Clover evokes spiritual and religious significance of divine triads and the Christian Holy Trinity.

Cypress branches are symbols of the immortal soul and the finality of death. To Greeks and Romans, the cypress symbolized the gods of the underworld and the nether gods, such as the Fates, who foretold the time of death, and the Furies, goddesses of vengeance not to be crossed.

Egyptians used the wood for mummy cases and Greeks to make coffins for their heroes. In a nice juxtaposition, the cypress is a symbol of joy and grace in the Far East.

Daisies represent purity, innocence, and loyal love. Interestingly enough, the flower was also considered an emblem of Aphrodite, Venus, and Freyja. Use their petals to represent a gentle woman.

Dandelion seed puffs blown into the wind will carry your thoughts to your sweetheart. Tuck a few into the potpourri of a husband, wife, or lover to do the same for you. It is a flower of faithfulness.

Dill is used to dull or lull. Use it only if your pain is especially sharp and likely to remain so over time. After all, you don't want to dull your memories too much.

Everlastings create never-ceasing remembrance for your loved one.

Forget-me-nots should be obvious as a symbol of remembrance. They represent faithful love and undying memory.

Hawthorn is representative of sweet hopes and marriage. Use hawthorn berries to represent a woman you consider a queen.

Heartsease brings happiness when remembering those we love who have passed on.

Irises were planted on women's graves to lead their souls to the Elysian Fields. Egyptians saw the flower as a symbol of life and resurrection. It can also signify faith, wisdom, valor, hope, light, and power.

Lavender was added to incense in order to see ghosts, but it also soothes the soul and signifies devotion and undying love. To Victorians, lavender sent a message of undying love.

Lemon balm provides comfort to the bereaved. It is an herb of sympathy.

Lotus flowers represent many different characteristics. Many cultures see it as representing great mysteries and truths. The Persians saw the Sun in it, not unlike the Egyptians, who considered it a symbol of creation and resurrection. To Buddhists, it is a symbol of heaven. The Chinese use it to symbolize perfection and purity, as well as summer. Finally, the Japanese see the past, present, and future within the symbol of a lotus.

Maize, the food of life, was placed in the mouth of a deceased Mayan commoner.

Marigolds are flowers of grief.

Marjoram comforts and consoles. According to the Greeks, when planted on graves it helps the dead sleep in peace. Add a pinch to your mixture for the same purpose.

Oak is symbolic of strength, masculinity, stability, and longevity.

Parsley increases or indicates strength and vigor, which could be evocative of a strong and vigorous personality.

Peaches, to the Chinese, are the fruits of eternal life.

Poppies bring eternal sleep and oblivion, allowing the dead to sleep in great peace.

Rosemary means the "dew of the sea." It has long been associated with friendship and remembrance and is an herb of Christmas, weddings, and funerals. It represents happy memories, fidelity, and love. In the seventeenth and eighteenth centuries, mourners began bringing sprigs of rosemary to funerals, dropping them into the grave.

Roses have always been associated with love, perfection, and the transient nature of things. Its blossoms were equated with love, beauty, youth, perfection, and immortality. A rose's thorns remind us of pain, while the fading flowers represent the fading nature of beauty and youth. A pink bloom represents simplicity and happy love. White is the color of purity and innocence. Yellow signifies perfect achievement, courage, and jealousy. Red roses are the color of passion, sensual desire, shame, blood, and sacrifice.

Rue is the "herb of grace."

Sage was considered by medievals to be a healing herb.

Sakaki branches were left by the Japanese as farewell gifts to the dead. In Shintoism, the sakaki is a sacred tree.

Sandalwood was used by Hindus and Buddhists for incense, embalming ingredients, and as wood for funeral pyres.

Sunflower petals or seeds would be a nice way to pay homage to Plains Indian tribes who valued the flower's seeds as a primary food source. Sunflower was so important to some Native American tribes that bowls of the seeds were placed on graves to serve as sustenance on their journey to the happy hunting ground.

Sweet peas symbolize departures, making them an excellent healing flower to add in a memorial mixture.

Vervain is thought to be tears wept by Isis over her dead husband.

Yarrow brings dreams of a loved one, perhaps in the form of happy memories.

Yew has long been associated with death, immortality, and resilience. It was often planted in graveyards and is a plant of grief, sorrow, faith, and resurrection.

The following ingredients obviously aren't even plants, but they have uses and connotations in common with our subject of death, remembrance, and burial. Any of these stones would make nice add-ins to your potpourri.

Amethyst is a healing stone excellent for a special potpourri.

Copal was burned as funerary incense by the Maya. It would make a nice, scented addition.

Coral is directly connected to the ocean and our Great Mother, which also connects it to the cycles of life and death. Pacific Islanders placed coral upon graves to protect the departed. Hindus used it in a similar fashion. A piece of naturally harvested coral placed near the top of your ivy jar would be beautiful, as well as soothing.

Jade was used by the Maya in a death ritual. Jade beads were placed in the mouth of the deceased, possibly to symbolize life or breath. It was included among Chinese grave goods for similar reasons.

Jet, a stone of protection, is also found among old grave goods. Victorians used the stone extensively in mourning jewelry, often incorporating locks of the deceased's hair into specially designed mountings.

Turquoise, one of my favorite stones, was used by some Native American tribes to guard their dead.

Remember above all else that this project is supposed to help you. It isn't just to keep your departed loved one's memory, but to help you continue on the path of healing.

The loss of someone we care deeply for is never an easy thing, and neither is healing from such a trauma. It takes time. Be patient. Take what I've written here and make it your own. Add whatever trinkets, herbs, flowers, and doodads you see fit to add. And remember, things will get easier with time.

Someday you'll look upon your ivy bowl of potpourri and mementos, and a smile will cross your face.

Celtic Herbal Incense and Gem Elixirs

❧ by Sharynne NicMhacha ❧

C eltic herb-lore is a treasure trove of mystical symbolism that can be used as an inspirational source for creating an array of magical herbal products and creations. Two of the most powerful ways to use the traditional Celtic associations of herbs and plants are in the production of herbal incenses and gem elixirs.

Herbal incenses are blends of herbs that, when burned at certain times of the year or for particular purposes, can have an effect on rituals, meditations, and ceremonies. Herb and gem elixirs are ritually created. They can be used in a variety of magical spells, healing rites, or dreamwork.

Guide to Celtic Herb-lore

First of all, we should become more acquainted with some of the most widely used and venerated herbs and plants in Celtic tradition. Here is a list of some of the most common plants in the folklore and mythology of the Celts.

Apple (Journeys, otherworld gifts, power)—The apple tree's symbolism speaks of gifts from the otherworld and, particularly, as a token of passage there. A silver apple branch with crystal blossoms on it was offered by a fairy woman to the voyager Bran. The white blossoms and red fruit made it an especially potent symbol of the otherworld, as red and white are two powerful otherworld colors in Celtic tradition.

Birch (Beginnings, awareness)—Birch was the first letter in the Celtic alphabet system known as *ogam*. The first message written in ogam was said to be a set of seven letter B's. This was a magical warning to the god Lug to protect his wife from straying or abduction.

Bog violet (Wisdom, protection, love)—The bog violet was used to encourage knowledge, wisdom, and eloquent speech, as well as protection from oppression or negative energies. It was also widely used in love spells.

Catkins (Abundance, success, friendship)—Catkins were used in magical charms to increase the powers and energies associated with fertility and abundance. They symbolized success and protection from the loss of friends.

Club moss (Vision, protection, power)—The Druids considered club moss a very sacred plant and gathered it for use in treating eye ailments and for its protective properties. Almost two thousand years later, people in Scotland use the plant for the very same reasons.

Elder (Healing, protection, vision)—The berries of the elder are used in a variety of healing charms and spells (as well as in folk medicine). It was also used for protection. If the juice of the inner bark was applied to the eyelids on quarter days, it was supposed to give one the ability to see through the veil.

Figwort (Life energy, joy, power)—This little known herb was used in Scottish folk magic and folk medicine. It was associated with an increase of fertility or life energies, as well as happiness, love, peace, and power.

Hawthorn (May Day, fairies, power)—The hawthorn tree is another sacred plant with white blossoms and red fruits. It was often associated with Beltane (May 1) and connected with fairy energies or powers.

Hazel (Divine wisdom, knowledge, problem solving)—The hazel tree and its nuts symbolized divine wisdom in Celtic tradition. The mythological well of wisdom was surrounded by sacred hazel trees that dropped their nuts into the water. The salmon of wisdom that lived in the water cracked the nuts to obtain the knowledge inside.

Ivy (Increase, protection, love)—Ivy leaves symbolized the manifestation of life energies, fertility, and abundance. They were also used in protective magic and in love divination done through dreams.

Juniper (Purification, protection, strength)—Juniper was used, much as sage is used in other cultures, as a purifying agent. It provided protection from negative events or misfortunes and from fear or fatigue.

Mistletoe (Healing, fertility, detoxification)—Mistletoe was gathered by the Druids of Gaul on the sixth day of the Moon. People in Celtic countries still gathered sacred plants during the waxing Moon in the last century. This plant was known as "All-Heal" in Gaulish. It increased fertility and was considered an antidote to all poisons.

Oak (Longevity, wisdom, strength)—The oak tree was well known in Celtic lore and has long symbolized longevity, wisdom, and strength. It was said that Druids considered it so sacred that they held no rites without using branches or foliage from the oak. It was often associated with the gods of the sky realm.

Rowan (Protection, magic, life energies)—The rowan, or mountain ash, was one of the most powerful Celtic herbs used in protective magic. Sacred fires used rowan wood. Its red berries were strung to make charm necklaces.

Saint John's wort (Success, abundance, protection)—This herb had many magical applications, including victory, good luck, abundance, increase, peace, and protection from all negative influences. It was believed to bestow spiritual power and was used in divination rites.

Yarrow (Healing, love, power)—Yarrow was used for many medicinal applications and brought beauty, swiftness, eloquence, and love. It was associated with personal power.

Celtic Herbal Incense Blends

Herbal incense is quite easy to prepare, but it does take focus, sincerity, and magical intent. Herbs should be selected based on their magical (and sometimes also medicinal) properties, as well as for your own personal connection with the plant. Try to gather or obtain organic herbs, as pesticides or other toxins will interfere with the plant's own natural energies and will be noxious. Get to know each herb intimately before using it in any magical preparations. Feel the herb, look at it, smell it, and become well acquainted with its physical properties and energy.

You may want to spend some time before any blending in meditation with each of the separate elements of the herbal blend. In this way, you ensure that you are in contact with the spirit of the plant, and that it is a correct ingredient for your work. You should also ascertain if the herbs you are considering will work well together. In my experience, Celtic herbs are happy to work in cooperation with other herbs from the tradition. In addition, it is important to begin establishing a relationship with each plant's spirit in order to work properly and effectively with its powers, wisdom, energies, and magical properties.

Once you have connected with the plants and are certain about the herbs you wish to work with, it is time to make the herbal blend. Take a wooden, glass, or metal bowl or dish dedicated for use in herbal magical preparations. Light a candle, and let your mind become calm. You may wish to play some calming or inspiring Celtic music while you work. Begin to focus on the work you wish to do. Handle the herbs, inhale their essence, and connect with them. Pass the herbs over or around the flame three times in a sunwise direction to bless and consecrate them.

When you are ready, take three pinches of the first herb, and place these in the dish. As you do so, recite or speak softly of the three properties (listed above) the herb will add to your magical blend. For example, if you are using yarrow in an herbal blend for love, you might say: "Love, beauty, and personal power." Say the words once as you put in the three pinches, or, if it seems appropriate, repeat the three words with each pinch of the herb. This makes a total of nine (three times three) repetitions, which is a powerful number in the Celtic magical tradition.

When all the herbs have been added, pass the dish over the flame three times in a sunwise fashion, and state calmly and clearly the magical purpose or intent of the herbal blend. Consecrate it in the presence of the spirits of the three worlds—the sky realm, the middle realm of earth, and the lower realm of the underworld—as well as the four directions. In Celtic tradition, the directions are not associated with elemental forces, but with specific powers or attributes. The main attributes of the directions are: east/prosperity, south/music, west/learning, and north/battle or conflict.

The herbal blend may be burned on a special incense charcoal or placed on top of salt or sand inside a metal or heat-proof dish or container. Offer the smoke to the spirits, and let yourself inhale a small amount of the smoke (indirectly) as you go on to perform any other meditation or magical rites that seem appropriate. If you are sensitive to smoke, you may offer the blend without burning it. I often place a dish of herbal blend on the altar or outside for the gods, the ancestors, or the spirits of the land. You can also carry some with you in a pouch or bag and offer it as seems appropriate. Store herbs in a glass jar with a well-fitting lid.

Here are some suggestions for Celtic herbal incense blends to get you started (organized by magical application or intent).

Love—Bog violet, ivy, yarrow

Strength—Oak, juniper, figwort

Wisdom—Hazel, oak, bog violet

Vision—Elder, club moss, birch, apple

Healing—Elder, yarrow, mistletoe, figwort

Success—Juniper, St. John's wort, catkins

Abundance—Catkins, figwort, ivy, St. John's wort

Magical power—Hawthorn, apple, mistletoe, yarrow, figwort

Protection—Club moss, rowan, juniper, St. John's wort, elder, ivy

Herbal Blends for the Wheel of the Year

You can also follow in the footsteps of the magical practitioners of Ireland and the British Isles by creating, using, and offering herbal blends on the four sacred holidays of the Celts: Imbolc on February 1, Beltane on May 1, Lammas on August 1, and Samhain on November 1. Here are some herbal incense blends using herbs and plants sacred to the Celts on these days.

Imbolc

This feast day was sacred to Bridget, triple goddess of healing, smithcraft, and poetry. The dandelion was associated with Bridget, as well as snowdrops, primroses, and other small flowers that herald the beginning of spring. Bridget's holiday was associated with the birth of lambs and the return of milk (abundance and plenty) after the long winter. There are a number of herbs associated with increase, plenty, and milk products in Celtic tradition, including milkwort, butterwort, ivy, honeysuckle, rowan, pearlwort, and figwort.

A straw doll symbolizing Bridget was placed in a basket decorated with stones and shells alongside a wand of sacred wood such as birch, broom, bramble, or willow. Here is a special herbal blend sacred to the goddess Bridget, which may be offered at Imbolc and used to promote abundance, life energies, warmth, strength, and protection. Seven magical herbs are given, which is a very sacred number in Celtic lore, symbolizing the meeting of the three worlds and the four directions.

Herbal incense blend for Imbolc—Dandelion, figwort, ivy, birch, willow, primrose, honeysuckle

Beltane

At Beltane, rituals protected herds and crops and ensured survival and increase in the summer months (after which the harvest would take place). Rowan wands and boughs were used. The house was decorated with hawthorn, and the blossoms of nettles and hawthorn were made into spring tonics. People carried vervain in fields, stopping in each of the four directions. Yellow flowers were especially sacred at Beltane. These included cowslips, buttercups, marigolds, furze, daffodils, and forsythia. Hazel, elder, ash, and holly were also used for abundance and protection. Purification rites included rowan, elder, and juniper. Yarrow was used in divination, and ivy was collected for health and beauty.

Herbal incense blend for Beltane—Rowan, hawthorn, vervain, elder, yarrow, buttercup, marigold

Lammas

The first ripe grain was ritually gathered around the time of Lugnasad, or the "assembly of the god Lug," which is also known as Lammas. The Celts grew oats, barley, wheat or spelt, and rye. Fresh fruit and berries were also gathered at this time of year. Sacred cakes made of barley were toasted over a fire made of rowan or other sacred wood. After Lammas, in some areas the heather bloomed, which was a beautiful sight all over the hills and mountainsides. Offerings of fruit or garlands made of seasonal flowers were made at holy places, including stone circles and standing stones.

Herbal incense blend for Lammas—Barley, oat, spelt, rowan, blackberry, heather, wild carrot (i.e., Queen Anne's lace root)

Note: This blend can be burned, but it is best done outdoors. It can also be offered in a vessel without burning it. In addition, by substituting some other kind of safe and edible berry for the rowan, the ingredients can be used to create a sacred cake.

Samhain

All crops had to be gathered by Samhain. Apples and hazelnuts were especially associated with this time of year, as they were the fruits of sacred trees associated with the otherworld. Divination was performed at the New Year using these two plants, as well as yarrow, ivy, flax or hemp seed, and oats. Torches made of heather or bog fir were carried around the fields. Some people feel that it is important to use oak, mistletoe, and club moss (the three most sacred herbs of the Druids) at this time of year. Juniper would also be appropriate for New Year purification.

Herbal incense blend for Samhain—Apple, hazel, yarrow, oak, mistletoe, club moss, juniper

Celtic Gem Elixirs

Another wonderful way to utilize Celtic herbs and plants is in the ritual preparation of gem elixirs. These consist of cauldrons or vessels of sacred water containing sacred herbs and gems (or charmstones). Use springwater that has been purified and consecrated or sacred water from a place that is spiritually resonant for you. To purify and consecrate springwater, pass it through the smoke of juniper or another cleansing herb. Then pass a large quartz crystal over the top and bottom of the vessel three times. Next, leave it in the sunlight and moonlight for three days and nights prior to use.

When you are ready to add the herbs, follow the same procedure as outlined above in creating Celtic herbal incense. Use only two or three herbs or plants, so as not to confuse or overcomplicate the essence or energy vibration that the plants will be imparting to the water. Sprinkle the herbs on the top of the sacred water, and let them rest gently on the surface. After this, add sacred gems or stones to the cauldron or container. Here are some stones that were traditionally used in Celtic magic and folk tradition, along with the properties and powers they possess:

White quartz (Healing, protection, success)—White quartz has been found at some Celtic sites. The Picts used white quartz pebbles painted with magical symbols for healing. In addition, spheres or egg-shaped objects made of quartz crystal were cased in silver housings and dipped in vessels of water to impart healing, protection, or wishes.

Rose quartz (Healing, cooling, protection)—Rose quartz were used in folk charms as "fever stones" to cool the heat of a fever. They were added to boiling water to lend their power, the water then being used to wash the arms and legs of those seeking healing.

Green stones (Healing, protection, loyalty, success)— Green stones were highly prized in Celtic tradition and used for healing, protection, victory, and oath-swearing. Green stones of various kinds, usually found in nature, were also set in silver and worn as amulets or talismans.

Garnet (Magic, witchcraft, women's power)—In Scotland, a group of Witches from Strathardle were said to have prized a garnet stone used in their magical workings. This stone is still on display in a Highlands museum.

Holed stones (Vision, power, prophecy)—Flat stones with naturally occurring holes were believed to impart the power of vision into the otherworld. In some legends, these stones were also associated with the gift of prophecy.

Other stones that were prized in various Celtic areas were black and white marcasite, agate (all colors, but especially blue and green), black and white marble, serpentine, amethyst, and variegated or mottled stones of all colors.

You may use small pieces or chips of quartz or other semi-precious stones, such as garnet, amethyst, rose quartz, peridot, or citrine, in your elixir. These look particularly beautiful when placed in a glass bowl.

Place the stone gently in the bottom of the vessel, focusing your intent on the powers or attributes you wish the stone to impart to the water. For new endeavors or beginnings, create your elixir at the New Moon. For increasing magic, prepare it during the waxing Moon. To add a boost of power to an elixir, make it at the Full Moon (keeping in mind that the Full Moon accentuates whatever powers are present, good or otherwise; it can be an unpredictable force). For decreasing or purifying magic, prepare the elixir during the waning Moon. To do deep inner work, create your elixir during the dark Moon.

Leave the herbs and the stones in the water for three days and three nights; then remove the stones and the herbs. Offer the herbs outside to the gods, ancestors, or spirits of the land. Bottle the water in a glass jar or container. It can be used right away for healing, magic, or other purposes, or kept for future use. The water can be used for anointing yourself or magical objects, cleansing or purifying, healing, or offering in ceremony. The powers of herb and gem elixirs are gentle and subtle, yet, if you take the time to become acquainted with the herbs, you are sure to experience their time-honored and powerful magical effects and energies of Celtic tradition.

Flower and Crystal Combinations

by Tammy Sullivan

For centuries, men and women have given beautiful stones and flowers as gifts and tokens of love. And such giving certainly involves the expectation of receiving a smile of delight in return. The way I see it, this constitutes a spell.

Emerson said: "The earth laughs in flowers." Flowers spread joy and healing. Shakespeare, meanwhile, spoke of the sermons in stones, alluding to their ancient wisdom and power.

Why are these items so potent as gifts? They are powerful magically. The oldest living thing on the planet happens to be a flowering bush that dates back over twelve thousand years. And the lifetime of stones is far longer than any living thing.

The custom of giving gifts to mark occasions also stretches back eons. For

example, ancient Romans presented good luck charms to the emperor to show their loyalty. Later, as the tradition evolved, flowers and crystals became an acceptable gift for any occasion.

Today, a man might present a woman with a diamond ring once it is agreed that they are to be wed. Historically, before the invention of jeweler's tools, people wore uncut diamonds on their person. The diamond was treasured for its beauty even in raw form.

Colored gemstones were assigned magical properties as early as 3000 BC. Most often, the attributes assigned to the gemstone took its cue from the ruling planet of that stone. Color played a part in this as well, because it was thought that the color unleashed the power within the stone. In the modern era, even the very young are gifted with colored gemstones associated with their month of birth.

When two people are still in the dating phase of a relationship, flowers are often given to the other as an expression of love. Flowers are also given if someone is sick or feeling under the weather, if someone has passed into the summerland, and basically anytime one wants to say "I'm thinking of you" to another.

Flowers have their own language. In the Victorian era, people expressed a huge range of meanings depending on which flower was sent. You could say almost anything you would want to say simply by sending a specific flower. You can also accomplish any spell goal you intend by using this flower language.

Combining Flowers and Stones

In magical work, people frequently use both crystals and flowers. As powerful as each one is on its own, they are unstoppable when combined. When you combine the two, the energies are doubled and the arrangements can be stunningly beautiful.

For example, when a member of my family is sick, I put red carnations (good health) and a carnelian stone (good health) in a vase to place near them as they rest. Not only will the sight cheer them up, but the flowers and stone will work together to bring good health to the person. A simple charging chant while changing the water keeps the flowers and the spell fresh.

If I were responding to a specific ailment, like a kidney infection, for example, I would add a sapphire as Libra rules the kidneys and sapphire is a Libra stone. You may also use deity-specific combinations as offerings and invocations. Below are some guidelines for working this beautiful form of magic.

Arrangement Tips

When designing your spell for a vase, let your instinct guide you. How many flowers and stones you add can be figured by your numerical correspondences, or you can just fill the vase. Both methods are acceptable. Just keep the shape and style of the vase in mind.

I also recommend that you use only glass or ceramic types of vases for spellwork. Glass will not interfere in any way with the goal and allows the magic to flow through it better than many metals or plastic. Also, many metals are damaging to delicate flowers. For the sake of beauty and to add extra color magic, you may use decorative glass marbles in the bottom of your vase.

If you are creating an arrangement to increase happiness in the home, and your heart guides you to add certain flowers, crystals, or herbs—just go with it. Being happy with the arrangement is the first sign that your spell is working.

When working with vines, such as honeysuckle or morning glory, know that they lend themselves to wreaths much more than to vases. You can easily tie in a few crystals. A wreath of honeysuckle with a few citrines tied in looks gorgeous on the front door and is reminiscent of old Greek customs. It is an easy way to weave a net of happiness over the whole household.

When the arrangement begins to wither and brown, it is of course time to remove it from the area. If you choose, you can hang the bundle of flowers upside down to dry, or you can add them to the compost pile. I like to burn my dried floral arrangements, ensuring that I get every drop of magical use from them. Cleanse the stone for reuse.

Magical May Baskets

Since medieval times, people have celebrated the return of spring by filling tiny baskets with flowers and secretly leaving them on a neighbor's doorstep. Why not add a beautiful crystal to the mix and increase the positive vibrations in this magical item?

The basket can be as simple as a doily rolled into a vase-like formation and secured with ribbon. Add a ribbon loop to the top for hanging. You can bind the crystal with the ribbon. Make certain to use a small or lightweight crystal so that the ribbon does not come undone as it hangs. You may also add greenery or herbs around the flowers for design harmony.

Magical May baskets do not have to be reserved for May Day. You can use them year round to send your good wishes to others. For a healing basket, try using heliotrope and topaz. If you want to wish someone good luck in the coming year, use an apache tear and daffodil combination. For a simple friendship basket, you can't go wrong with turquoise and sweet pea.

Potions, Elixirs, and Brews

Teas

The most delicious method of combining flowers and crystals is to brew a pot of floral tea and add a crystal to your cup. Brewing tea in the Sun adds a special magical zing. As you sip the tea, focus your mind on the goal.

When choosing your flowers for tea, make sure they are organic and edible. Also, be certain the flowers are properly identified and that you use only the petals. If you prefer a stronger drink, try chicory and dandelion coffee. The following flowers make good tea: marigold, carnation, chamomile, chicory, chrysanthemum, bachelor buttons, dandelions, honeysuckle, gardenia, geranium, hibiscus, jasmine, lavender, lilac, pansy, petunia, primrose, rose, snapdragon, sunflower, tulip, and violet.

When choosing your stone, make sure it is clean and has not previously been anointed with essential oils. Also, take note that certain stones should not be used, as they are toxic. Malachite, for instance, should never be taken internally. Popular magical crystals that cannot be used internally include: amazonite, amber, azurite, boji stones, crysocolla, emerald, garnet, iolite, kunzite, hematite, lapis lazuli, marcasite, magnetite, malachite, moonstone, opal, quartz, ruby, sapphire, sodalite, tiger's eye, topaz, tourmaline, and turquoise. Please note that this is only a partial list. Check any stone you are planning to use.

Also, you may also choose simply to place the stone in the saucer instead of in the tea. If you are in doubt about your stone's potential toxicity, it is best to use an indirect method of energy transfer. Simply place the stone in the general area.

Scrying Brew

Brew a cup of honeysuckle tea and place a clear quartz crystal inside it. Empty your mind and gaze into the tea, allowing visions to float through your mind.

Bath Potions

Nothing feels as soothing as a hot bath scented with relaxing aromas. Magical baths have a quality akin to healing hot springs. The warm water helps open the chakras and psyche. When you soak in a flower-strewn bath, you are soaking the attributes of the plant into your body. Adding a crystal imparts an additional vibration that works in harmony with the flowers to boost the power. Additional items, such as milk or honey, may be added if you'd like to take advantage of their skin-nourishing properties. And of course you may always add salt.

You can add the ingredients directly to warm bathwater, or you can premix them and store the mixture in a glass jar until you are ready to use them. If you prefer you can tie the flowers into a sachet for easier cleanup afterward.

I don't recommend using hematite or magnetite in the bath, as both can rust. It's also best to rinse the flowers in cool water before adding them to your bath to remove any pollen and tiny pests. Use organically grown flowers only. Bathing in water that may contain pesticide is not a good idea. Daffodil, morning glory, chrysanthemum, and rue should not be used in the bath as they can cause dermatitis.

Relax and unwind bath—Gardenia and quartz

Miracle bath (to heighten spiritual awareness)—African violet and amethyst

Beauty bath—Rose and rose quartz

Sacred Balms

Balm-making is simple, even when using crystals. It is best to use pure cocoa butter for balms, as it is good for the skin and holds scent well. Simply melt a stick of cocoa butter in a double boiler or in the microwave. Add the petals of your choice and one small crystal. Allow it to sit and harden.

Once the balm is set, apply it to your pulse points. Only use tumbled stones when making balms. Some raw stones and petals can irritate the skin, so check before use.

On the Body

In the past, young women wore flowers in their hair when they reached an age suitable for marriage. This custom is still alive in many parts of the world. If you dream of wearing flowers in your hair, it is said to foretell of your deepest wish coming to fruition.

Men and women both pin flowers onto outer garments at times. At one time it was quite fashionable to wear a single flower pinned about the breast area. Today, this custom is sadly reserved for special events, such as weddings, proms, and formal occasions.

In the South Pacific, people wove chain necklaces, or leis, from native flowers to mark important occasions. Leis are used to express emotion, such as grief, as well as to celebrate events like marriage, birth, and falling in love. They were thought to bring one closer to the great spirit. Accordingly, chanting and field blessings often took place while wearing a lei. In these tropical locations, it was considered wrong to let a beautiful flower wither and die unpicked. It should be used and celebrated.

Weaving daisy chain necklaces and circlets has long been a happy activity for many children. Any flower with a long stem may be used. Simply cut a small slit in the stem near the blossom, and loop the next daisy in the chain through the slit. At the end, tightly twist the remaining stem around the first. Wearing a daisy crown is reputed to attract love and to increase intuition. Wildflower crowns are traditionally worn by maidens to celebrate the changing of the seasons and to welcome spring.

Elixirs

Combining petals and stones in water will infuse the energies of the flowers and crystals into the liquid. You can then spray an area with this magical elixir to impart magical vibrations. It's best to let the liquid absorb the energies for a few days before use.

However, you may also use a brewing method to instill the plant properties into the liquid. This tends to add color to the water as well, which adds a boost in power. Be sure to let the brew cool before you use it. If the fragrance is not as strong as you like, add a drop or two of essential oil. Elixirs are often used in aromatherapy and also in vibrational medicine.

Peace Elixir

Place two cups of blue morning glory blossoms and an aquamarine in a shallow pan. Cover with water, and place on high heat. Allow the mixture to heat until just before it boils. Stir three times clockwise, and allow the elixir to cool. Pour it into a spray bottle, straining out the flowers and stone. The liquid now holds the properties of the plant and stone. Mist around the room when peace is desired. Do not take this elixir internally; it is toxic.

Sachets

Magical sachets can be placed almost anywhere. They can be used as dream pillows, room and car fresheners, or hung in the closet. Take a square of linen and place a tablespoon of flower petals and your chosen crystal inside. Tie the four corners of the material together to form a bundle. You can carry the sachets with you. Don't forget to add seeds. These future blossoms carry the same magical properties as the flower and represent fertility.

In the Garden

Many of us grow flowers in our gardens or own houseplants that flower. These can be living spells. For instance, placing rose quartz in the soil around your roses is a simple way to fill your home and gardens with loving vibrations. Another way to combine energies is to add a gemstone directly to your watering can.

Birth Month Correspondences

January—Carnation, garnet

February—Violet, amethyst

March—Jonquil, aquamarine

April—Sweet pea, diamond

May—Lily, emerald

June—Rose, pearl

July—Larkspur, ruby

August—Gladiolus, peridot

September—Aster, sapphire

October—Calendula, opal

November—Chrysanthemum, topaz

December—Narcissus, turquoise

Floral and Crystal Combinations

The following list incorporates my recommendations for tried and true combinations. However, if certain stones or flowers speak to you in a different way than they do to me, go with your instinct. This list is designed for simplicity's sake. It is perfectly acceptable to mix a wide range of flowers. Simply make sure the intent is harmonious to the vibrations of each flower you use.

To aid divination—Honeysuckle, cat's eye

For peace of mind—Blue morning glorys, amethyst

To increase happiness—Morning glory, amethyst

To release stress—Gardenia, malachite

To aid sleep—Chamomile, moonstone

To inspire creativity—Dandelion, clear quartz

To increase romance—Red rose, rose quartz

To aid meditation—Gardenia, sapphire

To calm arguments—Meadowsweet, carnelian

To remove hostility—Tiger lily, coal

To cleanse an area—Chamomile, clear quartz

To cleanse the body—Lavender, crysocolla

To cleanse the psyche—Chamomile, citrine

To increase love—Rose, rose quartz

To honor earth—Honeysuckle, emerald

To honor air—Lavender, aventurine

To honor fire—Sunflower, amber

To honor water—Jasmine, mother of pearl

To increase health—Rose, bloodstone

To search for truth—Daffodil, tiger's eye

To boost the memory—Periwinkle, fluorite

For balance—Honeysuckle, smoky quartz

To ground—Primrose, hematite

To increase intuition—Dandelion, moonstone

To increase wealth—Jasmine, emerald

To boost courage—Sweet pea, bloodstone

To stop nightmares—Morning glory, jet

To aid communication—Iris, amazonite

Complex Mixtures

When instinct takes over the design process of arranging flowers, we can often wind up with several different kinds of stones and blossoms. When using these combinations for spellwork, it is best to double-check the metaphysical properties of each ingredient to avoid conflict.

Full bouquets take many colors, shapes, and sizes of flowers to make them look complete. It is never necessary to go to such lengths for floral and crystal magic, but it is a thoroughly enjoyable method of spellcasting.

Final Tips and Tricks

To keep the flowers fresher longer, be sure to cut the stems at an angle. Make sure to allow plenty of length for the stem; you can do much more with a long-stemmed flower. Change the water every few days. While you do, recharge the spell by chanting.

The general rule is if the stone is unsafe for elixirs, it should not be placed in a water vase. Many of these stones contain copper, and copper will kill your flowers.

Floral and crystal combinations are a balm to the soul. The magical feeling created by them spreads not only to the recipient, but to the creator and others as well. It is a lighthearted, life-affirming practice. As you walk this garden path, may your life be blessed by the blossom and crystal.

Herb
History,
Myth, and
Magic

The Magic of the Morning Glory

by Tammy Sullivan

Few plants grow as quickly as the beautiful morning glory. In fact, the morning glory grows at a rate of up to five feet per month, making it one of the fastest-growing plants known. Officially called *Ipomoea*, this hardy flowering vine is an annual in most areas, although it will reseed itself and return year after year, depending upon the climate. In the tropical regions, morning glory growth is so lush they are considered pests. This plant prefers full sunlight, but will grow in a stunted manner in semi-shady areas.

The *Ipomoea* belongs to the family of *convolvulaceae*, which means "to twine around." This family includes over 1,600 species, one being the sweet potato—the most important root crop in the world. It is a dietary staple in tropical regions and an excellent source of vitamins and minerals. Sweet potato has been cultivated for well over ten thousand years.

Native Americans made use of another tuber root from the morning glory family, which they called the "man of the earth." Today it is called the wild potato. The taproot of this plant grows underground to between five to six feet long. It can weigh as much as thirty pounds. Tribal people would dig the root up and boil it to eat in emergency situations. The root was known to be bitter when raw. There were also medicinal uses for this root; it was smoked in a pipe to promote calmness and brushed on body parts to relieve pain. The most frequent medicinal use was to prepare a tea that would promote evacuation of the bowels.

The beautiful moonflower also falls under the same classification as the morning glory, even though it only blooms at night. It is pollinated by night-flying moths and, like most night bloomers, has an intoxicating aroma. Moonflowers are frequently used on altars and in sanctuaries. As they relate to the Moon, they are commonly associated with the feminine side of nature and are held as a sacred symbol of the goddess.

Bindweed, or wild morning glory, also belongs to the *convolvulaceae* family. It has arrow-shaped leaves and is considered dangerous to crops. It has an expansive root system that is almost impossible to get rid of, and it strangles out other plants.

Written records indicate that the European morning glory originated in China and was introduced in Japan as early as 710 AD. It was not until the seventeenth century that the morning glory was introduced to Europe. It is native to the Americas and many tropical regions. In Japan, its official name was *asagao*. The flower itself was called *kengo*, the seed *kengoshi*, and the vine *kuji-sou*.

The color of the flowers produced by the plant is varied—blue, pink, purple, red, and white. Growing the blue variety in one's garden is said to bring peace and happiness to the home, while all varieties are said to keep away hostile influences. An age-old practice of planting the morning glory in a pot placed in the garden is said to have the effect of warding off the evil eye.

Each flower blooms only once, then quickly closes and dies. It is replaced almost immediately by another colorful bloom, so that the vine blooms continually in the morning hours. The blossoms open from dawn to mid-morning daily. On cloudy days they often bloom for longer periods. Certain varieties of morning glory will hold their bloom until midday. The blooms range in size from four inches across to as large as eight inches.

Morning glory flowers can be a source of continual surprise to the gardener. You may plant seeds for a blue variety, yet next year it returns as purple. This is a natural hybridization process that has famously intrigued scientists. According to research, it is thought that the plant mutates in this way to attract new pollinators, such as hummingbirds, in order to survive.

The vine of the morning glory is beautiful in its own right. It produces large, heart-shaped leaves and most often grows in a clockwise spiral. An exception to this is the bedge bindweed, which will only grow in a counterclockwise manner. Morning glory is a climber and can grow to reach the top of fences, posts, or rooftops.

The intoxicating scent of the morning glory blossom attracts both butterflies and hummingbirds. It has long been a staple in the cottage-style garden. It provides shade and privacy along with its beautiful blossoms and aroma. The flowering of the vine usually begins around Midsummer and lasts well into the fall.

To propagate the morning glory, it is easiest to start from seeds. Soak the seeds overnight in warm water to soften the hull, and plant them in rich, well-drained soil. If the soil is too moist, the vine will not bloom as heartily as it will in well-drained soil. To encourage more flowers, add nitrogen to the dirt or plant them in poor-quality soil.

When placing morning glorys in the garden, care must be taken due to its invasive nature. The morning glory is a very aggressive plant and can easily smother out smaller plants. Also, it is best to place them where they have room to climb. You can use invisible fishing line to create a pattern on walls. The vines will grow along the string in a natural fashion, resulting in an enchanting flower-covered wall.

Morning glorys can be grown in hanging baskets but should be trimmed frequently. Trimming the vines back seems to encourage flowering. When grown in hanging baskets, the root systems have less room for expansion; however, this does not affect its fast growth rate or vigor.

The most popular choices of morning glorys today are the "heavenly blue," "pearly gates," "flying saucer," and "tie dye" varieties. There are hundreds of hybrids available, all beautiful.

As the vast majority of plants in the *convolvulaceae* family are poisonous, I do not recommend ingestion in any form. Certain varieties are edible, such as the sweet potato, the young shoot of the beach morning glory, and other varieties that are common ingredients in Asian cooking, but unless you are aware of which species you are dealing with, it is safer not to consume any portion of the morning glory. Because of its toxicity, morning glory carries the additional folk name of "devil's guts."

Although morning glory seeds are not safe for consumption, they have been ingested in religious rites for centuries. The ancient Aztecs often used the seeds in vision-seeking rites; unfortunately, many of them died during the process. As it is an unsafe practice, due to the poisonous nature of the plant, never ingest this plant. You can make use of the vision-invoking qualities of this plant in safer ways, such as weaving a boundary circle with the vines and performing a divination. Morning glory seeds now are treated with a chemical compound to prevent their abuse.

Ancient Aztecs thought of the morning glory as a key connector not only to their deity, but to occult knowledge in general. The morning glory gave extrasensory perception and the ability to visit spiritual guardians. An ancient statue depicts Xochipilli, the Aztec god of love, surrounded by five sacred plants, including the mushroom, tobacco, and the morning glory.

The morning glory was also thought to inhibit pain. Priests would smear themselves in a concoction containing ashes, tobacco, and morning glory before a ritual in an effort to numb the flesh and remove the fear of pain. Later, when Catholicism reached Mexico, the morning glory was all but extinguished. The church attributed its visions to Satan and warned against its use, but they were unsuccessful in their campaign to destroy this beautiful plant.

In the language of herbs, the morning glory flower represents the month of September, friendship, affection, and emotional bonds. In the language of flowers, it represents departures.

In parts of Holland, the trumpet-shaped flower of the morning glory was used by the Goddess as a glass. A charming tale relates that a winemaker's cart was stuck in the mud. A grandly dressed lady rode by and offered to help for a drink of the wine. She reached down and plucked a morning glory blossom to use as a glass. The winemaker agreed and filled the flower with his sweet wine. As soon as the lady drank the wine, the cart rolled free from the mud and she disappeared. Hence, the morning glory has the nickname of "our lady's glass" in this region.

A particular species of the morning glory plant, called bush morning glory or jalap, has a very important root known in magic circles as High John the Conqueror. So well known and powerful is this root that famed blues musician Muddy Waters sang of its attributes. In the lyrics to the song "My John the Conqueror Root," he proclaims that when he rubs his root, his luck cannot fail. In Voodoo and Hoodoo practices, High John the Conqueror relates to the Orisha Legba. When this root is first removed from the earth, it has an alluring spicy scent.

When it comes to magical use, the morning glory is very powerful, with a somewhat spotty reputation. Certain species of the morning glory family are known by the folk name of bindweed, a name which refers to its ability to bind problems or people. One old spell teaches that to assure fidelity one should knot the vine three times. According to European folklore, the morning glory has the attribute of being fully functional in any spell—so long as it's a wicked one.

This plant also has many positive uses. In the past, the morning glory was an important part of childbirth for the Hawaiians. No Hawaiian woman would allow herself to cry out in pain for fear of being ridiculed, so gathering of beach morning glory by the birth attendants was a necessary way for the mother to gain a bit of privacy. When the attendants returned with the blossoms and leaves, they were rubbed on the expectant mom's belly as she slowly chewed a few leaves. In another Hawaiian legend, a young man tried to rescue his lover from the land of the dead using swings made from the vines of the morning glory. It was also said that the Polynesian goddess Haumea created the morning glory by shredding her skirt on branches as she ran to save her husband. Wherever a scrap of cloth fell, a flower emerged.

The magical correspondences of the morning glory are: planet, Saturn; element, water; time of day, morning; affinity, masculine; month, September; deities, Haumea, Aztec sun gods. Its properties are peace, happiness, protection, cleansing, releasing, increase luck, success, and repelling fairies. A sprinkling powder made from blue morning glory blossoms picked at dawn on a New Moon and sprinkled in the home assures a Moon cycle of peace and happiness .

The properties and uses for the bush morning glory, or High John the Conqueror root, are a bit different. Its correspondences are: planet, Mars; element, fire; time of day, any; affinity, masculine; month, September; deity, Legba. Its properties are success, money, protection, binding, love, power, and luck. A powerful anointing oil can be made by scoring the root and soaking it in vegetable oil for several weeks. This oil can be used to anoint magical items, altar candles, and altars. It is an all-purpose anointing oil that packs a powerful magical punch.

The root of any morning glory can be used as a substitute for High John the Conqueror root. The entire plant can be powdered and sprinkled for travel protection. The morning glory is also useful in matters involving reproduction or fertility. It is representative of the male genitalia and can be used as a poppet (this is especially true of the jalap root). Burning any part of the morning glory plant produces a cleansing effect that rids the environment of negative vibrations.

Placing the seeds of the morning glory underneath a pillow or in a sachet is said to bind nightmares. The seeds are also reputed to ease childbirth when held. It also can divine a child's sex: Drop a morning glory seed in a glass of water. If it floats the child will be male; if the seed sinks, the child will be female.

To bind someone or something, you may wrap the vine around a poppet. The vine is also used to stimulate hair growth by rubbing it on the head or wrapping it around a candle. Celtic folklore relates that the vine of the morning glory is protective over children. To stimulate this protection for the child, the mother burns a section of the vine at both ends, then hangs the center portion above the child's cradle. The vines may be braided together for cord magic. The scent of the morning glory flower is used as an aromatherapy remedy to awaken the mind and add a spark to one's day. It is also helpful in overcoming addictions.

The flowers of the morning glory may be used as an attractant. They are frequently used as a natural dye and produce clear pastel shades. Moreover, the colorful blossoms possess the attribute of aiding divination. It has been said that the morning glory tucks in her blooms just before a rain.

The leaves are often used in love magic because of their heart shape, but they also have an ancient medicinal purpose. A light infusion of the leaves was once used to make a laxative drink, although today there are safer methods. As certain types of morning glory contain natural cyanide, it is not suitable as a medicine.

A most potent magical concoction can be made from the milky sap of the morning glory. Take a small amount of sap and mix it with a bit of amber powder. On a piece of paper, write a goal you are working to achieve; brush the sap and powder substance over the words you have written. You may burn or bury the paper. The sap of the morning glory is known to open doors and makes room for changes.

It has recently been discovered that it was morning glory sap that first gave "bounce" to rubber. Scientists recently analyzed the chemical composition of the ancient rubber of the Mayans and found that it was primarily made from the sap of the rubber tree plant and the juice of the morning glory flower. They used this recipe for the rubber balls used in their sporting games. Without the morning glory juice, there was no bounce.

There is also a little known species of the morning glory family that produces a seed called Mary's bean. This seed is most often found adrift in coastal waters. Mary's bean has a natural cross formation embedded within the seed. It also forms its own fuzzy winter coat and can remain viable after years of drifting in icy waters. In fact, it has been found to have drifted from Central America to the shores of Norway. The actual plant that produces the seed is known only in a few locations around the world, yet the seed has been found over fifteen thousand miles away floating along with the ocean tides. These drifting types of seeds are called sea beans.

Mary's bean is a good luck charm so prized that in the past they were actually passed down through families. It was thought to ease childbirth and cure both hemorrhoids and snakebites. These seeds are bursting with magical power and fertility. They also have the unique attribute of influencing time and can be used to speed things forward or to slow things down. It is best to keep the seed whole and intact.

No matter which species of morning glory you plant in your garden, you can count on a beautiful and magical experience. If you prefer constant blooms, plant several different cultivars so that you have flowers morning, noon, and night. Morning glorys can bring flowers to any garden.

The Magical Blue Lotus

✎ by Michelle Santos ✎

To the ancient Egyptians, there was no more magical flower than the blue lotus or water lily. *Nymphaea nouchali var. caerulea* (the scientific name for the Egyptian blue lotus) is actually more of a water lily than a lotus. It should not be confused with *Agapanthus africanus* (the blue lily) or *Nymphaea lotus* (the white lotus), both of which flourished in ancient Egypt. The blue water lily was prized for its beauty, fragrance, and mind-altering qualities when ingested. Used by pharaohs and priests, the blue water lily connected directly to the gods.

This flower thrived on the mud and muck at the bottom of the Nile. With its roots in the earth, its leaves floating in the water, and its flower reaching skyward, the blue lotus served as a natural symbol for the connection between gods and humans, between heaven and earth. The blue lotus seemed blessed by the gods, as its growth cycle represented hope for regeneration in the afterlife. In the afternoon of each day, the blue lotus disappeared, receding beneath the river water. Every morning the flower, with its light-blue petals and soft yellow center, emerged to greet the morning Sun.

Blue Lotus Mythology

The blue lotus was closely linked to the Sun and the story of creation. The god most associated with the blue lotus was the god of fragrance, beautification, and healing, Nefertem. He is often shown in pyramid texts as a man with a lotus blossom on his head, sometimes in two vertical plumes. Nefertem was associated with both the fragrance and the narcotic effect of the flower, which was often used as an anesthetic. Nefertem was said to dwell each day with the Sun god Ra, thus cementing his role as a solar deity. Nefertem played a central role in one Egyptian creation story from Heliopolis. In the story, a blue lotus appears in the watery abyss of chaos. Slowly, the petals of the flower pull back, one by one, to reveal a young god sitting in the center of the flower. This is Nefertem in his connection to Ra. The lotus child is the Sun god, the creator, the banisher of darkness. Becoming lonely, the child Sun god, in the center of the blue lotus, creates the other gods and everything else that exists today.

The ancient Egyptians associated the creative life force with sexuality and fertility. The blue lotus, therefore, is also a flower of sensuality and fruitfulness. Women were often wooed with gifts of the flower. Images of women holding the blue lotus or wearing it as a headdress on various papyri may be a reference to potent fertility or desire. Offerings to the goddess Hathor, who presided over sexuality, birth, regeneration, music, and dance (among other things), included bowls decorated with water lily designs. The goddess Heqet, a primordial goddess of birth, creation, and resurrection, was often depicted as a frog or a woman with a frog head sitting on a blue lotus.

Many other gods shared an affinity for the water lily. These deities were connected to the afterlife. Osiris, god of rebirth, is often depicted with a half-opened blue lotus. The four sons of Horus, who guard the canopic jars of the deceased and attend the judgment of his/her *ka* (soul) in the halls of Ma'ati, are depicted standing on Osiris's lotus. The connection of the blue lotus to resurrection was so great that a "Making the Transformation of the Lotus" spell was included in the *Book of the Dead*. It was said over the deceased:

> *The Osiris Ani, whose word is truth, saith—I am the holy lotus that cometh forth from the light which belongeth to the nostrils of Ra, and which belongeth to the head of Hathor. I have made my way, and I seek after him, that is to say, Horus.*

> *I am the pure lotus that cometh forth from the field [of Ra].*

Blue Lotus Horticulture

As may be surmised from its connection with ancient Egypt, the blue lotus grows best in warm climates. This beautiful, sky-blue flower is widespread across Africa, where wild and cultivated varieties can be found from Egypt to South Africa. The blue water lily prefers placid river and lake shoreline, but it can be nurtured for commercial production or private enjoyment.

Also known as frog's pulpit (possibly a connection to Heqet, the ancient Egyptian frog goddess), the blue water lily is a perennial aquatic plant. It anchors itself to the pond's muddy bottom with thick, dark, underground horizontal stems called rhizomes. These rhizomes produce shoots that develop into new plants. The blue lotus has large, flat, round leaves that float on top of the water. The leaves perform a very important function for the plant, allowing it to collect carbon dioxide through its tiny pores. The top of the leaf is coated with a fine waxy layer, forcing water to roll off and take away dust and debris. The blue water lily has a system of internal ducts that sends the carbon dioxide from the leaves down to the roots.

The flower of the blue water lily is its most noticeable feature. *Caerulea*, from its scientific name, references the sky-blue color of the flowers. *Nymphaea* refers to the nymphs of Greek mythology—semidivine mythic creatures with a loving, delicate, and beautiful nature. The flowers are held on strong stalks well above the water and are in constant bloom from the middle of spring to the end of summer. The petals of soft blue surround numerous golden yellow and blue stamens. The flowers open in mid-morning and close by early afternoon. This delicate flower is encased by four sepals (modified leaves in the outermost section of the flower) that control the opening mechanism of the flower.

The sweet fragrance of the blue water lily is a great attraction for bees, its prime pollinator. Once a flower is pollinated, it closes in upon itself and sinks under the water. On the soft, muddy bottom, the ovaries form a hard green oval fruit, that decays to release thousands of small seeds. The seeds are covered in a fleshy membrane that buoys them to the surface for a short while. They float away from the parent plant, dispersing before sinking back under the water and into the mud.

Growing these graceful, elegant plants is fairly simple, as long as you have plenty of Sun, good soil, and at least one foot of standing water. Full Sun is necessary for flowers to bloom and for the unique opening and closing of the flowers to occur. They do not flourish in swiftly moving water or in environments with high wind.

There are two methods for planting water lilies. For the first, simply cover your pond floor with a half foot of sand and compost mixture, and plant the flowers directly in the soil. The second technique involves putting the plants in a container that is sunk into the bottom of the pond. Container gardening is thought to be easier as the plants can be lifted out of the water for inspection and for cleaning the pond. Specifically manufactured water lily baskets are best and are available at most garden centers. Since they have latticework sides, line them with strong fabric made from jute or hemp (known in Britain as hessian) to prevent the soil from seeping into the pond water.

The best soil mixture to ensure good growth varies. However, sieved garden loam or pure, unwashed river sand are recommended bases. For artificial ponds, nutrients will have to be added to the soil for the water lilies to thrive. Artificial fertilizer can be mixed with loam to create a healthy environment. Use two parts loam to one part well-rotted cow manure, or equal parts loam, cow manure, and compost. Bone meal or coarse ground hoof and horn may also be added into the mix. Formulating the right nutrient mixture may take some time and several attempts. If too much nitrogen-rich material or fertilizer is used, the pond will be overrun with algae. If too little fertilizer is added to the soil mixture, the water lilies will appear sickly. To add more fertilizer afterward, you can use a slow-release fertilizer pill.

Once you've decided on a soil mixture, you will want to plant your adult lily flowers. (Growing from seed can take patience as the water lily takes three or four years to flower.) Place the crowns of the lily firmly into the soil, making sure they are just protruding from the ground. The soil should be covered with river sand or pebbles to keep the water clean. Tying a weight onto the plant is a quick and easy method to establish your loose plants in the pond. After tying on the weight, toss the plant into the pond. The leaves will float up, adjusting to the height, and the roots will extend into the soil within a few weeks. You can use this procedure with a cloth planting. Place the flower in the center of the material, tying it into place with the four corners of the cloth. Drop the flower into your pond. The cloth will disintegrate by the time the flower has connected to the pond's bottom.

Remember that the blue water lily prefers a water temperature of 70 degrees Fahrenheit or higher. However, it can tolerate winter lows of 30 to 40 degrees Fahrenheit. The blue lotus does go dormant in the winter, but should remain in water during this dormancy. If you live in a colder climate, remove your water lilies from the pond before the first hard frost. Store them in containers of soil in airtight bags in a cool, nonfreezing place. Make sure they do not dry out. Another method of winterizing these beautiful flowers is to wash off the soil, wrap the rhizomes in sphagnum moss, and store them also in an airtight plastic bag in a cool, nonfreezing area. If you have a greenhouse pond with a water temperature of 70 degrees Fahrenheit or above, you can transplant the flowers to that location as well.

Once the weather has gotten warmer, simply replant your water lilies and sit back to enjoy their beauty and fragrance.

Blue Lotus Medicine, Ancient and Modern

The priests and pharaohs of ancient Egypt prized the blue lotus for its healing and narcotic qualities when ingested. Ancient physicians claimed that the blue lotus stimulated blood flow, lessened aging, and increased the sex drive. Soaked in wine, the blue lotus brought euphoria, a sense of tranquility, and heightened awareness. Studies indicate it may contain the substances aporphine and nuciferine, which are soluble in alcohol and produce a relaxed, happy feeling in low dosages. Hallucinatory effects become prevalent in higher dosages.

Recent biochemical tests have determined that the blue water lily contains a flavonoid (a naturally occurring phenolic compound or resin that sets permanently when heated) similar to those found in ginkgo. Blue lotus is used currently to enhance the sex drive and to stimulate circulation. Other modern uses for this plant include relieving muscle spasms and pain. Blue lotus has shown the potential to treat Alzheimer's disease, migraines, and tinnitus (a continual ringing or roaring in the ear).

The easiest way to include blue lotus in your health regimen is through the purchase of a commercially prepared tincture, an alcohol-based liquid suffused with the plant's essence. The standard dosage of blue lotus tincture is six to ten drops in juice, water, or under the tongue, two times per day. To prepare blue lotus in a way similar to the ancient Egyptians, soak between three and five flowers in a bottle of wine for several hours before drinking. Do not add too many flowers as the wine will turn undrinkably bitter. You can also make a tea with the blue lotus flower by steeping the same amount of flowers in twenty-five ounces of water.

As blue lotus is a hypnotic sedative and (in higher doses) a hallucinogen, please don't drive or operate heavy machinery after drinking it. It is best to avoid blue lotus if you are pregnant or nursing, if you have a history of psychosis or depression, or if you are currently taking cardiac or psychiatric medication. As with alcohol, please use blue lotus responsibly.

Blue Lotus Spellwork

Today, we can use the restoring power of the blue lotus to move past current difficulties, dissipate depression, and be reborn anew. The blue lotus gives us the hope and knowledge that things will change for the better. To jump-start a new venture or life transformation or to internalize the lesson of the blue lotus, try this Blue Lotus Spell. It will help you be reborn anew.

Blue Lotus Spell

Gather two medium-sized bowls, some dirt (in a bag or bucket), water (in a pitcher or bottle), a picture of a blue lotus, a towel, and dried or fresh blue lotus petals (if possible).

This spell is best done during the New Moon, a time to begin new projects and welcome new life changes. Just as the Moon is born anew, so will you. You can do this spell as often as you like or you feel is necessary.

Create sacred space in whatever way feels best for you. You can cleanse the area with sage smoke, or you can do an elaborate cleansing with representations of the elements. You can also sweep out old debris with your besom or broom. Any type of cleansing is viable, so choose the one that most resonates with you. Create sacred space in the way you feel most comfortable.

Place all of your spell items in the center of your sacred space and sit in front of them. Pour a handful of dirt into one of the bowls, and fill both bowls with water. You will have one bowl with mud at the bottom of the water and one bowl that is clear.

Your muddy bowl should remind you of a river or lake. If you have blue lotus petals, add a few to the clean water.

Take your hands and plunge them into the muddy water, making sure to squeeze and kneed the mud at the bottom of the bowl. Looking at the blue lotus picture with your hands in the mud, say: "From chaos and darkness, the lotus emerged, bringing light and creation and growth. From the mud and muck of the Nile River, the lotus blossom blooms every day, reaching for the Sun and the light." Speak aloud what you feel is holding you back from your dreams and your desired transformation.

Let go of the mud and wipe off your fingers as much as possible before placing your hands in the clean water. Revel in the coolness of the water. If you were able to purchase the blue lotus petals, take time to breathe in the fragrance of the flower as it floats on the water. Close your eyes and take several deep, soothing breaths. Open your eyes, look at the blue lotus picture, and say: "The universe is golden, created anew by the Sun god. I reach for the warmth of the Sun as it enfolds around me. The rejuvenating power of the blue lotus is within me and all around me. The light is pure and life-giving." Now state any changes that you want to make. Don't limit yourself to just material objects. Consider your emotions and inner needs.

When you are done, take your hands out of the water, place them in a prayer position in front of your forehead, and thank the blue lotus for its healing energies. Place a few drops of water on your temples, heart, and feet. The power of the blue lotus will now be a part of your body and a part of yourself.

Dry your hands on the towel and carefully carry the bowls outside. Deposit the water and mud onto the ground in a sacred manner, asking the earth to recycle these powerful energies for the good of all creatures. You can put the blue lotus picture on your altar to remind you of your rejuvenating potential. Put all your other implements away and know that, like the blue lotus, a whole new day starts fresh for you tomorrow. Your transformation has only just begun.

The Saxon Nine Herb Charm

≈ by Sorita ≈

T he Nine Herb Charm comes from an ancient Saxon herbal often referred to simply as the "Spellbook," due to the range of herbal charms and spells it contains. The Saxons called their herb craft *wortcunning* or *lacnunga*, which is another title given to the herbal from which this charm comes.

The Nine Herb Charm is unique in its complexity among the healing spells from Saxon times. Its detailed instructions for the use of nine herbs for healing illness and disease combine herbal lore with magical practice and mythological symbolism. As such, it is an outstanding sample of ancient magical practice.

The form of this charm is akin to shamanic healing as practiced in parts of northern Europe by peoples like the

Lapps and Finns and may indicate a cross-fertilization of ideas regarding healing illness by holistic means. The presence of Woden and style of the words also suggest a strong Norse influence on the Nine Herb Charm.

This charm involves the healer fighting the spirit of a disease while calling on Woden for aid and preparing a healing salve for the infected wound. The infection is fought both on the spiritual and the physical level, and every possibility is covered by the healer to make sure it is overcome. The power of Woden as divine healer and master of the runes, combined with the inherent magic of the power plants, form a mighty charm to defeat the infection or disease—visualized as a poisonous snake.

The Nine Herb Charm

Forget not, mugwort, what thou didst reveal,
What thou didst prepare at the great proclamation.

You were called una, oldest of herbs,
Thou hast strength against three and against thirty,
Thou hast strength against poison and against infection,
Thou hast strength against the foe who fares through the land!

And thou, waybread [plantain], mother of herbs,
Open from the east, mighty within,
Over thee chariots creaked, over thee queens rode,
Over thee brides made outcry, over thee bulls gnashed their teeth.
All these thou didst withstand and resist;
So mayest thou withstand poison and infection,
And the foe who fares through the land!

This herb is called stune [cress]; it grew on a stone,
It resists poison, it fights pain.

Stide [nettle] it is called, it fights against poison.
This is the herb that strove with the snake;
This has strength against poison, and strength against infection,
This has strength against the foe who fares through the land!

*Now, attorlothe, conquer the greater poisons, though thou art
the lesser;
Thou, the mightier, vanquish the lesser until he is cured of both!*

*Remember, mægoe [chamomile], what thou didst reveal
What thou didst bring to pass at Alford:
That he never yielded his life because of infection,
After mægoe was dressed for his food!*

*This is the herb which is called wergulu [apple];
The seal sent this over the back of the ocean
To heal the hurt of other poison!*

*These nine sprouts against nine poisons.
A snake came crawling, it bit a man
Then Woden took nine glory-twigs,
He struck the serpent so that it flew into nine parts,
There wergulu brought this to pass against poison,
That she nevermore would enter her house!*

*Fille [chervil] and fennule [fennel], a pair great in power;
The wise Lord, holy in heaven,
Wrought these herbs while he was hanging;
He placed and put them in the seven worlds to aid all, poor
and rich.
It stands against pain, resists the venom,
It has power against three and against thirty,
Against a fiend's hand and against sudden trick,
Against witchcraft of vile creatures!*

*Now these nine herbs avail against nine evil spirits,
Against nine poisons and against nine infectious diseases,
Against the red poison, against the running poison,
Against the white poison, against the pale blue poison,
Against the yellow poison, against the green poison,
Against the dusky poison, against the dark blue poison
Against the brown poison, against the purple poison,
Against snake-blister, against water-blister,*

Against thorn-blister, against thistle-blister,
Against ice-blister, against poison-blister,

If any poison comes flying from the east, or any comes from
the north,
Or any from the west upon the people.
Christ stood over sickness of a cruel kind.
I alone know running water, and the nine serpents it
encloses;
May all weeds now spring up as herbs,
The seas, all salt water, be destroyed,
When I blow this poison from thee!

The healer prepares a salve of the nine herbs, pounded and mixed into a paste with old soap and juice from the crab apple. The healer encourages each of the herbs as they are added in sequence to the salve, reminding them of their powers and past victories. The whole charm was sung three times on each of the herbs before it was added. The charm was also sung into the mouth of the injured person, into each of their ears, and onto the wound, before the salve was applied.

When six of the herbs have been added, the healer sees the spirit of the infection approaching as a serpent. Water and ashes are added to the salve, it is boiled, and a beaten egg is added.

At this point the healer reenacts Woden's seizing of the runes when he hung on the world tree Yggdrasil, grabbing "nine glory-twigs." These were wooden sticks, each with the initial rune of the name of the herb cut into them. By doing so the healer is identifying himself with Woden, drawing on the power of the god and also the power inherent in the runes and the herbs. It is likely that the rune sticks would have been made from ash or yew whenever possible, to symbolize the power of Yggdrasil as the cosmic tree.

The runes used to aid healing are not mentioned by name in the charm, but two are mentioned in the final section as being averted by the charm. These are *thorn* (*thurisaz* in the Norse) and *iss* (*isa* in the Norse), being the thorn and ice protected against in the lines "thorn-blister" and "ice-blister." As the two runes most appropriate for embodying destructive and negative forces, it is highly appropriate that their influences should be warded against.

If we look at the Old English words in the charm, specifically the first letters, we can suggest what these nine runes were. *Mucgwyrt* (mugwort) and *mægoe* (chamomile) both begin with the letter M, which would give the rune *mann* (*mannaz* in Norse). *Wegbrade* (plantain) and *wergulu* (crab apple) both begin with the letter W, giving the rune *wynn* (*wunjo* in Norse). *Stune* (cress) and *stide* (nettle) both begin with the letter S, giving the rune *sigil* (*sowilo* in Norse). *Fille* (chervil) and *fennule* (fennel) both begin with the letter F, giving the rune *foeh* (*fehu* in Norse). The last herb is more problematic, as *attorlade* (attorlothe) begins with the letter A, which does not have a direct letter transliteration in the Saxon runes (the Norse *ansuz* became *os*, which corresponds to the letter O. Still, this is probably the best guess.

Looking at the powers of these runes we see the fiery might of feoh, the harmony of wynn, the solar power of sigil, and the conjoining force of mann all doubly emphasized. The magical rune power of Woden, as embodied by os, is the uniting force that brings together the four rune pairs. This brings to mind his eight-legged horse Sleipnir, with four pairs of legs. The ninth figure is Woden riding him, the whole symbolizing the nine worlds of creation.

This awesome combination of powers shatters the serpent into nine parts. We can see this as the Saxon equivalent of scattering something to the four winds, except this is more complete as it is being broken up and scattered throughout the nine worlds. The Saxons viewed serpents and their venoms as symbolic of diseases and illnesses, so when they are referred to it is often symbolically. The only poisonous snake the Saxons would have encountered in Britain, though, is the adder, whose bite is extremely unlikely to be fatal.

The nine worlds and the nine days that Woden hung on the world tree are emphasised by both the number of herbs in the charm and also by the text itself. It suggests each herb represents a day on the tree and one of the nine worlds. Three and nine were very powerful numbers within the Saxon worldview. Incantations were repeated in multiples of three to increase their power, drawing on the energy of beings associated with these numbers—like Woden and the three Wyrd sisters, who ruled the fate of all.

The "foe who fares through the land" is also a phrase that needs further consideration. This phrase has been translated as the "fairy who fare through the land." Protection from fairies, or elves as the Saxons called them, is a clear reference to the phenomenon of "elf-shot." The elves were considered to be agents of Wyrd and part of the flow of energy that surrounds us all and permeates everything.

Elf-shot were tiny invisible arrows that were fired by the elves and entered the body of the victim, causing them to become ill or even die. If we think of the modern views of bacteria and viruses—tiny, invisible, and airborne—we realize that the Saxon perception was far more advanced and appropriate than has been credited. Rather than being a quaint idea, "elf-shot" gains an entirely new and credible perspective as a way of describing the effects of illnesses and diseases too small to be seen.

This knowledge of the airborne nature of many illnesses, even if symbolically embodied by elf-shot, is made clear by the lines in the final section of the charm: "If any poison comes flying from the east, or any comes from the north, or any from the west upon the people."

The different colors of poisons referred to may have a dual meaning. Many of the colors could refer to physical appearance when ill—white (flushed), red or purple (suffused with blood), dusky, brown or green (bilious), yellow (jaundiced), pale or dark blue (cyanosed), and running (sweating or suffering from diarrhea). It is likely that this list also intends to cover all the options by dispelling poisons whatever their symbolic color. As the charm is designed to fight all "poisons," the healer would wish to be comprehensive in fending off all malefic influences.

The "blisters" that are averted by the charm again show the intention of the charm to prevent all forms of illness. "Blister" refers to the Saxon word *blaed*, which means "blast," as in blast of air or force. Here the emphasis is on the method of entry into the body by the illness. "Snake-blister" suggests bites, "water-blister" implies drinking something that is tainted and contagious, "thistle-blister" to stings and scratches from plants, and "poison-blister" to eating something that causes illness. The other two sorts of blister, thorn and ice, as has already been discussed, are likely to refer to negative magical energies, such as attack by a sorcerer, the evil eye, or the negative influence of creatures, such as elves or wights.

Another important reference comes at the end of the charm, when the healer says: "I alone know running water and the nine serpents it encloses," clearly referring to the property of running water to dispel enchantments and negative magic. The purifying quality of water makes it a very powerful force for dispelling negativity. By surrounding the power of the illness or disease, represented by the nine snakes, it is bound to prevent it from spreading and causing further illness. The distinction from still water, which can stagnate and harbor disease, is also implied by the emphasis on the "running" nature of water.

Water must be pure to be used in healing. This is referred to by the line: "The seas, all salt water, be destroyed," indicating an awareness of the fact that seawater has a very negative effect on the body when drunk, causing fever and delirium. Through sympathetic magic, these symptoms, associated with many illnesses, are dispelled, destroying the power of the negative magic or invading force that has entered the body.

The blowing away of the poison from the victim at the end of the charm also demonstrates the ability of the healer to overcome the illness. By air was it spread (elf-shot) and by air is it dispersed—via the power of the words uttered by the healer, the breath of life, and the inherent power in the runes that are used as part of the charm.

The reference to seven worlds can be interpreted in two ways. It could refer to seven of the nine worlds, probably omitting Hel as the world of the dead where nothing would grow, and Niflheim as the dark world where plants would not grow. Alternatively, it could refer to the seven classical planets that were known at the time—Sun, Moon, Mercury, Venus, Mars, Jupiter, and Saturn.

This charm was recorded at a time when the worship of the old gods was fading, and Christianity became the dominant religion. This is echoed in the text, with Christ being mentioned near the end almost as a placatory gesture to indicate the acceptability of the charm. The main deity of the charm is Woden, and his mastery of the runes is one of the major elements of the charm. The reference to "The wise lord, holy in heaven, wrought these herbs while he was hanging" is nicely ambivalent and could be taken as referring to either Woden hanging on the world tree or Christ on the cross. The serpents symbolizing illness and disease would also have been acceptable to Christians, as the symbol embodies the temptation and evil from the Garden of Eden.

When the properties of each herb in turn are explored, it becomes obvious that these were all widely regarded as having properties against poison and used to treat swellings and inflammations. Some of them also have the added benefit of being used to clean wounds and prevent the likelihood of infection. That many of these herbs are still used medicinally today is a testament to the knowledge of the old Saxon healers and the tradition they practiced.

Mugwort (*Artemisia vulgaris*) is the first herb mentioned in the charm; it has a long history of magical use. Mugwort was believed to protect against all poisons and remove tiredness; it also had the property of protecting the recipient from malevolent magic, including demonic possession and the evil eye. That mugwort is called *una* or "one" indicates the high esteem it was held in, as magically potent and "oldest" herb. Mugwort leaves have been widely used for their effects on the subtle body, helping to encourage psychism and lucid dreaming. Mugwort was used with chamomile as a decoction to take away pain from swellings and bruises.

The juice of plantain (*Plantago maior*) was used to treat inflammation. When extracted from the roots, the juice was used to treat wounds, to ease swelling, and against poisons of all kinds. The fresh leaves were also used as a compress for cuts and swellings. As the pulverized plant is an antibacterial agent, its use is entirely appropriate for healing infections. Plantain was thought to bestow powers of endurance on the recipient, a useful quality to have when fighting against illness. Plantain was called "way-broad," later "waybread," due to its wide leaves and its often being found by roadsides (ways).

Stune is the name given to watercress (*Nastrurtium officinale*), and is derived from the verb *stunan* meaning "to combat," which is what the herb does to pain from gout and rheumatism. The crushed leaves were applied in poultices. Watercress is a diuretic and so is ideal for flushing toxins out of the body. It was also used to treat skin ailments.

Stide, meaning "harsh," is a name for nettle (*Urtica dioca*). This is appropriate as nettle is itself an irritant by virtue of its sting. It was used as a remedy against the poisons of snakes, mushrooms, hemlock, and henbane, and it was also used as an herbal tincture for cleaning wounds and sores.

Attorlothe means "poison-hater" and may be one of two herbs. Opinion is divided as to whether this herb is betony (*Stachys betonica*), which was also called woundwort and used to treat wounds and ward off evil spirits, or black nightshade (*Solanum nigrum*). Black nightshade berries have a soporific quality and were useful as a sedative in herbal remedies. They are not poisonous like other members of the deadly nightshade family.

Chamomile (*Anthemis cotula*) flowers have been used since ancient Egypt for treating swellings. Chamomile speeds healing and reduces swellings and is also mildly sedative and soothes pain. The line "After mægoe was dressed for his food!" refers to the Saxon use of chamomile as a garnish for food.

Wergulu is the name for crab apple (*Pyrus malus*). Its pulp was widely used in poultices for fevers, being both antiseptic and antifungal. Many centuries later Culpeper records the use of crab apple in combination with plantain and fennel for inflammation, showing the enduring qualities of these combinations of herbs.

Chervil (*Anthriscus cerefolium*) is another herb widely used for treating swellings and congealed blood. The Saxons also used it to treat sore stomachs and aching joints. It stimulates perspiration, making it useful for sweating out a fever.

Fennel (*Foeniculum vulgare*) seeds were used for treating snakebites and as a purgative for people who had eaten poisonous mushrooms or herbs. They were also believed to ward off the evil eye, evil sorcerers, and elves.

Today we can still honor the Saxon healers of ancient times by reciting the Nine Herb Charm for healing. And as we do so we can reflect that in a changing world there will always be a need for healers and Witches.

Medicinal Herbs of the Northwest

❧ by Jonathan Keyes ❧

S heets of rain empty into rushing, winding rivers. Mountain valleys are lush with foliage. Tall cedars, maples, and hemlocks drip with florescent green moss. The scent of fallen wood, overripe huckleberries, and sweet salmonberries permeate the air. The sky is gray, tinged with blue streaks, and heavy with rain.

This is the landscape of the Pacific Northwest, a land that stretches from the foothills of the Cascade Mountains in northern California to the coastal regions of British Columbia. This is the land of woodpeckers, beavers, and brown bears.

Hiking through the woods or just strolling through a neighborhood park in this region, you can also find some very potent and effective herbal medicines. These medicinal plants can seem

mon—it is sometimes surprising how much we
ook these powerful herbs—but it can be very useful
se plants in their native environment. Many of these
so be grown in local gardens or bought as tinctures
ts of the country.

Native Herbs

Herbs gathered in their native habitat carry the energy and
beauty of the region they are found. Over hundreds of years they
will have adapted to a specific niche and created a mini-ecosys-
tem of plant colonies. In this way, the native plants end up thriving on just the right combination of moisture, light, air quality,
and soil.

This helps explain why wild herbs always carry a little more
potency and magic than cultivated herbs. Gathering and drinking Oregon grape tea, or taking a tincture of devil's club, brings
us not only the medicine of the combined chemicals from the
herbs, but the medicine of the land itself. This helps one heal at
a deeper level. Because of this, we always need to treat local
plants with care and respect, gathering only what we need and
leaving enough to thrive afterward.

Below I list seven native herbs that grow in the Northwest.
These are some of my favorites and the most powerful of herbs
in my region. There are hundreds more that I don't list, but I
always think it is smartest to get to know a few plants really well
than to know a lot only marginally well. If you live here or can
travel through, take time to sit with these herbs, draw them,
smell them, taste them, and give them thanks for their precious
beauty and magic.

Bleeding Heart (Dicentra formosa)

This gentle and fragile herb can be found at the edge of woods
where there is partial light and shade. Its characteristic drooping,
reddish-purple flower have led this plant to also be called
"Dutchman's breeches," due to the flower's similarity in appear-

ance to oversized pants. The flower also has the shape of a heart, giving it its common name.

The root of this herb is its potent medicinal part, containing strong alkaloids. When gathering this herb, I have cleaned a bit of the root off and nibbled a bit. It produces a calm, soothing effect when taken in this manner. Gather the root at the end of summer as the leaves start to color and become diminished. The energy of the plant will have descended inward at this time to be stored in the root for the winter.

As a tea or a tincture, this herb has analgesic (pain-relieving) and sedative qualities. If you are feeling nervous, uncentered, or have experienced shock or trauma in some way, bleeding heart is especially helpful.

Bleeding heart is also useful as an overall tonic. Like many roots, it helps to strengthen and nourish the very core of a person, building one's strength over time. It can help treat conditions of the liver and poor metabolism, as well as eczema, acne, depression, and anxiety. In Chinese medicine, one would recommend this for those with liver chi stagnation, who are suffering symptoms of frustration, sadness, bodily twitching and discomfort.

Finally, flower essence practitioners often recommend bleeding heart essence for those who have recently experienced trauma and shock, especially in the form of a broken relationship. I would recommend four drops of bleeding heart essence taken three times a day to help with the process of grief after a breakup or the loss of a lover or spouse due to illness and death.

As a tincture, I would recommend twenty to thirty drops up to three times a day as needed. As a tea, try taking one to three cups daily as needed.

Devil's Club (Oplopanax horridum)

This gigantic-leaved plant is sacred to many Northwest tribes, who revere it as medicinally potent and spiritually sacred. If you live or have traveled through the West Coast and its woods, you couldn't have missed this massive, prehistoric-looking plant. Towering sometimes ten to fifteen feet above the ground, its spiny wooden stems shoot up and end with wide drooping leaves that fan out from the center. Devil's club comes from the same family as ginseng (*Araliaceae*) and has some genetic and morphological similarities to that herb. Walking near it, you can smell its sweet, musky odor, although you will have to watch out for getting poked by its sharp thorns. Devil's club loves low-lying, damp places, and you can often find it growing near streams and rivers.

Unfortunately, the medicinal component of this herb is its root. Because of this, it means you have to dig up this massive, beautiful plant. Not only is this difficult (the roots are hard to dig up and the sharp spines may give some pause), but it is also slightly rare and should be gathered infrequently. It is best to gather this herb in the early fall. Some suggest gathering just the root bark, but the root is also medicinally potent and both can be used in tinctures and decoctions.

Like ginseng, devil's club is useful as a tonic, reducing the negative effects of stress and building the immune system. Because of this, it is helpful for offsetting autoimmune disorders, such as rheumatoid arthritis and asthma. It is also quite helpful as a respiratory stimulant and expectorant, pulling up mucus secretions and hard-packed phlegm. Its general sweetness points to its power in helping the pancreatic system. Native coastal tribes and some herbalists use it in treating diabetes.

Overall, devil's club is an herb to be revered and gathered and used infrequently. Its medicine is potent. Try taking twenty to thirty drops of the tincture three times a day or one to two cups a day as a decoction.

False Solomon's Seal (Smilacina racemosa)

This lovely plant grows from rhizomes in two- to three-foot stalks with lush alternating leaves ending in a raceme of small whitish flowers. From the lily family, false Solomon's seal has the beautiful look of a lily plant. It loves to emerge from moist dark spots dappled with a little sunlight. Like a number of other plants from the lily family, such as trillium, it has a soothing, relaxing quality that quiets the spirit and brings harmony and gentleness back to the soul.

As a medicine, the root is especially helpful for soothing, cooling, moistening, and relaxing the respiratory system and throat. Because of this, it is helpful for hot inflamed throats, dry, excitable coughs, and general bronchial infections. False Solomon's seal can also be used externally to heal inflammations, burns, and swellings.

Try taking thirty to fifty drops of the tincture up to three times a day, or drink two to three cups of the decoction a day for a good medicinal effect.

Oregon Grape (Berberis aquifolia)

Although this herb is known to many herbalists outside of the Northwest, I still like to include it here as part of my favorite Northwest herbs. There are actually a number of varieties of Oregon grape, of which the most common is *Berberis aquifolia*. This tall Oregon grape can grow to three to five feet tall and has alternating dark green, glassy leaves with sharp edges that can scratch and poke. With bright yellow clusters of flowers that bloom in the spring, you can often find this plant as an ornamental in garden beds throughout the West Coast and parts of the rest of the country. Although I prefer *aquifolia*, the low-growing variety found in the woods (*Berberis nervosa*) is also a strong medicinal herb.

I first discovered the wonders of this herb when I was trying to cure a very nasty case of psoriasis on my neck. The condition appeared as a two- to three-inch circular spot that would inflame, seep, and ooze from time to time. I finally decided to do something about it, making a formula with two parts burdock, one part yellow dock, and four parts Oregon grape with a pinch of licorice. After drinking several cups of this tea for a couple of weeks I noticed the psoriasis patch decreasing in size until after four weeks it was completely gone, never to return. Truly, I had learned the wonders and healing power of Oregon grape.

Like other bitter herbs, Oregon grape is very helpful at clearing out toxins, strengthening the digestive system, and encouraging the liver to function optimally. For those with poor digestion, bad skin in the form of acne, psoriasis, or eczema, fatigue, and even depression, Oregon grape will help stimulate the system to function better and so will relieve these complaints. I find it is especially useful for those who are overheated and tend to get stressed out and become anxious. Oregon grape can also be used for its antimicrobial properties, and I have heard of its usefulness in healing intestinal infections. As part of a skin cream, it can be helpful to heal rashes and abrasions.

To gather this herb, dig up the root and chop it up (very difficult as it is very hard). The root is beautifully yellow and can stain the skin when preparing it. Tinctures of Oregon grape should have a lovely golden-yellow glow. This is an herb generally to be taken over a long period of time for chronic complaints. Don't give up on it just because it tastes bitter and takes a while to work. Try two to three cups a day for several weeks to begin or take thirty to sixty drops of the tincture. I find that the tea works better.

Western Red Cedar (Thuja plicata)

Along with hemlock and douglas fir, the western red cedar is one of the most common and most beautiful trees one can find in the Northwest woods. With its gentle drooping branches, its pungent and stimulating aroma, and its deeply furrowed, chocolate-red bark, cedar has been hailed as the most sacred tree to many coastal tribes.

Cedar has a hypnotic beauty that is entrancing and somewhat feminine in nature. Spend time beneath her branches, and you will find yourself relaxed, peaceful, and uplifted at the same time. Native tribes worked cedar into canoes, longhouses, and magical totems, and they used cedar for smudging and for its medicinal properties.

Easy to spot and plentiful enough to harvest, one can gather a few branches and then remove the leaves from the stems. As with all these herbs, make a prayer of thankfulness and an intention to use cedar in a good way. Cedar is much more helpful if you've made good friends with her.

I often notice that herbs seem to help health conditions that tend to develop in the areas in which they grow. Cedar is a lovely antidote to the damp, wet conditions and the resulting fungal growth and respiratory diseases that often occur in the rainy, boggy Northwest. Cedar needles have antibacterial and antifungal properties and are quite useful externally in tincture form to heal ringworm, fungal infections of nail beds, and athlete's foot. This is a strongly sharp tincture and can be a little abrasive to tender tissue areas.

Because of its stimulating properties, the tea or tincture is quite helpful as an expectorant for sluggish coughs. Inhaling the steam of a drop or two of this oil in a hot pan of water can be quite effective for breaking up phlegmy respiratory conditions. Western red cedar is generally helpful in strengthening the immune system, clearing up infections in the body, and as a first line of defense against colds and urinary infections.

Try taking twenty to thirty drops twice a day or a cup of the tea once or twice a day. Avoid if pregnant or suffering from kidney disease. This is not an herb to use over a prolonged period of time. Use for seven to ten days at most.

Skunk Cabbage (Lysichiton americanum)

It's not too hard to recognize this pungent native Northwest herb. You can smell it from one hundred yards away. With its distinctive "skunky" odor and spiky yellow stalk emerging from lush wide leaves, skunk cabbage can be found in marshes, bogs, and near streams and rivers. In fact, this odiferous herb loves to grow wherever moisture is abundant.

Most herbalists I know are put off by collecting this local gem due to its smell and the difficulty of collecting it. The roots are the medicinal part and to gather them you need to be persistent and willing to get very muddy. Because skunk cabbage is found in damp places, it requires a great deal of effort to get a shovel to dig up the root—so wear your galoshes and your rain pants, and stick with it.

Skunk cabbage is a very effective medicinal herb for reducing spasms and painful muscle contractions, so it can be useful for stomach or uterine cramping. It is also effective for helping relax the bronchial membranes when they are congested or tight, as in a case of asthma. Because of its pungent aroma, skunk cabbage has an expectorant quality that makes it useful for healing damp phlegmy conditions.

In Chinese medicine, the element of water is associated with fear. I find that skunk cabbage is helpful to take for those experiencing unreasonable fear and paralysis, especially if these are occurring in conjunction with physical symptoms mentioned above.

Take thirty to fifty drops of this tincture two to four times a day or drink two to three cups of the tea each day to gain a medicinal effect.

Wild Ginger (Asarum caudatum)

I remember first falling in love with this plant as I trekked up a set of switchbacks to a lake nestled in the east side of the Olympic Mountains. Wild ginger isn't showy. It's pretty easy to miss unless you keep an eye out for it. First you'll notice the distinct heart-shaped velvety leaves emerging from short stalks low to the ground. Or, if it's springtime, you may notice something peeking out from the ground below the leaves. Keep looking for its delicate three-sepaled purple-brown flowers. Its sepals are elongated a good inch or two outside of the flower when in bloom.

Although it looks gentle and serene, this plant has fiery depths. Dig up the root of this plant and you'll see why it gets its name. The root has a distinct gingery flavor, and it has similar abilities to stimulate and heat you, bring on a sweat, get your digestion moving, clear your pores, and clear out toxins from your system.

This is a wonderful herb to use when you have a cold. Wild ginger will bring on a sweat and cool a fever. Ginger is also helpful for sluggish digestion and moving any stagnant food through the intestines. Wild ginger also helps those with slow, crampy, or spotty menstruation. It will help get the blood flowing, the body moving, and the energy circulating.

Wild ginger is used as an herb in many Chinese herbal formula compositions, because it helps to stimulate the body's digestive juices so that other herbs can be assimilated better. Wild ginger can also be used this way in combination with other medicinal herbal treatments.

Herbs affect the body but can also deeply affect the emotional body as well. This herb works well on a subtle level to move the energy when we get stuck in holding patterns and have a difficult time moving on. By sitting with this herb near a cool stream under tall cedars and douglas firs, you may feel yourself able to release old pains and stagnant ways of thinking.

Although the root is the most potent and long-lasting medicinally active part of the herb, the leaves can be used as well. Try drinking three cups of this tea a day, or thirty to fifty drops of tincture three times a day for the best effect.

Go North(west)

The Pacific Northwest is a unique and magical place. With abundant rainfall and towering evergreens, the region is perfect for a hike. Its mountain ranges sweep down majestically to dramatic ocean shores.

Cradled in this lush green land are some of the world's best herbal medicines. Although these herbs may seem abundant, we need to protect them and make sure they thrive within their ecosystem. Overharvesting has sometimes ravaged herbs from other locales when they become popular, such as goldenseal and lady slipper. Although I want to share the joy and wonder of these herbs with everyone, I also want to caution you against abusing this precious resource. Gather with care, don't take too much, and be sure to keep a healthy amount of the herb intact when picking.

And always remember, sometimes an herb's medicine can be discovered by simply being close to it in its native habitat. Many times I have found that simply sitting under the swooping boughs of a cedar tree or taking in the fragile beauty of bleeding heart will help bring me peace and reduce my stress. This in turn helps my mind and body to strengthen and heal.

If you live here or just want to come visit, I hope you can take the time to discover these healing herbs and their magical and medicinal value.

Birch:
The Tree of Beginnings

≈ by Sorita ≈

The birch (*Betula alba*) and the silver birch (*Betula pendula*) are among the most beautiful and easily recognized of trees. The silvery-white bark and slender branches give this tree an ethereal otherworldly appearance that is reflected in the qualities associated with it.

Birch grows quickly to a height of around fifty feet within twenty years. It can double this height by the time it reaches fifty years of age. Young trees have shiny reddish-brown bark, which become silver-white and peel with age, giving the characteristic appearance it is so famous for.

The birch tree gives us a whole range of colors as it grows through the seasons. In early spring the winter buds fill out and give the tree a purple sheen. In May the leaves unfold, turning the

overall appearance light green. In autumn the leaves turn bright yellow and fall to the ground.

Birch is one of the most important trees for the wildlife it supports, including 230 different species of insects. Its pollen is collected by bees in spring, and its seeds feed a wide range of birds in fall. The leaves rot quickly when they fall to the ground, producing leaf-mold that perpetuates the forest ecosystem.

Birch is symbolic of the seeds of conception. It is a pioneering tree, the first to grow back after natural disasters like earthquakes, volcanic eruptions, even the last Ice Age. Birch is also the first deciduous tree to put out its leaves in spring. It grows readily on the edges of forests, making it the first tree you encounter as you approach the forest.

In both the Celtic and Norse traditions, birch symbolizes birth and new beginnings. As birch contains both male and female catkins, it is able to self-propagate, emphasizing the ability of life to generate life. Our ancestors must have seen the success of birch in surviving and spreading and welcomed its new leaves as a sign of the coming spring and fertility in the land.

Birch is the first wood of the Ogham alphabet. The Ogham were said to have been given to men by the Celtic god of knowledge, Oghma, after whom they are named. An Ogham could represent a tree, a color, a bird, and also have symbolic meanings. The Ogham is still used today in Druidry, linking us back to our Celtic ancestors.

The Ogham *beith*, for birch, is associated with new beginnings, change, cleansing, and purification. Beith also represents the color white and the pheasant. As the first of the Ogham letters, beith is attributed to November, after the old Celtic New Year festival of Samhain.

Silver Birch

The silver birch was also seen in the Celtic world as an entrance to the fairy worlds. White and red were the colors of the underworld, hence the depiction of magical animals in these colors in

Celtic tales. The birch tree was known as the "Lady of the Woods" and often marks the beginning of the path for an adventuring hero, shaman, or magician. Spirits from the otherworld were sometimes described as coming out of the birch, dressed in birch caps and clothes. Traditionally, Russians dressed up a birch tree in women's clothes at Whitsun. Another Russian custom celebrated at this time was for the prettiest girl to be carried through the village in a mass of birch foliage.

In the runes, the birch is depicted by the rune *berkana* (*beork* in the Saxon), representing fertility, birth, and new beginnings. An Old English rune poem says of birch: "The birch though fruitless sends out countless shoots; leafy branches, high crowned reach to the sky." This verse implies not only the fertility of the birch, but also its subsequent use as the maypole representing the central column of the world tree connecting the worlds.

The goddess Berchta was associated with childbirth, and the birch was sacred to her. As with many of the old gods, we know very little about her except these associations. Meditating on the berkana rune and using it as an astral doorway to pass through may help you learn more of her mysteries.

Birch is also the traditional wood for making babies' cradles, so you can engrave berkana runes onto the cradle and embroider them on the expectant mother's clothes to encourage an easy birth.

With all its associations with goddesses, fertility, and childbirth, it is easy to see why the birch is ruled by the planet Venus. The Finnish goddess Aino, whose body becomes part of the landscape of nature at her death, is also symbolized by the birch. Cuckoos sit in birch trees and sing of the love that all animals bear Aino.

As the tree of beginnings, you can carve the beith Ogham or the berkana rune onto the end of a wand or rune staff to indicate the flow of energy from your will to create a new beginning.

Birch twigs have been widely used for flagellation—purifying the body by driving out negative energies. This is also seen in the use of birch twigs with leaves in saunas in northern Europe to stimulate the blood flow to the surface of the skin.

The use of birch twigs also occurred in ancient Rome in the festivals of Saturnalia and Lupercalia. At Saturnalia, around the time of Yule, young men would chase people through the streets, striking them with birch branches as an act of cleansing and purification. At Lupercalia, any woman struck with birch twigs was thought to become more fertile. This was done to encourage women to conceive. In Scotland, cattle were herded with birch branches to ensure their fertility. In medieval Russia, birch boughs were thrown on bonfires at Midsummer with the cry: "May my flax grow as tall as this bough!"

Bundles of birch twigs were used to beat the spirits out of the old year and bring in the new. As Samhain is the time of spirits as well as the Celtic New Year, this was very much a time for the birch. This practice developed into the Christian custom of "beating the bounds." It involved a procession around the boundaries of a particular area, such as a farm, manor, or church parish. At strategic points on the boundaries, particular objects like trees and walls would be struck with a birch besom or bundle of birch twigs. For private land this was usually carried out annually at Beltane. This served the purpose of driving away any evil spirits that had gathered at the boundaries of the land.

In medieval times birch was applied to purify criminals. The act of "birching" involved public whipping with a birch whip. Apart from the humiliation for having committed crimes against the community, this was a purificatory act, driving the bad habits out of the criminal and making them useful citizens.

Children were also punished in the Middle Ages with a birch rod, a practice mentioned by William Shakespeare in *Measure for Measure*. The maypole, center of the Beltane celebrations through the Middle Ages, was often made of birch. The maypole can be seen as the axis mundi, the central column of creation that joins the different worlds together. It was also a symbol of fertility. The shape of the maypole also embodies the combined energies of the male—the phallic pole was male, and the garland of flowers placed around the top was the embracing vulva. The use of red and white ribbons on the maypole further emphasizes this theme, representing the sexual energies of women and men. In parts of Europe, hanging a red ribbon around the stem of a birch tree was thought to avert the evil eye from a home.

In Wales there is a summer counterpart to the maypole. On Midsummer Eve the "summer birch" was raised and decorated with garlands and wreaths of flowers. Groups of men would guard the summer birch to stop men from other villages stealing it. Any village that lost its birch could not hoist another one until they had stolen or destroyed the birch of another village. In extreme cases, villagers in the eighteenth century were known to guard the tree all night with guns.

Another May custom that drew on the qualities of the birch was the placing of a birch twig over the door of a prospective or actual sweetheart on May Day morning. As the tree of beginnings, the birch symbolized a couple's desire to be together. It is interesting to see that the birch was central to ceremonies marking the turning of the light and dark halves of the year.

When we look at the birch we must also mention the fly agaric mushroom (*Amanita muscaria*). This highly hallucinogenic and toxic mushroom grows at the base of certain trees, especially silver birch. The fly agaric has been widely used in northern magical traditions—mentioned in the Norse tradition and appearing in shamanism in such regions as Siberia, Finland, and Lapland. The fly agaric was prepared and used to engender "spirit flight." The birch was often seen as the world tree that the shaman could travel along to encounter spirits and other worlds.

The idea of spirit flight in connection with birch is further emphasized by the use of birch twigs to make the besom, or Witch's broom. The broom was seen as the transportation for a Witch going to the sabbat after having rubbed flying ointment onto her body. Hallucinogenic plants like fly agaric were used in making the flying ointment that would enable the spirit flight. Birch sap can also be tapped for making wine, leading to another form of flight for the tree.

Birch bark and birch wood also have a wide range of uses. Birch bark was used by early man to make buckets and receptacles by sewing strips together. In Scandinavia, strips of bark were wrapped around the legs to keep them dry. This is the origin of the wearing of gaiters.

When collecting the bark, take from branches and not the trunk. Removing trunk bark can affect the tree's nutrient flow. The bark is waterproof and useful in making canoes and roofs.

The fresh wet inner side of the bark can ease muscular pain if placed against the skin. The pitch gathered from the tree has also been used for treating skin complaints since ancient times, and modern research indicates that two of the constituents, betulin and betulinic acid, may inhibit skin cancer. Once again we see the wisdom of our ancestors born out by modern science.

Birch bark contains about 3 percent tannic acid, and it has been widely used in the tanning process. An extract of pale color is beneficial for the early and final stages when tanning leather.

Another use of birch bark is to make paper. It has been suggested that the name birch was derived from the Sanskrit word *bhurga*, meaning "tree whose bark is used for writing on." Birch bark can be used as the basis for amulets and talismans, as it is ideal to carve runes or sigils into. In Norse mythology, birch is sacred to the thunder god Thor. It was believed that bark should never be collected from a birch tree unless it had been "kissed by Thor." This meant that the tree should have been struck by lightning. It was thought then that Thor had claimed the spirit of the tree, and it was now available for human use.

Pitch from the birch tree was made into glue, which could be used to fix flints to arrows and spears to give them their sharp points for hunting. As well as being used in besoms, the birch twigs lent themselves to making baskets and thatching roofs. Birch wood is tough and easily worked and was used to make furniture and utility items like spools and bobbins.

The sap of the birch should be collected when it is still rising, in early March. This is done by making a hole about one inch deep in the trunk about three feet off the ground. A tube is placed in the hole, and the sap is allowed to run into a container. Remember to ask the tree's permission first, and put the bark back over the hole afterwards.

If you are going to make wine, collect the sap from a number of trees, so as not to overtap any individual trees and harm them. You need eight pints of sap to make a gallon of wine. As soon as you have collected the sap, boil it, add four cups of sugar, and simmer for ten minutes. Put one cup of raisins into a bucket, pour in the boiling liquid, then add yeast and the juice of two lemons when the mixture has cooled to body temperature. Cover the bucket and leave to stand for three days, then strain into a clean demijohn and seal with an airlock. Once fermentation is complete, rack the wine into a clean jar and allow the sediment to settle. Then bottle the wine and store in a cool place for a minimum of two months before drinking.

You can also make tea from birch leaves. This is an old remedy for treating urinary problems, cystitis, gout, arthritis, and rheumatism. Collect fresh leaves and dry them. Add boiling water to two teaspoons of leaves in a cup. Let stand for ten minutes and strain.

A more modern use of birch is as an aromatherapy oil. Birch oil is analgesic, anti-inflammatory, and reduces fevers. It is very good for muscular pain, particularly tendon problems, and for treating arthritis and rheumatism. This is a very strong oil and should be handled with care and used in very small quantities.

Birch bud oil has somewhat different qualities from birch oil, and it is very good for treating skin conditions, such as dermatitis, eczema, and psoriasis. It is also used in treating cellulite and edema.

From the dawn of time to today, the birch has been with us, symbolizing fertility and new beginnings. Birch provides us with a whole range of useful products and beverages. So when the wheel turns and the seasons change around us, remember the Lady of the Woods. Her benevolent power is as accessible to us today as it ever was.

The Quarters and Signs of the Moon and Moon Tables

The Quarters and Signs of the Moon

Everyone has seen the Moon wax and wane through a period of approximately twenty-nine-and-a-half days. This circuit from New Moon to Full Moon and back again is called the lunation cycle. The cycle is divided into parts called quarters or phases. There are several methods by which this can be done, and the system used in the *Herbal Almanac* may not correspond to those used in other almanacs.

The Quarters

First Quarter

The first quarter begins at the New Moon, when the Sun and Moon are in the same place, or conjunct. (This means that the Sun and Moon are in the same degree of the same sign.) The Moon is not visible at first, since it rises at the same time as the Sun. The New Moon is the time of new beginnings, beginnings of projects that favor growth, externalization of activities, and the growth of ideas. The first quarter is the time of germination, emergence, beginnings, and outwardly directed activity.

Second Quarter

The second quarter begins halfway between the New Moon and the Full Moon, when the Sun and Moon are at right angles, or a ninety-degree square to each other. This half Moon rises around noon and sets around midnight, so it can be seen in the western sky during the first half of the night. The second quarter is the time of growth and articulation of things that already exist.

Third Quarter

The third quarter begins at the Full Moon, when the Sun and Moon are opposite one another and the full light of the Sun can shine on the full sphere of the Moon. The round Moon can be seen rising in the east at sunset, and then rising a little later each evening. The Full Moon stands for illumination, fulfillment, culmination, completion, drawing inward, unrest, emotional expressions, and hasty actions leading to failure. The third quarter is a time of maturity, fruition, and the assumption of the full form of expression.

Fourth Quarter

The fourth quarter begins about halfway between the Full Moon and New Moon, when the Sun and Moon are again at ninety degrees, or square. This decreasing Moon rises at midnight and can be seen in the east during the last half of the night, reaching the overhead position just about as the Sun rises. The fourth quarter is a time of disintegration, drawing back for reorganization and reflection.

The Signs

Moon in Aries

Moon in Aries is good for starting things, but lacking in staying power. Things occur rapidly, but also quickly pass.

Moon in Taurus

With Moon in Taurus, things begun during this sign last the longest and tend to increase in value. Things begun now become habitual and hard to alter.

Moon in Gemini

Moon in Gemini is an inconsistent position for the Moon, characterized by a lot of talk. Things begun now are easily changed by outside influences.

Moon in Cancer

Moon in Cancer stimulates emotional rapport between people. It pinpoints need and supports growth and nurturance.

Moon in Leo

Moon in Leo accents showmanship, being seen, drama, recreation, and happy pursuits. It may be concerned with praise and subject to flattery.

Moon in Virgo

Moon in Virgo favors accomplishment of details and commands from higher up, while discouraging independent thinking.

Moon in Libra

Moon in Libra increases self-awareness. It favors self-examination and interaction with others, but discourages spontaneous initiative.

Moon in Scorpio

Moon in Scorpio increases awareness of psychic power. It precipitates psychic crises and ends connections thoroughly.

Moon in Sagittarius

Moon in Sagittarius encourages expansionary flights of imagination and confidence in the flow of life.

Moon in Capricorn

Moon in Capricorn increases awareness of the need for structure, discipline, and organization. Institutional activities are favored.

Moon in Aquarius

Moon in Aquarius favors activities that are unique and individualistic, concern for humanitarian needs, society as a whole, and improvements that can be made.

Moon in Pisces

During Moon in Pisces, energy withdraws from the surface of life, hibernates within, secretly reorganizing and realigning.

January Moon Table

Date	Sign	Element	Nature	Phase
1 Sun. 7:14 am	Aquarius	Air	Barren	1st
2 Mon.	Aquarius	Air	Barren	1st
3 Tue. 7:43 am	Pisces	Water	Fruitful	1st
4 Wed.	Pisces	Water	Fruitful	1st
5 Thu. 9:44 am	Aries	Fire	Barren	1st
6 Fri.	Aries	Fire	Barren	2nd 1:56 pm
7 Sat. 2:09 pm	Taurus	Earth	Semi-fruitful	2nd
8 Sun.	Taurus	Earth	Semi-fruitful	2nd
9 Mon. 8:58 pm	Gemini	Air	Barren	2nd
10 Tue.	Gemini	Air	Barren	2nd
11 Wed.	Gemini	Air	Barren	2nd
12 Thu. 5:50 am	Cancer	Water	Fruitful	2nd
13 Fri.	Cancer	Water	Fruitful	2nd
14 Sat. 4:31 pm	Leo	Fire	Barren	3rd 4:48 am
15 Sun.	Leo	Fire	Barren	3rd
16 Mon.	Leo	Fire	Barren	3rd
17 Tue. 4:49 am	Virgo	Earth	Barren	3rd
18 Wed.	Virgo	Earth	Barren	3rd
19 Thu. 5:49 pm	Libra	Air	Semi-fruitful	3rd
20 Fri.	Libra	Air	Semi-fruitful	3rd
21 Sat.	Libra	Air	Semi-fruitful	3rd
22 Sun. 5:28 am	Scorpio	Water	Fruitful	4th 10:14 am
23 Mon.	Scorpio	Water	Fruitful	4th
24 Tue. 1:00 pm	Sagittarius	Fire	Barren	4th
25 Wed.	Sagittarius	Fire	Barren	4th
26 Thu. 5:31 pm	Capricorn	Earth	Semi-fruitful	4th
27 Fri.	Capricorn	Earth	Semi-fruitful	4th
28 Sat. 6:09 pm	Aquarius	Air	Barren	4th
29 Sun.	Aquarius	Air	Barren	1st 9:15 am
30 Mon. 5:32 pm	Pisces	Water	Fruitful	1st
31 Tue.	Pisces	Water	Fruitful	1st

February Moon Table

Date	Sign	Element	Nature	Phase
1 Wed. 5:46 pm	Aries	Fire	Barren	1st
2 Thu.	Aries	Fire	Barren	1st
3 Fri. 8:31 pm	Taurus	Earth	Semi-fruitful	1st
4 Sat.	Taurus	Earth	Semi-fruitful	1st
5 Sun.	Taurus	Earth	Semi-fruitful	2nd 1:29 am
6 Mon. 2:32 am	Gemini	Air	Barren	2nd
7 Tue.	Gemini	Air	Barren	2nd
8 Wed. 11:33 am	Cancer	Water	Fruitful	2nd
9 Thu.	Cancer	Water	Fruitful	2nd
10 Fri. 10:44 pm	Leo	Fire	Barren	2nd
11 Sat.	Leo	Fire	Barren	2nd
12 Sun.	Leo	Fire	Barren	Full 11:44 pm
13 Mon. 11:13 am	Virgo	Earth	Barren	3rd
14 Tue.	Virgo	Earth	Barren	3rd
15 Wed.	Virgo	Earth	Barren	3rd
16 Thu. 12:09 am	Libra	Air	Semi-fruitful	3rd
17 Fri.	Libra	Air	Semi-fruitful	3rd
18 Sat. 12:11 pm	Scorpio	Water	Fruitful	3rd
19 Sun.	Scorpio	Water	Fruitful	3rd
20 Mon. 9:38 pm	Sagittarius	Fire	Barren	3rd
21 Tue.	Sagittarius	Fire	Barren	4th 2:17 am
22 Wed.	Sagittarius	Fire	Barren	4th
23 Thu. 3:16 am	Capricorn	Earth	Semi-fruitful	4th
24 Fri.	Capricorn	Earth	Semi-fruitful	4th
25 Sat. 5:14 am	Aquarius	Air	Barren	4th
26 Sun.	Aquarius	Air	Barren	4th
27 Mon. 4:56 am	Pisces	Water	Fruitful	New 7:31 pm
28 Tue.	Pisces	Water	Fruitful	1st

March Moon Table

Date	Sign	Element	Nature	Phase
1 Wed. 4:18 am	Aries	Fire	Barren	1st
2 Thu.	Aries	Fire ·	Barren	1st
3 Fri. 5:22 am	Taurus	Earth	Semi-fruitful	1st
4 Sat.	Taurus	Earth	Semi-fruitful	1st
5 Sun. 9:37 am	Gemini	Air	Barren	1st
6 Mon.	Gemini	Air	Barren	2nd 3:16 pm
7 Tue. 5:38 pm	Cancer	Water	Fruitful	2nd
8 Wed.	Cancer	Water	Fruitful	2nd
9 Thu.	Cancer	Water	Fruitful	2nd
10 Fri. 4:42 am	Leo	Fire	Barren	2nd
11 Sat.	Leo	Fire	Barren	2nd
12 Sun. 5:23 pm	Virgo	Earth	Barren	2nd
13 Mon.	Virgo	Earth	Barren	2nd
14 Tue.	Virgo	Earth	Barren	Full 6:35 pm
15 Wed. 6:12 am	Libra	Air	Semi-fruitful	3rd
16 Thu.	Libra	Air	Semi-fruitful	3rd
17 Fri. 5:59 pm	Scorpio	Water	Fruitful	3rd
18 Sat.	Scorpio	Water	Fruitful	3rd
19 Sun.	Scorpio	Water	Fruitful	3rd
20 Mon. 3:43 am	Sagittarius	Fire	Barren	3rd
21 Tue.	Sagittarius	Fire	Barren	3rd
22 Wed. 10:36 am	Capricorn	Earth	Semi-fruitful	4th 2:10 pm
23 Thu.	Capricorn	Earth	Semi-fruitful	4th
24 Fri. 2:21 pm	Aquarius	Air	Barren	4th
25 Sat.	Aquarius	Air	Barren	4th
26 Sun. 3:33 pm	Pisces	Water	Fruitful	4th
27 Mon.	Pisces	Water	Fruitful	4th
28 Tue. 3:31 pm	Aries	Fire	Barren	4th
29 Wed.	Aries	Fire	Barren	New 5:15 am
30 Thu. 4:00 pm	Taurus	Earth	Semi-fruitful	1st
31 Fri.	Taurus	Earth	Semi-fruitful	1st

April Moon Table

Date	Sign	Element	Nature	Phase
1 Sat. 6:49 pm	Gemini	Air	Barren	1st
2 Sun.	Gemini	Air	Barren	1st
3 Mon.	Gemini	Air	Barren	1st
4 Tue. 2:15 am	Cancer	Water	Fruitful	1st
5 Wed.	Cancer	Water	Fruitful	2nd 8:01 am
6 Thu. 12:25 pm	Leo	Fire	Barren	2nd
7 Fri.	Leo	Fire	Barren	2nd
8 Sat.	Leo	Fire	Barren	2nd
9 Sun. 12:58 am	Virgo	Earth	Barren	2nd
10 Mon.	Virgo	Earth	Barren	2nd
11 Tue. 1:46 pm	Libra	Air	Semi-fruitful	2nd
12 Wed.	Libra	Air	Semi-fruitful	2nd
13 Thu.	Libra	Air	Semi-fruitful	Full 12:40 pm
14 Fri. 1:08 am	Scorpio	Water	Fruitful	3rd
15 Sat.	Scorpio	Water	Fruitful	3rd
16 Sun. 10:19 am	Sagittarius	Fire	Barren	3rd
17 Mon.	Sagittarius	Fire	Barren	3rd
18 Tue. 5:13 pm	Capricorn	Earth	Semi-fruitful	3rd
19 Wed.	Capricorn	Earth	Semi-fruitful	3rd
20 Thu. 9:56 pm	Aquarius	Air	Barren	4th 11:28 pm
21 Fri.	Aquarius	Air	Barren	4th
22 Sat.	Aquarius	Air	Barren	4th
23 Sun. 12:43 am	Pisces	Water	Fruitful	4th
24 Mon.	Pisces	Water	Fruitful	4th
25 Tue. 2:12 am	Aries	Fire	Barren	4th
26 Wed.	Aries	Fire	Barren	4th
27 Thu. 3:27 am	Taurus	Earth	Semi-fruitful	New 3:44 pm
28 Fri.	Taurus	Earth	Semi-fruitful	1st
29 Sat. 5:58 am	Gemini	Air	Barren	1st
30 Sun.	Gemini	Air	Barren	1st

May Moon Table

Date	Sign	Element	Nature	Phase
1 Mon. 11:17 am	Cancer	Water	Fruitful	1st
2 Tue.	Cancer	Water	Fruitful	1st
3 Wed. 8:18 pm	Leo	Fire	Barren	1st
4 Thu.	Leo	Fire	Barren	1st
5 Fri.	Leo	Fire	Barren	2nd 1:13 am
6 Sat. 8:20 am	Virgo	Earth	Barren	2nd
7 Sun.	Virgo	Earth	Barren	2nd
8 Mon. 9:10 pm	Libra	Air	Semi-fruitful	2nd
9 Tue.	Libra	Air	Semi-fruitful	2nd
10 Wed.	Libra	Air	Semi-fruitful	2nd
11 Thu. 8:24 am	Scorpio	Water	Fruitful	2nd
12 Fri.	Scorpio	Water	Fruitful	2nd
13 Sat. 4:56 pm	Sagittarius	Fire	Barren	Full 2:51 am
14 Sun.	Sagittarius	Fire	Barren	3rd
15 Mon. 10:59 pm	Capricorn	Earth	Semi-fruitful	3rd
16 Tue.	Capricorn	Earth	Semi-fruitful	3rd
17 Wed.	Capricorn	Earth	Semi-fruitful	3rd
18 Thu. 3:19 am	Aquarius	Air	Barren	3rd
19 Fri.	Aquarius	Air	Barren	3rd
20 Sat. 6:39 am	Pisces	Water	Fruitful	4th 5:20 am
21 Sun.	Pisces	Water	Fruitful	4th
22 Mon. 9:24 am	Aries	Fire	Barren	4th
23 Tue.	Aries	Fire	Barren	4th
24 Wed. 12:00 pm	Taurus	Earth	Semi-fruitful	4th
25 Thu.	Taurus	Earth	Semi-fruitful	4th
26 Fri. 3:19 pm	Gemini	Air	Barren	4th
27 Sat.	Gemini	Air	Barren	New 1:25 am
28 Sun. 8:33 pm	Cancer	Water	Fruitful	1st
29 Mon.	Cancer	Water	Fruitful	1st
30 Tue.	Cancer	Water	Fruitful	1st
31 Wed. 4:51 am	Leo	Fire	Barren	1st

June Moon Table

Date	Sign	Element	Nature	Phase
1 Thu.	Leo	Fire	Barren	1st
2 Fri. 4:17 pm	Virgo	Earth	Barren	1st
3 Sat.	Virgo	Earth	Barren	2nd 7:06 pm
4 Sun.	Virgo	Earth	Barren	2nd
5 Mon. 5:08 am	Libra	Air	Semi-fruitful	2nd
6 Tue.	Libra	Air	Semi-fruitful	2nd
7 Wed. 4:41 pm	Scorpio	Water	Fruitful	2nd
8 Thu.	Scorpio	Water	Fruitful	2nd
9 Fri.	Scorpio	Water	Fruitful	2nd
10 Sat. 1:05 am	Sagittarius	Fire	Barren	2nd
11 Sun.	Sagittarius	Fire	Barren	Full 2:03 pm
12 Mon. 6:19 am	Capricorn	Earth	Semi-fruitful	3rd
13 Tue.	Capricorn	Earth	Semi-fruitful	3rd
14 Wed. 9:32 am	Aquarius	Air	Barren	3rd
15 Thu.	Aquarius	Air	Barren	3rd
16 Fri. 12:05 pm	Pisces	Water	Fruitful	3rd
17 Sat.	Pisces	Water	Fruitful	3rd
18 Sun. 2:54 pm	Aries	Fire	Barren	4th 10:08 am
19 Mon.	Aries	Fire	Barren	4th
20 Tue. 6:23 pm	Taurus	Earth	Semi-fruitful	4th
21 Wed.	Taurus	Earth	Semi-fruitful	4th
22 Thu. 10:49 pm	Gemini	Air	Barren	4th
23 Fri.	Gemini	Air	Barren	4th
24 Sat.	Gemini	Air	Barren	4th
25 Sun. 4:48 am	Cancer	Water	Fruitful	New 12:05 pm
26 Mon.	Cancer	Water	Fruitful	1st
27 Tue. 1:09 pm	Leo	Fire	Barren	1st
28 Wed.	Leo	Fire	Barren	1st
29 Thu. 12:15 pm	Virgo	Earth	Barren	1st
30 Fri.	Virgo	Earth	Barren	1st

July Moon Table

Date	Sign	Element	Nature	Phase
1 Sat.	Virgo	Earth	Barren	1st
2 Sun. 1:06 pm	Libra	Air	Semi-fruitful	1st
3 Mon.	Libra	Air	Semi-fruitful	2nd 12:37 am
4 Tue.	Libra	Air	Semi-fruitful	2nd
5 Wed. 1:13 am	Scorpio	Water	Fruitful	2nd
6 Thu.	Scorpio	Water	Fruitful	2nd
7 Fri. 10:13 am	Sagittarius	Fire	Barren	2nd
8 Sat.	Sagittarius	Fire	Barren	2nd
9 Sun. 3:25 pm	Capricorn	Earth	Semi-fruitful	2nd
10 Mon.	Capricorn	Earth	Semi-fruitful	Full 11:02 pm
11 Tue. 5:46 pm	Aquarius	Air	Barren	3rd
12 Wed.	Aquarius	Air	Barren	3rd
13 Thu. 6:59 pm	Pisces	Water	Fruitful	3rd
14 Fri.	Pisces	Water	Fruitful	3rd
15 Sat. 8:39 pm	Aries	Fire	Barren	3rd
16 Sun.	Aries	Fire	Barren	3rd
17 Mon. 11:44 pm	Taurus	Earth	Semi-fruitful	4th 3:12 pm
18 Tue.	Taurus	Earth	Semi-fruitful	4th
19 Wed.	Taurus	Earth	Semi-fruitful	4th
20 Thu. 4:38 am	Gemini	Air	Barren	4th
21 Fri.	Gemini	Air	Barren	4th
22 Sat. 11:28 am	Cancer	Water	Fruitful	4th
23 Sun.	Cancer	Water	Fruitful	4th
24 Mon. 8:24 pm	Leo	Fire	Barren	4th
25 Tue.	Leo	Fire	Barren	New 12:31 pm
26 Wed.	Leo	Fire	Barren	1st
27 Thu. 7:36 am	Virgo	Earth	Barren	1st
28 Fri.	Virgo	Earth	Barren	1st
29 Sat. 8:27 pm	Virgo	Earth	Barren	1st
30 Sun.	Libra	Air	Semi-fruitful	1st
31 Mon.	Libra	Air	Semi-fruitful	1st

August Moon Table

Date	Sign	Element	Nature	Phase
1 Tue. 9:08 am	Scorpio	Water	Fruitful	1st
2 Wed.	Scorpio	Water	Fruitful	2nd 4:46 am
3 Thu. 7:13 pm	Sagittarius	Fire	Barren	2nd
4 Fri.	Sagittarius	Fire	Barren	2nd
5 Sat.	Sagittarius	Fire	Barren	2nd
6 Sun. 1:19 am	Capricorn	Earth	Semi-fruitful	2nd
7 Mon.	Capricorn	Earth	Semi-fruitful	2nd
8 Tue. 3:47 am	Aquarius	Air	Barren	2nd
9 Wed.	Aquarius	Air	Barren	Full 6:54 am
10 Thu. 4:10 am	Pisces	Water	Fruitful	3rd
11 Fri.	Pisces	Water	Fruitful	3rd
12 Sat. 4:22 am	Aries	Fire	Barren	3rd
13 Sun.	Aries	Fire	Barren	3rd
14 Mon. 6:00 am	Taurus	Earth	Semi-fruitful	3rd
15 Tue.	Taurus	Earth	Semi-fruitful	4th 9:51 pm
16 Wed. 10:07 am	Gemini	Air	Barren	4th
17 Thu.	Gemini	Air	Barren	4th
18 Fri. 5:03 pm	Cancer	Water	Fruitful	4th
19 Sat.	Cancer	Water	Fruitful	4th
20 Sun.	Cancer	Water	Fruitful	4th
21 Mon. 2:33 am	Leo	Fire	Barren	4th
22 Tue.	Leo	Fire	Barren	4th
23 Wed. 2:08 pm	Virgo	Earth	Barren	New 3:10 pm
24 Thu.	Virgo	Earth	Barren	1st
25 Fri.	Virgo	Earth	Barren	1st
26 Sat. 3:01 am	Libra	Air	Semi-fruitful	1st
27 Sun.	Libra	Air	Semi-fruitful	1st
28 Mon. 3:56 pm	Scorpio	Water	Fruitful	1st
29 Tue.	Scorpio	Water	Fruitful	1st
30 Wed.	Scorpio	Water	Fruitful	1st
31 Thu. 3:00 am	Sagittarius	Fire	Barren	2nd 6:56 pm

September Moon Table

Date	Sign	Element	Nature	Phase
1 Fri.	Sagittarius	Fire	Barren	2nd
2 Sat. 10:34 am	Capricorn	Earth	Semi-fruitful	2nd
3 Sun.	Capricorn	Earth	Semi-fruitful	2nd
4 Mon. 2:15 pm	Aquarius	Air	Barren	2nd
5 Tue.	Aquarius	Air	Barren	2nd
6 Wed. 2:56 pm	Pisces	Water	Fruitful	2nd
7 Thu.	Pisces	Water	Fruitful	Full 2:42 pm
8 Fri. 2:23 pm	Aries	Fire	Barren	3rd
9 Sat.	Aries	Fire	Barren	3rd
10 Sun. 2:30 pm	Taurus	Earth	Semi-fruitful	3rd
11 Mon.	Taurus	Earth	Semi-fruitful	3rd
12 Tue. 4:59 pm	Gemini	Air	Barren	3rd
13 Wed.	Gemini	Air	Barren	3rd
14 Thu. 10:53 pm	Cancer	Water	Fruitful	4th 7:15 am
15 Fri.	Cancer	Water	Fruitful	4th
16 Sat.	Cancer	Water	Fruitful	4th
17 Sun. 8:15 am	Leo	Fire	Barren	4th
18 Mon.	Leo	Fire	Barren	4th
19 Tue. 8:07 pm	Virgo	Earth	Barren	4th
20 Wed.	Virgo	Earth	Barren	4th
21 Thu.	Virgo	Earth	Barren	4th
22 Fri. 9:06 am	Libra	Air	Semi-fruitful	New 7:45 am
23 Sat.	Libra	Air	Semi-fruitful	1st
24 Sun. 9:54 pm	Scorpio	Water	Fruitful	1st
25 Mon.	Scorpio	Water	Fruitful	1st
26 Tue.	Scorpio	Water	Fruitful	1st
27 Wed. 9:16 am	Sagittarius	Fire	Barren	1st
28 Thu.	Sagittarius	Fire	Barren	1st
29 Fri. 6:01 pm	Capricorn	Earth	Semi-fruitful	1st
30 Sat.	Capricorn	Earth	Semi-fruitful	2nd 7:04 am

October Moon Table

Date	Sign	Element	Nature	Phase
1 Sun. 11:24 pm	Aquarius	Air	Barren	2nd
2 Mon.	Aquarius	Air	Barren	2nd
3 Tue.	Aquarius	Air	Barren	2nd
4 Wed. 1:33 am	Pisces	Water	Fruitful	2nd
5 Thu.	Pisces	Water	Fruitful	2nd
6 Fri. 1:32 am	Aries	Fire	Barren	Full 11:13 pm
7 Sat.	Aries	Fire	Barren	3rd
8 Sun. 1:04 am	Taurus	Earth	Semi-fruitful	3rd
9 Mon.	Taurus	Earth	Semi-fruitful	3rd
10 Tue. 2:06 am	Gemini	Air	Barren	3rd
11 Wed.	Gemini	Air	Barren	3rd
12 Thu. 6:21 am	Cancer	Water	Fruitful	3rd
13 Fri.	Cancer	Water	Fruitful	4th 8:25 pm
14 Sat. 2:38 pm	Leo	Fire	Barren	4th
15 Sun.	Leo	Fire	Barren	4th
16 Mon.	Leo	Fire	Barren	4th
17 Tue. 2:15 am	Virgo	Earth	Barren	4th
18 Wed.	Virgo	Earth	Barren	4th
19 Thu. 3:19 pm	Libra	Air	Semi-fruitful	4th
20 Fri.	Libra	Air	Semi-fruitful	4th
21 Sat.	Libra	Air	Semi-fruitful	4th
22 Sun. 3:54 am	Scorpio	Water	Fruitful	New 1:14 am
23 Mon.	Scorpio	Water	Fruitful	1st
24 Tue. 2:53 pm	Sagittarius	Fire	Barren	1st
25 Wed.	Sagittarius	Fire	Barren	1st
26 Thu. 11:47 pm	Capricorn	Earth	Semi-fruitful	1st
27 Fri.	Capricorn	Earth	Semi-fruitful	1st
28 Sat.	Capricorn	Earth	Semi-fruitful	1st
29 Sun. 5:17 am	Aquarius	Air	Barren	2nd 4:25 pm
30 Mon.	Aquarius	Air	Barren	2nd
31 Tue. 9:10 am	Pisces	Water	Fruitful	2nd

November Moon Table

Date	Sign	Element	Nature	Phase
1 Wed.	Pisces	Water	Fruitful	2nd
2 Thu. 10:46 am	Aries	Fire	Barren	2nd
3 Fri.	Aries	Fire	Barren	2nd
4 Sat. 11:05 am	Taurus	Earth	Semi-fruitful	2nd
5 Sun.	Taurus	Earth	Semi-fruitful	Full 7:58 am
6 Mon. 11:46 am	Gemini	Air	Barren	2nd
7 Tue.	Gemini	Air	Barren	2nd
8 Wed. 2:46 pm	Cancer	Water	Fruitful	2nd
9 Thu.	Cancer	Water	Fruitful	2nd
10 Fri. 9:34 pm	Leo	Fire	Barren	2nd
11 Sat.	Leo	Fire	Barren	2nd
12 Sun.	Leo	Fire	Barren	4th 12:45 pm
13 Mon. 8:18 am	Virgo	Earth	Barren	4th
14 Tue.	Virgo	Earth	Barren	4th
15 Wed. 9:14 pm	Libra	Air	Semi-fruitful	4th
16 Thu.	Libra	Air	Semi-fruitful	4th
17 Fri.	Libra	Air	Semi-fruitful	4th
18 Sat. 9:46 am	Scorpio	Water	Fruitful	4th
19 Sun.	Scorpio	Water	Fruitful	4th
20 Mon. 8:15 pm	Sagittarius	Fire	Barren	New 5:18 pm
21 Tue.	Sagittarius	Fire	Barren	1st
22 Wed.	Sagittarius	Fire	Barren	1st
23 Thu. 4:25 am	Capricorn	Earth	Semi-fruitful	1st
24 Fri.	Capricorn	Earth	Semi-fruitful	1st
25 Sat. 10:41 am	Aquarius	Air	Barren	1st
26 Sun.	Aquarius	Air	Barren	1st
27 Mon. 3:20 pm	Pisces	Water	Fruitful	1st
28 Tue.	Pisces	Water	Fruitful	2nd 1:29 am
29 Wed. 6:30 pm	Aries	Fire	Barren	2nd
30 Thu.	Aries	Fire	Barren	2nd

December Moon Table

Date	Sign	Element	Nature	Phase
1 Fri. 8:26 pm	Taurus	Earth	Semi-fruitful	2nd
2 Sat.	Taurus	Earth	Semi-fruitful	2nd
3 Sun. 10:05 pm	Gemini	Air	Barren	2nd
4 Mon.	Gemini	Air	Barren	Full 7:25 pm
5 Tue.	Gemini	Air	Barren	3rd
6 Wed. 1:00 am	Cancer	Water	Fruitful	3rd
7 Thu.	Cancer	Water	Fruitful	3rd
8 Fri. 6:52 am	Leo	Fire	Barren	3rd
9 Sat.	Leo	Fire	Barren	3rd
10 Sun. 4:31 pm	Virgo	Earth	Barren	3rd
11 Mon.	Virgo	Earth	Barren	3rd
12 Tue.	Virgo	Earth	Barren	4th 9:32 am
13 Wed. 5:00 am	Libra	Air	Semi-fruitful	4th
14 Thu.	Libra	Air	Semi-fruitful	4th
15 Fri. 5:42 pm	Scorpio	Water	Fruitful	4th
16 Sat.	Scorpio	Water	Fruitful	4th
17 Sun.	Scorpio	Water	Fruitful	4th
18 Mon. 4:10 am	Sagittarius	Fire	Barren	4th
19 Tue.	Sagittarius	Fire	Barren	4th
20 Wed. 11:39 am	Capricorn	Earth	Semi-fruitful	New 9:01 am
21 Thu.	Capricorn	Earth	Semi-fruitful	1st
22 Fri. 4:49 pm	Aquarius	Air	Barren	1st
23 Sat.	Aquarius	Air	Barren	1st
24 Sun. 8:43 pm	Pisces	Water	Fruitful	1st
25 Mon.	Pisces	Water	Fruitful	1st
26 Tue.	Pisces	Water	Fruitful	1st
27 Wed. 12:04 am	Aries	Fire	Barren	2nd 9:48 am
28 Thu.	Aries	Fire	Barren	2nd
29 Fri. 3:08 am	Taurus	Earth	Semi-fruitful	2nd
30 Sat.	Taurus	Earth	Semi-fruitful	2nd
31 Sun.	Taurus	Earth	Semi-fruitful	2nd

About the Authors

ELIZABETH BARRETTE is the managing editor of *PanGaia* and assistant editor of *SageWoman*. She has been involved with the Pagan community for more than thirteen years and lives in central Illinois. Her other writing fields include speculative fiction and gender studies. Visit her website at: http://www.worth-link.net/~ysabet/index.html.

CHANDRA MOIRA BEAL is a freelance writer who divides her time between Austin, Texas, and London, England. Chandra is Sanskrit for "the Noon." She has written three books and published hundreds of articles, all inspired by her day-to-day life and adventures. Chandra is also a massage therapist and Reiki practitioner. To learn more, visit www.beal-net.com/laluna.

STEPHANIE ROSE BIRD is an artist, writer, herbalist, healer, mother, and companion. She studied art at the Tyler School of Art and at the University of California at San Diego, and she researched Australian Aboriginal art, ritual, and ceremonial practices as a Fulbright senior scholar. Currently, she leads herbcraft workshops at the Chicago Botanic Gardens. Her column "Ase! from the Crossroads" is featured in *SageWoman*. Her book *Sticks, Stones, Roots & Bones* was published by Llewellyn in 2004.

DALLAS JENNIFER COBB lives an enchanted life in a waterfront village and writes about what she loves most: mothering, magic, gardening, and alternative economics. Determined to love what she does, she is forever scheming ways to pay the bills. Her essays have appeared in numerous publications. This year her video documentary "Disparate Places" was produced on TV Ontario's

Planet Parent. She is a regular contributor to Llewellyn's almanacs and can be contacted at gaias.garden@sympatico.ca.

ELLEN DUGAN, also known as the Garden Witch, is a psychic-clairvoyant and a practicing Witch of more than seventeen years. Ellen is a master gardener, and she teaches classes on gardening and flower folklore at her local community college. Ellen is the author of *Garden Witchery* (Llewellyn, 2003). She and her husband raise their three magical teenagers and tend to their enchanted gardens in Missouri.

MAGENTA GRIFFITH has been a Witch for more than twenty-five years, and she is a founding member of the coven Prodea. She leads rituals and workshops across the Midwest and is the librarian for the New Alexandria Library, a Pagan and magical resource center (http://www.magusbooks.com/newalexandria/).

JAMES KAMBOS is a writer and painter who has had a lifelong interest in folk magic. He has written numerous articles concerning the folk magic traditions of Greece, the Near East, and the Appalachian region of the United States. He writes and paints from his home in the beautiful Appalachian hills of southern Ohio.

JONATHAN KEYES lives in Portland, Oregon, where he likes to fiddle around in the garden and play with his cat. Jon works as an astrologer and herbalist and has written an astrological health book titled *Guide to Natural Health* (Llewellyn, 2002), as well as an herb book titled *A Traditional Herbal.* He is currently working on a book titled *Healers*, a series of interviews with various herbalists, *curanderos*, and medicine people from around the United States.

SHARYNNE MACLEOD NICMHACHA is a Celtic priestess and Witch and a direct descendant of Clan MacLeod—long recorded in oral tradition as having connections with (and the blood of) the *sidhe*, or fairy folk. Sharynne has studied Old Irish, Scottish Gaelic, and Celtic mythology through Harvard University where she has published a number of research papers. She teaches workshops and sings and plays bodran, woodwinds, and stringed instruments with the group Devandaurae. She recently published her first book, *Queen of the Night: In Search of a Celtic Moon Goddess* (Red Wheel/Weiser, 2004).

LEEDA ALLEYN PACOTTI practices as a naturopathic physician, nutritional counselor, and master herbalist.

LAUREL REUFNER has been a solitary pagan for more than a decade. She is active in the Circle of Gaia Dreaming and is often attracted to bright and shiny ideas. Southeastern Ohio has always been home. She currently lives in Athens County with her husband and two adorable heathens, er, daughters. Her website may be found at www.spiritrealm.com/Melinda/paganism.html.

SHERI RICHERSON has more than twenty years of experience in newspaper, magazine, and creative writing. She is a longtime member of both the Garden Writers Association of America and the American Horticultural Society. She is also a member of the Tropical Flowering Tree Society, the North American Rock Garden Society, and the American Orchid Society. Her favorite pastimes are riding her motorcycle, visiting arboretums, traveling, horseback riding, and working in her huge garden. Sheri specializes in herb gardening and in growing tropical, subtropical, and exotic plants. For more information, visit her website at: http://SheriAnnRicherson.exotic-gardening.com.

MICHELLE SANTOS has been a practicing Witch for over eight years and has been working with the fey since she was a child. Founding member of the Sisterhood of the Crescent Moon, she is active in the Pagan community in southeastern Massachusetts. Michelle presents various workshops, classes, and apprenticeship programs near her home. She is an ordained minister through the Universal Life Church and performs legal handfastings, weddings, and other spiritual rites of passage. She shares her home with elfy husband Michael and little Witch-in-training Neisa.

LYNN SMYTHE is a freelance writer living in Delray Beach, Florida, with her husband and two children. She spends too much time playing outside in the dirt where her main gardening passions are attracting butterflies and growing organic herbs and vegetables. She is a member of the Evening Herb Society of the Palm Beaches, and she writes a monthly column for their newsletter *The Herbin' Times*. Additional information can be found on her website: http://users.adelphia.net/~lynnsmythe.

SORITA has been a Wiccan for more than a decade, during which time she has worked within a variety of traditions and groups. She is the high priestess of a number of covens and groups in the London area, along with her partner, David Rankine. She is a fulltime writer, contributing to a number of publications on a regular basis. In addition to writing, she also leads regular workshops on witchcraft, astral projection, psychic development, and healing. When she is not working, she loves traveling to some of the forgotten sacred sites of Wales and Cornwall. To find out more, visit her online at www.avalonia.co.uk.

TAMMY SULLIVAN is a fulltime writer and solitary Witch who writes from her home in the foothills of the Great Smoky Mountains. Her work has appeared in the Llewellyn almanacs and *Circle* magazine.

S. Y. ZENITH is three-quarters Chinese, one tad bit Irish, and a lifelong solitary eclectic Pagan. She has lived and traveled extensively in Asia to such countries as India, Nepal, Thailand, Malaysia, Singapore, Borneo, and Japan for over two decades. She is now based in Australia where her time is divided between writing, experimenting with alternative remedies, and teaching the use of gems, holy beads, and religious objects from India and the Himalayas. She is also a member of the Australian Society of Authors.